Growing Up
Crooked

by
Wilbur Rees

Copyright © 2004 by Wilbur Rees

ISBN 0-7414-2304-9

Published by:

INFIN∞ITY
PUBLISHING.COM

1094 New De Haven Street, Suite 100
West Conshohocken, PA 19428-2713
Info@buybooksontheweb.com
www.buybooksontheweb.com
Toll-free (877) BUY BOOK
Local Phone (610) 941-9999
Fax (610) 941-9959

Printed in the United States of America

Printed on Recycled Paper

Published November 2004

Dedicated to my wife, Reba,
who was not afraid to "kiss a camel."

TABLE OF CONTENTS

FOREWORD

My backbone is spliced together with prayer, perversity and scar tissue. That gives a certain cant to my posture and warp to my soul. Mix that with a family as disaster-prone as the Hindenburg, a catastrophic economic depression, two world wars and a heavy dose of fundamentalist religion, bake it all in the hot, Southern California sun for a quarter of a century and you have the formula for a Roman candle kind of life—colorful, fiery and sometimes dangerous.

To begin with, let me tell you about Percival Pott, an eighteenth century English surgeon who was the first to correctly describe the nature of a spinal deformity know as "kyphosis." In non-medical terms, that's "humpback." In honor of Dr. Pott's work, they called the malady "Pott's Disease." He didn't get the disease; just the honor. I got the disease.

Pott's Disease is tuberculosis of the spine. The disease is rare now, except in third-world countries, but used to be seen most frequently in children as an infection and destruction of the vertebrae resulting in severe deformity. The two missing vertebrae in my own particular spine resulted in a backbone angled at 90°. Now you can curse a hump like that, laugh at it, cry about it or thumb your nose at it, but you cannot remain indifferent about it. It's there and you have to deal with it. Everyone around you has to deal with it too.

How I caught the disease is somewhat of a mystery. The most likely theory is that the germ came from the unpasteurized milk of a tubercular cow. My grandmother had a less complex answer. She simply said it was "God's will." You can see why I was not overly fond of God for awhile. For the first three years of my life I was normal enough. Unfortunately, I don't remember them. What I *do* remember are the decades that followed.

I was part of a family which had other kinds of twists and bends to contend with in addition to my obvious physical ones. A crooked spine is easy to see, but contorted personalities are more difficult to detect and analyze. During the 1920's, Psychology was in its infancy. The term "dysfunctional family" had not yet been coined. Sigmund Freud was not given much credence in small, Southern California towns like ours, so treatment was scarce. Families dealt with their problems as best they could and strove mightily to hide behind the mask of normalcy.

The pages that follow span the first twenty-five years of my existence within this twisted household, straining to uphold the facade of plumb-line rectitude while grappling with all the bent contours and angled planes of our tangled relationships. The sequence of vignettes that follow are not necessarily in chronological order, but rather are arranged according to theme and the accumulation of persistent memories.

The verbal dialogue recorded here may not always be the verbatim documentation of actual conversation, but it is true to the essence of remembered communication. Others who have been involved in some of these events will, of course, have their own perspectives. I leave it to them to write their own stories.

I have called these experiences "Growing Up Crooked." This is a book about scars.

While that may sound morbid, it is not intended to be, for in the final analysis, it is scar tissue that holds us all together.

CHAPTER 1

ALMOST PARADISE

"Every history has one quality in common with eternity. Begin where you will, there is always a beginning back of the beginning."

-Edward Eggleston

The wiry young man burst into the dentist's office unannounced. This was no time for formalities. The man's name was Harry Peet Rees and he had a clear mission; tell the dentist he was never again to see the girl he had been dating. No one was more surprised than the hapless dentist as Harry tossed him the tennis racquet which the dentist had just given to his girl friend as a gift. The girl's name was Cora Matilda Raymond and Harry had decided that Cora belonged to him. He staked out his claim on her as some miner might do with a promising lode.

I suppose Cora could have refused Harry's proposal of marriage, but she was not a forceful woman, and it was not in Harry's makeup to take "no" for an answer to any proposition – never was, never would be. She saw in Harry's flashing, dark eyes a strength and stability that she must have admired. He was an intrepid gamecock type of man who could stare down a lion, a bear – or a dentist. He possessed unbounded ambition, endless self confidence, intelligence, education and came from a fine, proud family. All of these attributes must have boded well for the future.

The wedding was a small, but gala affair with a flamboyance that surely was an embarrassment to Cora. Harry, having just graduated from Pratt Institute in New York with a degree in Electrical Engineering, felt obliged to display his electrical prowess by lacing the arbor under which the ceremony took place with braided strands of electric light bulbs. Such galvanic ostentation was rarely seen in 1913. It was bright, gaudy and a prelude of things to come.

Soon after the ceremony, Harry whisked away his bride to a foreign country – Brazil, to be exact, where he had just secured a position as Instructor at "Instituto de Electro-Technica" in Rio de Janeiro. Although the school was not a "university" in the U.S. sense of the word, it was much to Harry's liking, for all of the students stood at their desks when he entered the classroom and repeated in unison, "Bom dia, Doctor Rees."

Cora was not so enamored with her new location as was Harry. Beetles the size of dates kept dropping from the ceiling, alligators thumped around under the house, she didn't speak a word of Portuguese and, to top it all off, she was pregnant. No matter. At the first of the twentieth century, a woman went with her husband – no question, no discussion, no complaint. Happiness or contentment was not part of the equation.

On Monday, October 13, 1913, Dona Clara, a Brazilian mid-wife and new-found friend, scurried to the Doctor Rees residence to assist in the delivery of Raymond, Harry and Cora's firstborn. It was a time of celebration and congratulations all around. While Cora sorely missed her friends and family at home, she now had a healthy, happy baby upon whom to focus all of her attention. Poor baby Raymond did not have an inkling that his future sister and brother would forever call him "Brazil nut" and remind him at every turn that

2

he could never become the President of the United States, because he was born in a foreign country. Later in his life, that rule perhaps would be changed by Congress, but not until any childhood aspirations had long disappeared.

Not many years passed before a dark cloud cast a shadow over this Brazilian utopia. Harry's mother, Elvina Peet Rees, suffered a heart attack. There was no alternative but to abruptly resign his position at the Institute and book the first passage home. All of his three brothers and his sister would join their father at a bedside vigil, and he must be there too. Cora bade a hasty farewell to Dona Clara, placed Raymond in a basket and headed back to the states with Harry. Packing and traveling were not her favorite pastimes, but she looked forward to returning to the familiar surroundings of home. After the crisis passed, Elvina would go on to live another thirty years or so until she was ninety two, but no one guessed it at the time.

When Harry's mother had recovered, it was time for another adventure that would test the mettle of Cora and her four year old son. Heeding Horace Greeley's advice to "Go West, young man, and grow up with the country," Harry landed a job in Los Angeles teaching in a high school. Again, with no option but to follow along, Cora packed what she considered to be the bare essentials, added them to Harry's cots, water can, tool boxes and tent and started out on the arduous trek to Southern California. Never mind that there was a World War going on, or that the hundreds of miles of roads were unpaved and little more than wagon trails, Harry was up to the challenge of it all and Cora and Raymond had better be too.

The sturdy pioneers started out from Boston on September second, 1918, with more fortitude than finances and more pluck than practice. They nestled Raymond into the back seat of their Willis Overland along with his stuffed toy dog and a mountain of bedding, food and cooking utensils, only guessing

3

at what lay ahead of them. A few of the roads were paved in some parts of the country and Harry wrote in his diary, "Our speed was only limited by the power of the motor." For most of the way, however, the roads were mere wagon ruts and in some places they didn't exist at all. Harry writes that at one point in New Mexico, they traveled twenty miles off the road without even knowing it. There were wash-outs galore, mud slides, sand drifts, steep hills, blind curves, rattlesnakes, cactus beds and hazards enough to give second thoughts to a Sir Edmund Hillary explorer. Since all of this was before my time, I can only guess at the weariness, short tempers and recriminations that occurred, but knowing well the Harry and Cora of later years, I am sure that road obstacles and mechanical breakdowns were not the only hazards on the trip.

Over a month later, on October 12th, 1918, the exhausted travelers arrived in Los Angeles. It seemed like paradise, graced with palm trees, beautiful homes, paved streets and, as Harry noted, "nearly 800 miles of sewer lines." Harry wasn't one to rent or buy a ready-made house, however. He was a builder. It would be foolhardy to rent a house when you could build one and own it.

The first house he built was in San Pedro, a suburb south of Los Angeles. Point Fermin was the site, close to a military installation where target practice was frequent and the cannons rattled the windows and shook the foundation. Did he take into account the proximity to the fort when he built the house? I don't know. There was something about the roaring cannon, however, that fit his personality. Harry heartily endorsed anything loud, explosive and earth shaking.

It was here, in the shadow of the mighty shore weapons that a second child was born to Cora and Harry, a baby girl they named Mildred, after Harry's sister. Mildred was born July 7th, 1920, and like her parents, had dark hair and brown eyes and a determined disposition. She would need that disposition as she grew up in a family whose daily interactions sometimes rivaled the firing of the shore batteries.

The unnerving noise of cannon fire eventually wore down even Harry. He picked out another building site on a main north-south artery running through another city, Alhambra, situated on the outskirts of L.A. The acquisition of land was no problem in the mid-1920's, so Harry secured two huge lots with plenty of room to expand, build on and garden. The house he built on Atlantic Boulevard was a carbon copy of the one he had built at Point Fermin, only larger. A beamed ceiling in the living room symbolized the rock-solid construction of the house and complimented the massive brick fireplace. The double garage just to the rear was nearly as big as the house. In addition to space for two cars (we almost never had more than one), there was a workbench and tool area to the side, another wide storage room to the rear with another large tool space in back of that. Overhead, he had included a full-length attic for the storage of keepsakes, mementos and seasonal decorations. The attic also had storm-type doors that opened outward to allow for sun bathing au naturel. Unless someone climbed onto the roof with a ladder, the sunbather felt his or her privacy was secure.

This house was home to me for the first twenty one years of my life. I was born in this house in mid-May, 1925. I was not exactly planned, but hey, here I was. It was a promising beginning. My mother told me that I weighed a hefty ten pounds at birth and gave every indication of being a robust, active, and perfectly normal youngster. And so it seemed that this healthy family of five, with a large, sturdy house, amidst the snow capped mountains and orange groves of Southern California had finally arrived in paradise. But neither the house, the family nor the new arrival would turn out exactly as they seemed.

5

CHAPTER 2

THE LITTLE BROWN JUG

"Two old chairs, and a half a candle,
One old jug without a handle
These were all his worldly goods."

-Edward Lear

For sheer terror and sadistic torture, nothing could match the hospital which formed my earliest memories. When I entered the hospital, in 1929, I had not yet reached my fourth birthday. I had no way of understanding it at the time, but I would be there for a whole year. From a tall, brick tower nearby, the Westminster chimes tolled out their mournful tones like a funeral dirge. At my age, I didn't know any big words – hardly any words at all – but I sure knew about big feelings and these were big feelings. I've heard it said by the experts that kids three years old don't remember much, but believe me, those dreary chimes wrapped me in an isolation as permanent as the skin on my body. I remember nothing of my life before that time.

I'm sure my mother explained to me as best she could why I had to be in the hospital, but at my age, feelings ran stronger than logic. If I had a sick backbone, why couldn't I just stay home with it? Had I done something so wrong that I had to be taken away from my family? Why couldn't Mama and Papa stay with me? And why did they have to dress up in white like ghosts every time they came to see me?

There were no understandable answers, but through all of the gnawing questions, those incessant bells kept bonging away to remind me of my abandonment. Would I ever be able to leave this chamber of horrors? The disconsolate tattoo of the bells seemed to say no. One small comfort was the little brown jug which sat defiantly by the white enameled urinal on the night stand. The jug was ridiculously small, like a charm for a bracelet, less than half an inch tall. The fact that it survives today, with no more damage than a broken handle, gives testimony to the fierceness with which I guarded it over more than seven decades. It has nothing to do with the "Little Brown Jug" in the drinking song, but is a small icon of affection – a link to the world of the caring.

Hospitals were grim affairs in the late twenties – walls painted battleship-gray, large wards with rows of beds lined up like file boxes, and a great catalogue of senseless rules which must be followed to the letter. The staff at the hospital where I was seemed far more interested in uniformity and discipline than in curing the sick. The Children's Orthopedic Hospital in Los Angeles was something straight from the pages of a Dickens novel.

One of the strictly enforced rules of the hospital was that visitors, including parents, must don sterile gowns with long sleeves and thick, white mittens. These strange costumes made them look like participants in a Ku Klux Klan rally. I didn't know much about germs and microbes and I'm not sure that the doctors did either. All I knew was that now my mother's gentle touch was shielded from me by a bulky cloth covering. To make matters worse, visiting privileges were limited to an hour, two or three times a week. Every time a visiting period ended, I was not sure when or if I would ever seem them again.

One more annoying rule had to do with toys and play-things. If a toy was brought to a child, he or she could view it from a distance, but then it must be whisked away to the hospital roof for a twenty-four-hour decontamination period in the hot, Southern California sun before it could be returned to the child. Why the nurses didn't have to dress in gowns or bake in the sun was more than I could ever understand. The only explanation seemed to be that they were somehow immune to the dirt and filth of the world, while parents and visitors were not.

One nurse stands alone in my memory. She was the one with the white, pointed hat. She was the absolute authority on our floor. Her stern eyes blazed like acetylene torches, igniting guilt in all tender souls. The expertise of this white clad commandant seemed to lie more in the area of correction and control rather than medicine. Years passed before I finally learned that witches wore black pointed hats rather than white ones. Her methods of maintaining law and order in the hospi-tal ward would hardly pass pediatric standards today, but at the time they were quite acceptable, and they certainly were effective.

One efficient tool at her disposal was the "tin mitt." Tin mitts were ingenious devices probably first invented by Spanish Inquisitors. They consisted of metal cups, large enough to fit over a child's hands, with cloth sleeves attached which could be tied to the child's arms with drawstrings. The dents and scrapes on the tin mitts bore evidence to the mad-dening effect on children as they attempted to free their hands by banging them on walls, bed frames and each other. The offending patients had their hands tied in the tin mitts for whatever length of time the nurse deemed appropriate to the crime. The offense might be anything from refusing to eat your oatmeal mush or making noise during nap time to wetting the bed.

I don't remember wetting the bed all that often, but I must have. One day the witch with the pointed hat marched over to my bed with a large pair of shears. She unceremoniously held up the small appendage between my legs, inserted it between the blades of the shears and threatened to cut it off if I wet the bed one more time. I never did.

It was always hard for me to tell the difference between discipline and medical procedures. They all seemed to be connected to punishment. A Bradford Frame, for example, was a simple rectangle pieced together from ordinary plumbing pipe with a heavy canvas stretched taut over the surface. Being strapped to this apparatus day in and day out was like being stretched over the surface of a kettle drum. This treatment was alternated with being tied into a body cast while iron weights pulled your head north as similar weights pulled your hips south. This twenty-four-hour-a-day treatment went on for a year in the hospital and four years at home. All of this did little to straighten my spine, but it was quite effective in providing a certain distortion to my outlook on life.

The year confined to the Children's Orthopedic Hospital at the age of three seemed like ten years in a medieval dungeon. There were few bright spots, but they did occur. The weekly religious service was one. Volunteers from some area church could come in to belt out gospel songs and see that we three-year-olds were all saved from sin. This early introduction to religion was, undoubtedly, the first shove that got me started on the long road from simple fundamentalism to sanctified agnosticism. At the tender age of three and four, I never did understand why God wanted to send us all to hell, but even so, the prospect seemed better than where we were. I remember being wheeled into the service while strapped to a gurney. When the question was asked, "How many of you want to go to heaven?" I fervently raised my hand. I would have raised it just as fervently had the preacher asked how many wanted to go to Piggly Wiggly. I just wanted out of there.

The infrequent visits from Shrine Circus clowns provided a welcome relief, too. Their high jinks were like an oasis in an emotional desert. They never stayed long enough to suit us, but their outrageous red noses and baggy pants always ignited laughter and helped to ease the sense of isolation. One clown even wore a pointed hat like the head nurse. I especially enjoyed seeing him get hit in the face with a cream pie.

But the warmest impression of all didn't come from a program or show, but from a person dressed in hospital garb. She was probably not a full-fledged nurse, because she wore a different colored uniform. Likely she was a nurses' aide. She was quite young, I thought, although three year olds are unpracticed at judging age. Was she seventeen? Nineteen? Twenty five? It didn't really matter. Her name was Miss Rose; that I will never forget. She stands out in my mind because out of all the nurses, orderlies, doctors and aides, there was a caring in her eyes. When she entered the ward, I changed from a patient with a number to a real, live human being. I don't remember her giving shots, taking temperatures or doling out pills, but as I look back on it, she was the most valuable member of the hospital staff.

Whatever her age, she was wise enough to bend the rules in favor of compassion. There was healing in her touch – a touch unobstructed by gowns or rubber gloves. When she stroked my forehead or smoothed the sheets, it was a real hand she used.

I was in love with Miss Rose. She didn't make me answer "Fine" like the other nurses did whenever they asked how I was feeling today. She let me be honest. Even at the age of three and four, that seemed important. If I felt bad, it was okay to say so. I could even cry without having the tin mitts put on me.

She took time to read to me and play small, silly games:

"Itsy Bitsy Spider" and "I'm a Little Teapot." When she was there, I didn't even hear those cursed bells in the tower. She wasn't Mama, but she could spend more time with me than Mama because the hospital rules said she could.

It was Miss Rose who gave me the little brown jug, not big enough to hold anything, but just right to circle with my fist and feel its glow radiate like a chunk of pitchblende. I couldn't give her anything in return, but she knew I would have if I could.

That the little jug has survived to this day seems like some sort of miracle. Sometimes I wonder why. Children's toys have a way of disappearing, especially if they are small, but this one didn't. It was different. It seemed to have an ability of its own to survive. When Miss Rose gave it to me, I don't think she stopped to analyze her action, but now that ceramic jug has become a symbol of a covert alliance between two people against unspeakable loneliness and loss. The tiny jug was a gift she dared to give without first having it sanitized on the hospital roof. It survived and so did I.

CHAPTER 3

THE DEADLY BATH

"Cleanliness is, indeed, next to godliness."

-John Wesley

One of the best things about coming home from the hospital was the weekly bath in the tub – with help, of course. Bath time was one of the rare events when I was permitted to escape the plaster cast that held my body like a clam in the half-shell. Mama would unbuckle the straps that kept me from rolling off the gurney that my Papa had built, lift me out of the cast and place me in the tub. It didn't happen often. Saturday night was the traditional bath night.

One bath in particular stands out in my mind. I was five or six at the time. From my position strapped into the cast, I could see the gas flame under the boiler over my head as it licked the hot metal base. The water heater was attached to the wall several feet off the floor. Papa had put me under the water heater over an hour ago while he went to the laundry room to work on the washing machine. Mama and Papa used to move me around the house on this made-over baby carriage so that they wouldn't have to carry me in the tortoise shell cast, which must have weighed a ton.

Papa had showed me many times how the water heater worked and he had explained the dangers about it in a stern voice. "Fire under the boiler creates steam," he said, "and steam builds up pressure. If the pressure increases, it will eventually blow up the boiler." My imagination filled in the rest; a big boom that would raise the house off its foundation flying pieces of hot metal boiling water and steam gushing everywhere. The gas flame must be turned off before that ever happened. It was time to turn off the flame now, but no one was coming to do it.

Strapped tightly into the cast, there was no way I could reach the gas valve. Neither was there any escape from the bottom side of the boiler. I was stuck. Where was everybody? Why didn't somebody come? Papa had long ago left the laundry room and was in the front room with Mama. I could hear their voices raised like screeching birds. I couldn't make out all of the words, but I understood enough of them.

"I work like a Trojan all day for you," Papa said. I didn't know what a Trojan was. Maybe a horse. Maybe a football player I had heard my brother, Raymond, talk about. "What do I get in return?" Papa yelled.

"I try to do my part," Mama said. "I take care of the children. It's not easy, you know. It's certainly not easy." I knew that I was the one that took most of her time and energy. She cooked and cleaned house for everybody, but I was the one that really drained her strength. My twinge of guilt didn't last long. The boiler was beginning to sing like a teakettle up and down in a sort of rhythmic hissing.

"Papa!" I called. "The water heater is boiling. It's boiling, Papa."

"I've been a good wife and a good mother," Mama sobbed. "You can't say I haven't. I work hard, you know. I just don't get any pay for it."

The voices moved closer, into the kitchen. That was closer to the laundry room, too. Maybe they were coming. Surely someone would come. Raymond wasn't home. Neither was my sister, Mildred. But why would Papa put me there under the water heater and just go off and forget me?

The voices grew louder. "If you loved me . . . " Mama said. "If you loved me . . ." The boiler continued to hiss at me like some flame-breathing dragon. Soon it would spew out scalding water and boil us all to death.

"Papa!" I yelled. "Don't forget the water heater. It's gonna explode. You better come, Papa."

"I deserve better," I heard him say. "Don't I provide for you?" Papa's voice was loud and angry. "Is there anything you want that you don't have? Clothes? Food? A decent place to live?"

"That's not it, Harry. You buy things, yes, but I never have a say in any of it. You buy things and bring them home, but I never have a say."

"For crying out loud, Cora. That's because I drive the car. I suppose you want two cars now. What do you think we are, movie stars?"

"We wouldn't have the car we have now, Harry, if I hadn't put up the money for it. Now I have nothing. Not even a penny."

"Oh, so that's it? You resent my driving the car, do you?"

I began to shake. What they were talking about had nothing to do with water heaters. The world was about to end with a big bang and they were talking about silly, stupid things that didn't matter. Why did they always get mad about stuff like that?

"Mama!" I yelled. "Someone come quick and turn off the boiler! It's gonna explode!"

"Who do you think puts gas and oil in that car?" Papa's booming voice sounded like a bass drum. "Who keeps it up, Cora? Could you change the plugs or put in an oil filter? You can't even drive, Cora. You don't know how. So don't boo-hoo to me about how you paid for the car."

14

Mama's high pitched sobs mingled with the high pitch of the steam in the boiler.

"I don't want to drive," Mama said. "I just would like a little say in things, Harry. I make no choices. I cook what you bring home to cook, I wear what you give me to wear, I read what you bring me to read. I feel like a trained seal – an animal in the zoo. I don't have ten cents of my own to spend. Is it too much to ask to have a little change so I can buy some rouge once in a while? Some talcum powder? I'm not extravagant, Harry."

"Money! It always comes down to money, Cora. I can never make enough money to suit you. The stock market crashed. Or haven't you heard? Times are bad and they're going to get a hell of a lot worse. You ought to be glad I have a job and bring home the bacon instead of whining about how little you have. You're an ungrateful – "

"Don't say it, Harry! Don't you say that hateful word!" Mama's sobs were muffled, like she was crying into her apron. "You'll never understand."

"No, I guess I won't," Papa shouted.

Bits of metal on the underside of the boiler were beginning to glow, awash in blue-yellow flame from the gas jet. If I could only roll over, maybe I could crawl away, but the straps held me firm. I remembered the story of the three little pigs and how the big, bad wolf came to an untimely end as he dropped down the chimney into a vat of boiling water. In spite of his evil heart, I always felt sorry for him. I wondered how it would feel to drown in boiling water. I would soon know. Death would come, but would I have to suffer long, or would I go to be with Jesus right away, the way the preacher at the hospital service said? Why couldn't Jesus come right now and get me with a couple of angels instead of drowning me first in boiling water?

The water heater could not hold out much longer. It was

sizzling and crackling, the ugly flames dancing up and down against the hot metal in a small preview of hell. Mama and Papa's voices kept on shouting, oblivious to the boiler and to me. I was a stranger looking in. I didn't exist. Soon I would be blown away and no one would even miss me.

"Dear God," I prayed. "Why are you doing this to me?" Mama and Papa could fight well into the night. I knew that. They would quit eventually, but what if that didn't happen until the boiler blew off the roof?

I looked around the laundry room, trying to keep my mind off the terror overhead. The washing machine stood at my feet, a huge wooden drum nestled in a metal tub. If I could somehow get to the other side of that monstrous machine, it might shield me from the blast, but I couldn't reach the wheels to push them forward. I looked at the battleship-gray floor, chipped and pitted like the surface of the moon. Papa said it needed painting. It didn't matter now. It would all be gone soon, made into splinters and sawdust by the blast.

"Somebody!" I screamed again. "Somebody get me out of here. The water heater's going to blow up. Can't anybody hear me? We'll all be killed and especially me!"

"It's all I can do to bring home enough to feed this family," Papa yelled. When he said, "This family," it sounded distant, like we were a family from a foreign country that Papa just took pity on because no one else would help us. I wondered if maybe that were true. Maybe we weren't Papa's real family at all.

"But you all have it a damsite better than most families around," he said. When Papa said "damn," I knew he was really mad. But why couldn't he take out just two seconds to come turn off the water heater? It added its high scream to the quarrel like a third voice.

"Don't I leave you money for the milk man every morning, Cora?"

"Yes, but—"

"And the ice man?"

"Sure, but—"

"Then why do you complain all the time? You're an ungrateful woman, Cora. Damned ungrateful!"

The statement had a finality about it. I could tell the fight was over. The verdict was in and Mama was guilty. Papa stomped out of the kitchen into the laundry room. Good. Mama was ungrateful, but at least Papa would turn off the water heater now and we would be spared being boiled alive.

Papa's angry strides shook the house as he marched toward the back door. I reached out to grab his shirt-sleeve, but he continued his mad dash for the door as though I were only a small part of the washing machine.

"Papa! The water heater!"

The screen door banged shut and Papa was gone. The boiler kept sizzling like the fuse of a bomb.

"Mama!" I called. "Come quick! Hurry up!"

Now that Papa was gone, I couldn't imagine why Mama didn't come. Had she gone deaf? Finally, she shuffled out to the laundry room, wiping her nose with a piece of crumpled toilet paper.

"What is it, dear?"

"The water heater. It's about to blow up."

She reached up and twisted the valve and stared at the boiler as though she had never seen it before – as though she didn't even know what it was.

"Could you get me out of here, Mama? I'm scared."

"It's all right, dear. Everything's all right." The gurgling, snapping boiler contradicted her words.

"Just move me outa here, Mama. The water heater could explode any minute. Papa said so."

"Papa says a lot of things," Mama said. She lifted me up, cast and all and carried me into the bathroom. "It's time for your bath, anyway." I had forgotten it was Saturday night. That's the reason the water heater was turned on in the first place. It was a risky business just to stay clean. Was it really worth it? Besides, I didn't seem all that dirty.

Mama lifted me out of the cast and turned the spigot at the end of the tub. The water spilled out in a torrent of steam. "Where did Papa go?" I asked.

"I don't know, dear. It doesn't matter. He'll be back."

"Did he hurt you, Mama?"

I watched her face twist and her eyes fill with tears again. "No. No, he didn't hurt me. Don't you worry about anything."

The steam from the tub collected on the enameled walls and dribbled down in little rivulets, carving shiny pathways, just like the tears on Mama's face.

"Mama."

"Yes, dear."

"I'm glad the boiler didn't blow up."

"I am too, dear." She answered as though she were only commenting on the weather.

"Don't ever put me under the water heater again, okay? Okay, Mama?"

"What dear?"

"Mama, you're not listening. What if the boiler had burst? We'd all be burned – boiled – maybe even dead. It could have happened, you know. We could all be dead. Papa said so."

Mama didn't answer. She tested the temperature with her elbow and let the tears from her face drip down and mingle with the bath water. I loved Mama – but sometimes home didn't seem much better than the hospital.

CHAPTER 4

HOW DID I GET HERE?

"Amoebas at the start
Were not complex;
They tore themselves apart
And started sex. "

-Arthur Guiterman

"What in the world is wrong with that lady?"

I was staring at a woman across the street, waddling down the sidewalk with her back arched, trying to support the biggest belly I had ever seen in my life. The word "pregnant" was never mentioned at our house. I would not have known what it meant anyway.

"She ate too many potatoes," my sister, Mildred, said. My brother, Raymond, agreed with her. Both my sister and my brother were good at keeping straight faces while fibbing, though, so I could never be completely sure of their telling the truth. But just in case, I refused to eat my potatoes that night.

The woman with the huge belly became part of a mysterious puzzle about where I came from – where anybody came from. I suspected that there was something inside of her besides potatoes. "How did I get here, anyway?" I used to ask. Responses to the question gave me some interesting things to think about, but no facts. However I got here, it was a shameful process that only adults talked about in whispers. Sometimes the question brought smiles or giggles, too, and there were jokes about whatever people did to have babies. I didn't understand all that. It must be a little funny as well as being somewhat wicked. Everybody seemed to know the answer but me.

"You'll know soon enough," the older ones would say, or "You'll understand when you grow up." But when would I grow up? My brother, Raymond, was grown up. He was almost twenty and grew hair on his chin, but I knew that he wouldn't tell me, because I was only eight. My sister, Mildred, was grown up enough, too, although she was only thirteen.

"C'mon, Mildred, how do babies get born?" I asked. If I teased enough, maybe she'd give me a straight answer. "I know babies come out of mothers, but how do they get in there? How did I get inside of Mama and how did I get out?"

Mildred knitted her brow together in a serious scowl. She brushed her long, dark hair back over her shoulders, pausing to hunt for appropriate words. At last, I was going to get an answer.

"Well," she said, "two people have to love each other. If they love each other, they have babies."

Was that it? Was that all she was going to tell me? It sounded like we were on the right track, all right, but hardly the detailed answer I was looking for. "You mean, just by loving each other, Mamas and Papas have babies?" Mildred nodded her head, but looked away as though she were not telling me the whole story. "I know lots of people that love each other," I reasoned, "and they don't have babies."

"Well, in the first place, you have to be married," she said, "and then you have to love each other a lot."

I thought of the Simons, just to the north of us. They didn't have any children. Maybe that was because they didn't really love each other. They were Jewish, too. Maybe only Christians knew how to love that much. But then, of course, some Jewish couples had babies, so at least some of them knew how to love. There must be more to it.

Mrs. Doyle, next door, ran a small chicken farm. She raised Rhode Island Reds and fattened them up on corn and table scraps. I took a special liking to those chickens and hated it whenever one ended up as a fryer. One day I watched horrified as a rooster attacked one of the hens. He jumped on top of her in a merciless frenzy of dust and feathers. I screamed through the wire fence and threw clods of dirt to scare him away, but he was so intent on his mission that all of my efforts to distract him were wasted. I ran to the house and yelled at my mother. "Come quick! One of the roosters is killing one of the hens!"

How could she remain so calm? Here was a murder taking place in the hen yard and she didn't even stop washing the breakfast dishes. "Roosters do that sometimes," she said. "He's not really hurting her."

"Not hurting her?" I wailed. "He's killing her! He's on top of her – her wings are spread out like they're broken – it's awful!"

"It looks awful," Mama smiled, "but he has to do that or there wouldn't be any little chickens. Ordinary eggs, like we eat for breakfast, don't hatch all by themselves. Before little chickens are hatched, the rooster has to do that to the hen."

"The rooster puts chickens in the eggs?"

"Something like that."

"Oh," I said, feeling foolish. I should have known that roosters put chickens in eggs. Otherwise, what were roosters for, except waking everybody up in the morning? But how did the roosters put chickens in the eggs? The question remained unanswered and I dared not ask.

I went out to the backyard again and peered through the wire fence to Mrs. Doyle's chicken yard. The abused hen did not seem worse for her ordeal. She calmly scratched and pecked at the ground like nothing had happened. The proud rooster strutted in satisfaction. He had put a chicken inside an egg. I wished I knew how he did it. If only I could get hold of a book that would tell me these things.

I didn't have a Bible of my own, but Mama's was always available. I didn't look at it much because I didn't understand it. It was full of mysteries about terrible things that would happen in the future and strange stories that taxed even my imagination. It took special people to understand what the Bible was talking about. There was a lot in it about heaven and hell, but at the time, I was a lot more interested in where I came from than where I was going.

Then I heard Mama reading the Christmas story from Luke. "And in the sixth month, the angel Gabriel was sent from God to a virgin espoused to a man whose name was Joseph . . ."

"What's a virgin?" I asked.

"A virgin is a girl who isn't married and hasn't had a child."

Aha! I was onto something. Maybe the Bible had the answer to what I was looking for.

"Can virgins have children?" I asked.

"No," Mama said, "virgins can't have children."

"Well then, how come Mary did? She was a virgin."

"That's different," Mama said. "That was a miracle."

"Was the angel Gabriel a rooster?" I asked.

Mama smiled and shook her head."

"I don't understand that story at all," I said.

"Just listen," Mama said.

I could tell that Mama didn't want to talk about it by the way she sighed and shifted in her chair, but why was she reading it, if she didn't want to talk about it? It seemed to me that adults did that sort of thing quite often – bring up a subject and then refuse to talk about it. One thing was pretty clear. The Bible had some things to say about how babies got here and how I got here, so maybe I had better start reading the Bible on my own.

Mama was pleased to see me reading the Bible, although she didn't know why I was reading it. Genesis, the very first book in the Bible, gave some hints about how babies come to be, but they weren't clear to me at all. "Lay" was one of the clue words. Some man by the name of Shechem took some woman by the name of Dinah and "lay with her." Is that what makes babies? If lying down with a girl or woman makes babies, then I would never lie down with my sister, Mildred, again – not even on the lawn in the front yard. Even especially in the front yard. What if she had a baby right there in our yard facing Atlantic Boulevard in front of the whole world?

Another word in the Bible was "know." In the fourth chapter of Genesis it said, "And Adam knew Eve his wife; and she conceived, and bare Cain . . ." So that's how babies came. You had to know someone. Well, that seemed pretty obvious. You wouldn't just lie down with a total stranger. You'd have to know them first. There must be some missing pieces to the puzzle, but I didn't know what they were. Why did everyone have to be so secretive?

The most bewildering information of all came from a trip I made with Mama to downtown Los Angeles to visit a "home for unwed mothers." The home was sponsored by one of the radio evangelists that Mama listened to every day. Mama had no money to give, but her heart was touched, so she resolved to bake some cookies and deliver them to the home in person. Having no choice, she took me along with her.

The building was old and in a run-down section of the city. It was cold, dark and smelled of disinfectant. By keeping my eyes and ears open, I gathered lots of clues to the mystery of birth, but none of them made any sense; they only added to my confusion.

I saw several other ladies with big bellies, so I got the idea that having babies made you enormously fat. That story about eating too many potatoes was just a big fib. I saw a lot of ladies with babies, too, but Mama and the evangelist talked in voices barely above a whisper, so I gathered that there was something shameful going on here. Why were all these women living together in this big old building? Where were their husbands? Were they all virgins visited by the rooster Gabriel? Why would anybody want to have a baby in this big, old, broken-down building rather than at home, like where I was born?

"What does 'un-wed' mean, Mama?" I asked.

"It means that these girls aren't married. They don't have husbands."

"If they don't have husbands, are they virgins? Like Mary?"

"No dear, they're not virgins," Mama said, trying to avoid the discussion by opening her purse and looking for something that I suspected didn't exist. "They just don't have husbands."

"Then if they don't have husbands and the Angel Gabriel didn't visit them, how come they're having babies?" I persisted.

"Don't worry about it. You'll understand it all someday," Mama said.

It was the answer I always got from grown-ups. How would I ever know if they never answered my questions? I felt dumb. It was an adult secret that I was supposed to figure out all by myself. When I got smart enough to know the answer, then I would be an adult. It was a maddening sort of game like "twenty questions" that I played with my brother and sister sometimes. Grown-ups dropped little hints, but it was up to me to figure out how I got here from the hints they gave. Would I ever grow up? I pictured myself getting married and never knowing how to have babies.

If these "unwed" ladies were all having babies without husbands, maybe just loving someone wasn't enough. After all, the rooster wasn't exactly loving that hen when he was putting the chicken inside the egg. Maybe somebody jumped on top the these ladies and beat them up like the rooster did to the hen. But how did the baby get inside the woman? It had something to do with men and something that the ladies weren't at all proud of. Mama didn't want to talk about it, so I was left with my picture of a man sitting on top of a lady, rooster style, and making the feathers fly.

For years I wrestled with the problem, fitting one clue with another, trying various combinations of what I had learned in winks and whispers. Nothing seemed logical. When the truth did come, it was not from my parents, or my sister, or my brother, or my teachers, or the radio evangelist, or even the Bible. It came from that universal lodge of schoolboys who struggle with the day-in-day-out, difficult task of growing up. We huddled in our underground cave which we had dug in the vacant lot just west of Atlantic Boulevard. A single candle glowed in the center of the circle while we smoked hand-fashioned cigarettes made from ruled paper and pencil shavings. We repeated the ribald stories overheard from our elders, pretending to understand what made them funny and trying desperately to pass the invisible barrier into adulthood.

"Well, I know where babies come from," said one of the boys. The sly grin on his face was clear evidence of his inside information. "And I know what a guy has to do to a girl."

"So do I," rose in a chorus from the gathered brotherhood, no one wishing to acknowledge his ignorance.

"I don't think you really know," I said, testing. "Whisper it to me so I know that you know."

"Well, a guy has to take his . . ." He leaned over and whispered the dark secret into my ear. The dim candlelight danced along the earthen walls of the cave as all fell silent, trying to overhear the hushed words of his disclosure. My eyes widened in fascination. He was telling the truth. I knew it because no one could dream up such an unthinkable process on his own. Suddenly, everything seemed answered like finding the final clue in a riddle – Adam knew Eve, virgins, unwed mothers, fat ladies and even the rooster and the flying feathers.

"Yeah," I said. "You know it, all right."

The secret information was shared about the circle. Most said that they knew it already, but some of their remarks showed otherwise.

"That's nasty!" the youngest member said.

"I would never do that," volunteered another.

We sat in the circle, drawing on our acrid, pencil-shaving cigarettes, silently digesting the truth we had just been told. If it was factual, and I had no reason to doubt it, then it meant that this was what Papa had done to Mama, not once, but three times, since there were three of us children. As preposterous as it might seem, I knew it was how I came to be.

CHAPTER 5

SWEATER GIRL

"Distrust any enterprise that requires new clothes."

-Henry David Thoreau

"Who's that working out in our backyard?" I asked Papa.

"Some poor fella out of a job," Papa said. "I put him to work chopping weeds. Told him if he'd work for a couple of hours, I'd give him enough to at least buy a meal for his family."

"Why is he out of a job?" I asked.

"The depression we're in. Lots and lots of people don't have jobs these days. He used to work in a bank, but the bank had to let him go."

"Will you ever be out of a job, Papa?"

"Not likely. They'll always need teachers." Papa didn't want to worry me by telling me that there were already 200,000 teachers out of work and 2000 schools in the country couldn't afford to open. Papa scowled then. "Just because I have a job doesn't mean we can throw money around, mind you. We have to be very careful how we spend what we've got. Money doesn't grow on trees." That last little cliche was one I had heard often and would continue to hear for a long time to come. I didn't think we were poor, but we saved everything: string, rubber bands, tinfoil and even the card boards in cereal boxes so that we could put them in our shoes when the soles got holes in them. But then, everybody I knew scrimped in the same way. Thrift was more than a social quirk in the early 1930's, it was synonymous with patriotism and essential to survival. The lean days of that time surely affected Papa's penny-pinching ways, but they didn't explain his taste in clothes.

Papa was no couturier. He leaned – nay, leaped – toward the practical and utilitarian rather than the stylish. Since he was the sole purchaser of clothing for the Rees household, our appearance ran to the frumpy. He bought clothes only when he thought we needed them and then shopped exclusively at the Bankrupt Stock Liquidators in downtown L.A. Bullocks or May Company Department Stores were just not his style. You could always get bargains at the Liquidators and, if nothing else, Papa was a bargain hunter. Not only did he buy at mark down prices, he bought in quantity as well. Bulk was always cheaper. That meant if women's cotton house dresses were on sale, buying two or three was better than buying one. No matter that they all had the same cut and sported pink flamingos all around. Style was unimportant. Price and quantity were what mattered. We had plenty of trunks and storage space along with enough moth balls to rid the city of moths forever.

Mama never had ten cents to spend on her own wardrobe. I'm sure that she complained about that and it is probably one of the many subjects for the turbulent arguments which occurred every Saturday morning with the regularity of the sunrise. I didn't keep notes on the topics of these shouting matches. They tended to ramble from one theme to another anyway. My own stance was to simply accept what could not be changed. Papa was the unquestioned quartermaster for our little battalion of stalwarts and to complain would be as pointless as rafting down the dry Los Angeles River bed. Papa's tenacious hold on the family income was unyielding and cloaked in secrecy. I learned the hard way about the secrecy part. Papa wanted no one in the family to be privy to his financial affairs and most certainly he wanted no one outside our buttressed walls to learn of his credits and debits.

It was the summer of 1933 when I stumbled onto a veritable treasure trove of material for my world of make believe. Papa had dumped several months worth of check stubs out onto the trash pile in our backyard. I found them before the flames of the bonfire did. With creative abandon, I invited my friends over to "play banker," freely tearing out the stubs and distributing them liberally in the yard, up and down the street, across the neighbors' front yards to waft in the breeze to unknown destinations. After all, they were just trash, weren't they? Why not use them creatively. As a result, most of the neighbors knew Papa's bank balances better than the members of our own family. When Papa discovered my transgression, the ensuing lecture was a loud and long lambast designed to correct my complete lack of judgement. The lesson I learned was, perhaps, not the one Papa intended to teach. Money took on a shameful face – something to be hidden and spoken of only in whispers. To show your bank balance was like dropping your pants in public. Nice people didn't do it. I knew nothing about money laundering in those days, but learned to believe that money was, at best, nasty business. "Filthy lucre" took on a whole new meaning for me.

Nasty or not, Papa was the family comptroller. About the only cash I ever actually saw was what Papa left in the milk bottle on the back porch for the milkman to pick up when he delivered the milk. That is not to say that Papa was not a good provider, but simply to point out that we never had a say in what was provided. The clothing we wore is a case in point. We all tended to look like museum pieces from the generation just past. My brother wore knickers long after they were no longer in vogue. Probably Papa had brokered a terrific deal on these knee-length remnants and purchased enough to carry over into the next century. This aberrant fashion statement did little for his self confidence, but what could he do? Papa guarded his purchasing prerogative like a pit-bull.

For my part, bib overalls were the costume of the day. What others might be wearing was of no consequence. Bib overalls were sturdy, practical, easy to wash – and cheap. The one other advantage was that I never had to choose what to put on in the morning. It didn't matter whether I was going to a party or a mud fight, bib overalls were all I had to wear. Long underwear completed the outfit. This serviceable undergarment, complete with pearl buttons and generous drop seat, provided no end of conversation opportunities among my playmates. No one I ever met among my circle of acquaintances even owned, let alone wore, a pair of long johns. This was Southern California, after all. If the temperature ever dropped into the forties, it made the headlines. Nevertheless, long underwear was my fashion for the fall, winter and spring. Papa, no doubt, had found half a truck load at a give-away price.

My sister, Mildred, suffered the most under our curious clothing curse. As a budding teenager, she was the most conscious of the inadequacies of our wearing apparel. Even in the hard times of the depression, girls her age had some variety in the outfits they wore to school. For Mildred, it was always the same, the changeless red sweater that had the durability of armor plating. You always knew who it was walking home from school, even at a distance. If the figure wore a bright red cardigan, it had to be Mildred.

It was fall, winter and spring – sweater weather – that Mildred hated the most. Her friends poked fun at that sweater which never seemed to wear out. When it became a little thin at the elbows, the next day it was as good as new again. It seemed miraculous.

"I'm not going to wear that darn sweater," Mildred fumed. It was the first football game of the season and Mildred was going to walk over to Moore Field with her friends.

"Now don't be silly, dear. You'll get cold before the game's over," Mama said.

"I don't care if I freeze. I'm not wearing that sweater." Mildred's black eyes were ablaze with defiance.

"I know you don't like it," Mama said, "but it's the only one you've got. Maybe you'll get a new one at Christmas time. A different color."

"Hah! Fat chance! I thought I had worn this one out a year ago – a hole in the pocket and two buttons missing. So what did I get for my birthday? The same sweater all over again – same cut, same weave, same ugly red – just a size larger. The school colors are blue and gold, Mama, not red. I wouldn't be caught dead in this old red rag of a sweater."

"Try to understand, dear. Papa means well. It's a good, serviceable sweater and it will keep you warm. That's the main thing."

"It's not the main thing, Mama. That's just what it is not. The main thing is that it's ugly and red and my friends never see me in anything else. I look like an idiot. That's the main thing. Don't you understand?"

"I do understand, dear," Mama said, "but I can't do anything about it. Maybe you could wear your yellow scarf or something to make it look a little different."

"Oh, Mama. There isn't anything I can do to make it look different! The guys at school have started making jokes about it. One of them calls me 'red' all the time because of it. As soon as I get to school, I ditch it in my locker, so why wear it in the first place? I hate it."

"Well," Mama sighed, "I guess you'll just have it put up with it. It's the only sweater you have and I don't want you catching cold. Just ignore what people say and try to have a good time at the game."

Mildred went to the game all right, but I had a sneaking suspicion that if I went out and looked, I'd find her red sweater stuffed under the red berry bush in the front yard.

Mildred fretted out the year with her red sweater and now it was Christmastime. Christmas morning dawned clear and bright under the Southern California sun. The tree in our front room, as always, was decorated by Papa, a tall scraggly evergreen wrapped in silver tinsel as though it might escape unless it were bound tightly. Unlike other households, there were presents piled high under the tree. Santa had been good to us, even in depressed times. The "presents" ran to the practical – tooth paste, shoe polish, that sort of thing – but it was still exciting, even though we knew that Santa gave only "useful" gifts. By this time, we all new that "Santa" was really Papa and so we directed our appreciation in his direction.

"And here's one for Mildred," Papa said, laying a brightly wrapped package in her lap. Mildred carefully undid the paper, folding it to use for next Christmas. As she lifted the lid to the box, the unmistakable odor of moth balls filled the living room. She slowly lifted out another red sweater for all to see.

"How nice," Mama said, as though repeating lines from a rehearsed play. "You really needed that, didn't you dear?"

Even at eight years old, I could recognize the dark glaze of disappointment that clouded her eyes. "Thank you, Papa," she said. "I really needed that."

CHAPTER 6

SOMEPLACE TO HIDE

"What! Must I hold a candle to my shames?"

-William Shakespeare

"The Merchant of Venice"

The world looked a whole lot safer, more secure, from under the bed, but even then, sometimes I wanted to turn myself into a dust ball and disappear altogether. I would hide there whenever the doorbell rang. Down under the springs, I could escape from strangers who wanted to sell us things, and from the doctors who wanted to hook weights to my head and feet and stretch out my backbone and I could escape from Papa.

Mama used to explain to people that I was shy. She said that was the reason I hid under the bed, but that wasn't it at all. "Shy" was too weak a word. "Shy" meant a mild uneasiness about unfamiliar faces, but to me it was a lot more intense than that. I was scared. I was both scared and ashamed, but maybe shame was the strongest feeling I had.

For one thing, I knew that I could never be what Papa wanted me to be. I couldn't understand pi squared or speak Spanish and I had a zig-zag spine. I was the imperfect member of the family and Papa couldn't stand imperfection. Not that I wasn't loved, mind you, but it was the kind of love that you give to a broken teapot when you can't exactly throw it away, but you know it will never be handsome or useful again, so you stick it on the shelf and put a flower in it.

Papa was not a tall man, but he made up for his abbreviated size with bluster, the way a bantam rooster does. When he walked through the house, he never stepped softly, but thundered like a locomotive crossing a trestle, rattling the dishes and making the furniture bounce about on the floor. When Papa entered a room, everything else got sucked out except tension and the odor of the bay rum that he used for shaving lotion. He had a sense of humor, but only used it when company came, as though it might be wasted on the rest of us.

I was ashamed not only of myself, but I was ashamed of Papa, too, most of the time. Not because of the way he looked, although that was pretty funny sometimes, with sleeve garters to hold up his oversized sleeves and colored yarn tied around his fingers and toes to keep them from cracking, but the way he acted. The Chow dog that once bit my leg seemed to have a sweeter personality than he did.

Because of Papa, we were never on good terms with the neighbors. One day, when Papa went on a wild rampage, Mister Hooper, who lived two doors down, stepped in to quiet Papa and stop him from killing somebody. Papa was waving his .38 around out in the front yard, threatening to kill Mama or himself. Today, most people would call the police, but there was no 911 in those days. I was glad that Mister Hooper stepped in. To me, it seemed a reasonable thing to do, but from then on, Hooper became "the old fossil."

Widow Doyle, next door, killed a chicken and threw the head into our yard for our three cats to devour. Papa told her in words unprintable that our yard was not her garbage dump. From then on, Widow Doyle wouldn't speak to us and stopped sharing the Sunday funnies with us. I didn't miss the Widow Doyle so much, but I sure missed "The Katzenjammer Kids" and "The Toonerville Trolley."

Mrs. Simon, on the other side of us, would speak to Mama, but not Papa. That's because she heard him tell Mama to go to hell once and took it as a personal assault against all women.

The Shannons, down on the corner, wouldn't have anything to do with us either because Papa told their kid, Bertram, to stay away from our house. Bertram had punched me in the nose and knocked me into a drainage ditch once. After I got the mud out of my ears and nostrils, Bert and I were good friends again, but that didn't settle it with Papa. I think that if I had broken Bert's nose and won the fight, everything would have been all right, but since I lost, Bert was forever banished to the other side of Atlantic Boulevard. Papa could not abide the defeat of anyone with the name Rees.

From under the bed, I used to watch Papa sometimes, the light bouncing off his bald head, his generous lower lip protruding like a bulldog's, and think that he was the smartest, most talented, most two-fisted man on the face of the earth. He was also as cold as an arctic winter and no more predictable than a California earthquake. That's why I was under the bed instead of on his lap.

Papa wasn't the only reason I hid under the bed. It seemed to me that our whole family stood out in the neighborhood like a cockroach on a table napkin. We were different from everybody else. The way we dressed was odd – Mama's frumpy dresses, my brother's knickers, my sister's never-ending red sweaters, my bib overalls and long underwear –nobody else dressed quite like we did. On top of that, we kids all had the same haircuts – the inverted bowl, Oriental style. Papa cut each head of hair with such circular precision that it looked like he had used a compass with the pivot planted squarely in the centers of our skulls and a razor at the end of the radius to inscribe the circumference.

I would never have admitted to being ashamed of Mama, although I could see as plainly as anyone that she was different from other women. Her shapeless, old dresses hung like windless sails on her tired body and added ten years to her looks. She did the best she could with the dresses Papa brought home to her, but they were drab and outdated. Her hair was graying fast and she kept it swept back in an unflattering bun punched together with bone hairpins. She bulged in some places where other women didn't bulge and looked pale and drawn all the time. Her nails were split like rotten wood and the ends of her fingers were cracked and stained in a criss-cross pattern.

Mama's religion was something else that set her apart. Papa didn't believe in church – at least not when I knew him. He believed in a man named Darwin and said that the Bible was just a collection of stories and fairytales that were full of lies and contradictions. That's why we never went to church as a family.

But Mama was a believer. She tuned in to every radio evangelist from each station that had enough kilowatts to get through our Philco. The Bible was more than just a collection of stories; it was a guidebook for the future as well as the past and every word of it was to be literally believed. Perhaps because she had no job, no bank account and no money, she believed in streets of gold and gates of giant pearl. Perhaps because there was so little justice here, she believed there had to be justice somewhere. While she hunched over the wooden bowl chopping coleslaw or bent over the ironing board ironing Papa's shirts, she believed in heavenly rewards because there were so few here on earth. As she battled to stay on her feet through her own incessant hemorrhaging and tried to cope with my illness as well, she believed that Jesus might come and take her away tomorrow. That's how she got through the day. Because Mama believed, I believed too, but I was ashamed that I couldn't out argue Papa about religion. Sometimes I wished that I could be like some of my brother's or

36

sister's friends – Methodist, or even Catholic. They didn't speak in tongues or clap their hands when they sang hymns, they didn't believe that the world would end any time soon and they didn't plead for money the way Mama's evangelists did.

Part of the fuel for my shame was the constant tension between Papa's intense desire to be known as the first in the neighborhood with new inventions and also his fierce frugality. The two inconsistencies seemed to make us the oddest family in the whole city. We had an electric lawnmower, but no telephone; an electric phonograph with a record changer, but only an old treadle sewing machine; the best equipped and only gymnasium in town, but no bicycle.

That's not exactly true. We had a bicycle, but it was an antique. I should have been proud of it, but wasn't, primarily because of the laughter it aroused from the kids who saw me ride it. The bike had been in the family for a long time. Papa and my Uncle Clayton had built it themselves for my Aunt Mildred many years ago. The bicycle was a "girl's" bike, of course. That was the first strike against it, as far as I was concerned. The back wheel sported a wooden fender with a fancy skirt guard made from heavy twine. It had old-fashioned cork handle grips and a narrow, leather seat with an oblong hole right in the middle of it. I never could figure out why the hole was there, unless it was to accommodate the rider's flatulence. That's what my friends said it was and howled in derision.

The biggest drawback to the bicycle was that it had no coaster-brake. In fact, it had no brakes at all. My Aunt Mildred, for whom it was made, rode it and survived into adulthood. It was passed on to my brother, who learned to ride on it and he, too, survived. It then went to my sister. She rode it and lived to tell about it also. Then it came down to me. I was not permitted to attend public school until I reached the ninth grade because the rough-and-tumble of the school-yard might do injury to my crooked spine, but I could ride out into the world on a bicycle with no brakes. I never questioned this inconsistency, nor did anyone else in the family. Papa simply could not afford to buy a new bicycle.

A favorite pastime among my friends and me, during those adventurous years when we were eleven or twelve, was to take our bicycles up to the top of the Granada Park hill in Alhambra, push off from the brink and see if we could exceed the speed of sound. The road was not paved and was deeply rutted by the roots of trees and Southern California rain storms, but this only added to the challenge. Even with the sturdy tires and efficient brakes on the new bikes of my friends, it was hazardous enough, but on the antique contraption under my legs, it was an absolute flirtation with death.

I might have stayed at home, left the shameful machine parked in the garage and crawled under the bed again, but my longing for adventure exceeded my feeling of humiliation. Time after time, I hauled the primitive bone-shaker to the top of the hill, straddled the ventilated leather seat, spread my legs wide to clear the spinning pedals, and flew down the ruts and gullies like a tercel after a titmouse. The fact that I made these perilous runs with nothing more than abrasions and contusions is a testimony to the possibility of guardian angels. I survived. To my continued shame, so did the bicycle.

We always seemed to be way behind everyone else in the city as far as modern equipment was concerned. While other families had vacuum cleaners, for example, we took our rugs out to the clothes line and whaled away at them with brooms and wire beaters. Eventually, Papa bought a vacuum cleaner – a Eureka, which meant, "I have found it!" or so Papa said. It had been years, though, before Papa "found it," or felt we could afford our "Eureka." I rationalized it away. I knew that we didn't clean our carpets quite as often as the neighbors, but what did it matter? Who would get down on their hands and knees to examine the dirt in our carpet? Besides, none of the neighbors ever came into our house anyway.

As the great depression began to lose its grip on the country and the calendar edged toward the forties, an increasing number of salesmen came to our door, despite the large sign which read, "No solicitors or agents." These salesmen (there were never any women) hawked everything from Fuller Brushes to encyclopedias. We never bought anything from them, because Mama didn't have any money, but she was always courteous enough to answer the door and she liked to talk to them. I think it took her mind off her troubles and broke up the monotony of the day. I knew that they only made money when they completed a sale, but she examined each product as though the salesman made a commission just by discussing the virtues of the product.

One day two men came by selling vacuum cleaners – not the Eureka brand – and offered to give Mama a "free demonstration." She told them that we had just had the carpets out for a beating, so there couldn't be much dirt left in them. They smiled in their most friendly way and assured her that it didn't matter. They could prove to her that their machine was powerful enough to pull out dirt that she didn't suspect was there. She had nothing to lose because it was all "free."

It was the "free" part that finally persuaded her. What could she lose by having these nice young men come in and give her front-room carpet a free cleaning? She wiped her hands on her apron and opened the door to let them in.

It seemed like a mistake to me – strangers coming into our house – seeing the way we lived – looking at the clutter piled everywhere – noticing the furniture that didn't match and the holes in the knees of my overalls. They were aliens from another world – the world of normal people who had telephones and vacuum cleaners and didn't listen to radio evangelists begging for money. I sat against the wall away from the carpet, folding my arms against this invasion of our privacy.

The younger man of the two removed his suit coat and looked for a place to lay it.

"Just put it over the back of the morris chair," Mama said. Other mothers might have offered to hang it in the closet, but I knew that all of our closets were full to the ceiling and it would be impossible to hang anything in any of them.

The older man kept his coat on and began telling of the wonders of his machine while the younger man hunted for an electrical outlet. I pointed to one. The man smiled at me like I was a trained animal and plugged in the cord.

The machine roared to life, its canvas bag ballooning out from the handle like it might explode. The young man pushed the vacuum back and forth over the carpet with one hand. He looked like a dancer with a mechanical partner. He obviously enjoyed his work while the older man shouted above the noise, telling Mama about horsepower, suction and electric motors.

Finally the racket ceased and the older man lowered his voice to a mellow, medical kind of tone, explaining to Mama the importance of cleanliness and sanitation in the home. I felt like we were natives in the presence of patronizing missionaries. To my horror, while the older man continued his condescending lecture on hygiene, the younger man unhooked the bag from the back of the cleaner and dumped the contents out in the middle of the carpet. Mama's eyes grew large, but she didn't complain. After all, the demonstration was free. I noticed that Mama's right shoulder began to rotate in a slightly circular motion, the way it did when she became agitated.

The pile of dirt in the center of the rug was impressive; more than enough to fill the grass catcher on Papa's lawnmower. How could that much dirt remain in a rug we had beaten until it was nearly threadbare? While the older man lectured, the younger man took a small whisk-broom and spread the ugly heap in an ever-widening circle, as a child might do with sand at the beach.

"You don't want your family to live in this kind of dirt, do you?" The salesman looked at Mama with the accusing eyes of a government health inspector. "You don't want your precious little boy playing on a carpet that hides this kind of dirt . . . "

Precious little boy? I hunched my shoulders and shrank against the wall.

"Think of the germs, the disease, the sickness that lurks out of sight just beneath the surface of your rug." The man leaned forward to emphasize the filth of our house while the younger salesman drew his whisk-broom over the gray mass spreading out before him.

"All that you say is true," Mama said, "but we just don't have any money at present."

"What is money compared to the health of your family?" the man asked.

"Nothing, of course, but . . ." Mama was stammering and I could see the moisture in her eyes. Shame welled up within me again. We were poor, we were dirty, I was sick, too, and it was probably all because of the dirt in the rug. There it was, all in front of us, a big, flat circle of grit deep enough to plant radishes – although who would want to plant radishes in such foul stuff?

"We can manage the finances," the man said. "Think of your family. Just think of your children."

They were torturing Mama. She loved me. I knew that for a fact. She loved us all, but she had no money. Get out of here, I wanted to scream, but I just watched the younger man making designs in the pile of gray dust.

"I can't buy it just now," Mama said. "I want to. It's really a good machine I like it but you have to understand. I really don't have the money for it now."

"How can you live on top of dirt like this?" the younger man broke in.

"Maybe later," Mama said. "Later. Yes, I'm sure later but not just now."

I couldn't take it. I felt naked before the world. These ugly men were exposing our filthiness – our dirt – before the whole universe. I ran to the sleeping porch at the back of the house. I could still hear them talking. Talking, talking, talking! Would they never leave us alone?

At last I heard the front door close and Mama's footsteps coming closer. She got down on her hands and knees by the bed and peered under.

"You can come out now," she said. "They're gone."

I looked from under the bed-springs into her brown eyes.

"You'll have to help me roll up the carpet and take it out," she said. "We'll have to be careful not to spill all that dirt they left. And then you'll have to beat the carpet again."

I did. Oh yes, I did. I put both hands to the broom and swung with all my might. "Take that!" I screamed. "And that! And that!" Clouds of dust exploded into the air with every swat of the broom. "You dirty bums!" I yelled. "Call my Mama dirty, will you? Take that!"

CHAPTER 7

THE DAY THAT MAMA SCREAMED

Peter, Peter Pumpkin-Eater
Had a wife and couldn't keep her.
He put her in a pumpkin shell,
And there he kept her very well.

-Mother Goose

Mama saved things. Everybody saved things during the depression – string, rubber bands, tinfoil. But Mama went beyond saving what everybody else saved. For Mama, everything came to have value: empty spools, butter wrappers, avocado pits, egg shells even cardboard bottle caps. "I can plant something in that," she'd say, holding up an empty soup can like it was a Grecian urn, or "That probably belongs to something important," she'd say about some odd shaped piece of metal with a hole in it. It was quite clear that Mama couldn't tell the difference between treasure and trash.

She had no organized way of storing the things she saved, so they simply piled up on any empty surface at hand or any dark space with a door on it. Soon every shelf, cupboard and closet was stacked high and deep with what any sane person would call garbage. Even Mama's bedroom was not spared from the ever multiplying mounds of useless junk. After a while, she could not find her way to the bed and took to sleeping on the front room couch. The creeping debris in our house seemed to take on a life of its own, multiplying during the night like some odious phalanx of malevolent organisms.

Papa's complaint about Mama's poor housekeeping seemed reasonable to me. I was embarrassed by it, too. Who wants to invite a friend over when there isn't even a place to sit down? When Papa said we lived in a "pig-sty," he was pretty much right. In today's psychological lingo, Mama would, no doubt, be diagnosed as "obsessive compulsive." But even at ten years old, I didn't need a psychologist to tell me why Mama did what she did. I knew. It all started back before I was even born.

Mama's aforementioned trip to Brazil at the beginning of her marriage and the subsequent cross-country trip to California were episodes she never would have chosen for herself. She was simply given no choice. Papa was absolute captain of the ship and Mama was the crew. She cooked his meals, scrubbed and ironed his clothes, washed his dishes and took care of his children. It didn't seem so unusual at the time. That was the way families functioned.

But in addition to all this, Mama was poor. She was poor because Papa kept all the money. He was the only one wise enough to spend it the right way. That, I believed, was why Mama got into the habit of saving everything. She didn't have bus fare because Papa said she didn't need to go anywhere. She didn't have money to go to the beauty parlor because Papa said that was frivolous. Whatever we were, we were not frivolous. She had no money for gifts to give to friends or relations because, if gifts were needed, Papa could go out to the garage and get something out of the moth-balled trunks. When it came time for my sister Mildred to get married, Mama wrote back to a cousin in the east and borrowed money for the wedding dress. To Papa, buying a wedding dress for his daughter was a senseless squandering of hard-earned money. Money was reserved for needs, not frivolity. Papa was rich; Mama was poor.

Sometimes Mama conducted her own private mutiny, like borrowing money for the wedding dress. Sometimes, too, I was co-conspirator in her schemes. After I had learned to walk again, at eight years old, Mama would bake cookies with coconut frosting and little jellybeans on the top. Steeling myself against the temptation to eat them myself, I peddled these delicacies door to door to earn a few pennies for Mama's purse. It was a daring thing to do. I knew that if Papa ever found out about it, he would unleash a tornado of verbal violence followed by weeks of icy silence. Sometimes Mama and I shelled walnuts from our big tree in the backyard, packaged them in small bags and sold them for a nickel apiece. At times, I would sneak raisins out of our pantry, wrap them in wax paper, and sell them at a fraction of what Papa paid for them. The neighbors were always glad to get them. Keeping some dimes and nickels in Mama's purse was always a challenge for her and for me. I was painfully aware that no one else saved old cereal boxes and stale bread crusts, but at the same time, I understood why she did it.

Papa used more than drying up the money supply to keep Mama trapped in her own house. Getting rid of the ice-man is a case in point. Every other day or so, the ice-man came to deliver our twenty five pounds of ice. He would lope up the back steps, the dripping block of chiseled ice flung over his shoulder and announce in a loud voice, "Ice-man!" before he entered through the back door. His entrance was not unusual. Our house was no different from other houses on the block. This was the way he stepped into every kitchen. It was a more trusting age, and the ice-man was expected and welcomed. Once inside, the young man smiled and exchanged a few pleasantries with his customers. Mama would usually be standing by the sink peeling potatoes or shelling peas when the ice-man entered. Their meeting and conversation was as chaste as the ring of a church bell, but for Mama this was one of the few fresh touches with the outside world that was permissible. For Papa, it grew into a serious invasion of his domain. Thus, we were one of the first families in the city to buy a Kelvinator refrigerator. Under the pretext of securing avant-garde electrical equipment, Papa got rid of the ice-man forever. While I liked the idea of owning the only refrigerator in the neighborhood, I knew I would miss the friendly banter of the ice-man and especially the refreshing ice chips he let me glean from his truck.

While Mama had no opportunity for male companionship outside the family, Papa felt at liberty to enjoy female companionship. Mama made no attempt to hide from us children those times when he went up to our mountain cabin to be with one of the secretaries at the school where he taught. At the time, I had no understanding of the deep mysteries of sexual liaisons. I presumed that he went up in the hills to get away from our "pig-sty" and have conversation with one of his fellow workers. From appearances, Mama wasn't resentful. In fact, during those absences, there was a sense of relief which came over all of us. Perhaps if there had not been a friendly secretary available, Mama might have supplied one just to get Papa out of the house.

When Papa and Mama were not yelling at each other, they were not speaking to each other. Sometimes the deafening silence would go on for weeks at a time. The noiseless anger was almost worse than the yelling. We had ceased eating together as a family long ago. Papa ate in his room. Mama, of course, had to take his meal to him, or else send Mildred or me to carry in the plate before the food got cold.

Papa's room was sealed off from the rest of the house by an invisible wall of fear and secrecy. The door was always closed when he was inside. The room was filled with radio tubes, resistors, wires and electrical gadgets of all sorts, to say nothing of the books, office supplies, cameras, developing chemicals and a bottle of port wine hidden on the top shelf of the "dark room" closet where he developed photographs. Everyone in the family knew where he kept the port wine, but no one dared to shatter his delusion of concealment. A casual observer might consider that his private quarters were the habitat of some mad scientist. The truth is, these unusual accouterments were merely accessories to his hobbies: radio, electronic research, photography and science. The wine, of course, was kept for "medicinal purposes."

I dreaded taking his dinner to him. When it was my turn, I was filled with all of the angst of a criminal approaching the judge's bench. To burst into the room unannounced would be a cardinal sin. Each of us children, and even Mama, must stand outside the door and knock, waiting for his growled "Come in," before entering.

"Here's your supper, Papa," I would say and then scoot back to the kitchen before he could answer. He didn't believe in opening a window, so his room always smelled like the inside of my Keds. I never wanted to linger.

Mama's pleasures were simple and widely spaced. She could play the piano, but had no time for it. Once in awhile she would sit down at the piano and play the whimsical ditty, "Today Is the Day They Give Babies Away With a Half a Pound of Tea" just for the entertainment of her children, but most of the time the piano stood as a silent reminder of past melodies and vanished leisure. There were other hints of former creativity as well. Mama was a painter of fine china and pastel landscapes, but now there was no time and no money for such luxuries. If she could sit down for a few minutes in our old morris chair and sip a cup of cambric tea, it seemed to be enough to sustain her. Much of the time she was even too busy for that.

A good part of the hard labor which kept Mama exhausted was a result of my illness. Five of the first eight years of my life were spent flat on my back staring at the ceiling while strapped to a Bradford frame or the cast that extended from my head to my thighs. This, for Mama, meant that I had to be lifted, carried, turned, exercised, fed, bathed, educated and entertained. She enlisted the help of my sister and brother, but when they were in school, it was all up to her. At the time, I had little appreciation for this unbearable drain on her physical and emotional energy. All I knew was that she was always there with gentle strength and inexhaustible love.

Mama was sick, too. Desperately sick. By the time I could walk again, somewhere around seven and a half years old, I knew that something was terribly wrong with Mama. She was pale, drawn and subject to fainting spells. What was worse, she was bleeding to death in some mysterious way that I could not understand. At times, while she was going about her chores, great splotches of blood would appear on the floor where she was standing. While I sat terrorized, Mama would stagger cross-legged to the bathroom, trailing blood all the way. She never would tell me why this happened, only that I must help her clean it all up before Papa came home. Papa must never know. I always felt guilty about these times, because it seemed such a shameful thing to Mama and I imagined that in some mysterious way, I was responsible for it. If I had not been born, Mama would not be as sick as she was – would not be bleeding to death. Somewhere deep inside her, I had broken something, torn something, that let loose an awful river of blood that was taking away her life. Fervently I scrubbed at the dark, red spots on the floor and carpet while Mama lay down on the couch. Papa would never know.

One morning I pulled the blanket over my head as I heard Papa shouting at Mama again. If I could just ignore it, he would have to go to work soon. Then it would be quiet again.

Before long, I heard the door slam and our 1928 Buick careening out the driveway in reverse gear. I tiptoed out to the kitchen.

"I'm sorry, Mama," I said.

Mama didn't answer, but stood by the kitchen sink staring at a piece of paper, tears splashing down like the blood sometimes did. I didn't know what to say, so I got my toy lead soldiers and brought them to the kitchen, arranging them in battle lines for a make-believe war. It was quiet, except for my own subdued imitations of exploding shells and battle cries.

I had never heard Mama scream in my whole life. She was too quiet, too reserved ever to scream. I supposed she would scream if cornered by a bear or chased by a bandit, but right in our own kitchen? With no one around but me? Never. I was dumbfounded when, without warning, Mama threw her head back and screamed a scream that sounded like it would shatter every window in the house. It was loud, long and steady. I was paralyzed by the piercing sound. When she stopped, she closed her eyes and hung her head like she had just finished the solo in an opera. I sat shivering on the floor. I wondered if the neighbors had heard. I wondered it the police had heard. I wondered if Papa had heard, wherever he was.

Finally I scrambled to my feet and ran to her side. "Mama, what's the matter?" I asked. She didn't answer me. I put my arm around her waist as I looked at the piece of paper she had been studying. It was the head of a devil with its tongue sticking out. Papa had drawn it. I knew that because he had signed it "Harry." There was no writing or message; just this ugly, little picture.

"Are you all right, Mama?" I asked.

"I'm angry," Mama said. "I'll be all right in a minute."

"You scared me."

"I'm sorry, dear. It'll be okay."

"Do you need to lie down on the couch?"

Mama ran her fingers through my hair and moved toward the stove. "No," she said. "I think I'll just fix myself a little cambric tea."

CHAPTER 8

THE CONDUCTOR

"Heaven is under our feet
as well as over our heads."

-Henry David Thoreau

Papa was mad. I could tell by the way he drove our 1928 Buick out of the driveway, zig-zagging backward like a marble in a pin-ball machine. Sometimes when he was mad at Mama, he stayed away for days at a time. Not that I cared, mind you. When he was gone, we got to go places and do things that we couldn't do when he was home, like riding the "Big Red Cars" of the inter-urban trolley.

Whenever Papa was gone, Mama took me down to hear Aimee Semple McPherson in Los Angeles. Aimee was a faith-healer and evangelist who had built a 5000-seat temple and a Bible School. She was a mesmerizing speaker and a "must see" attraction for tourists coming to Southern California. I was eight years old at the time, was free of my cast and had learned to walk again. I still had to wear a brace, which was a miserable meld of leather and rebar, but nonetheless, I could navigate on my own. I wasn't particularly religious, but I would endure both the brace and the Bible just to ride into L.A. on the trolley. Papa got mad often enough for us to make the trip six or eight times a year. On those special occasions,

Mama packed enough bread and peanut butter into a shopping bag to last the day and we walked the few blocks down to Midwick station, the small track-side shelter where the trolley stopped.

From the station platform, I could see far down the track and watch the massive red front of the trolley loom larger and larger like a beet-colored behemoth rising from a desert mirage. My chest swelled with pride and importance as I watched the long, three-car commuter train grind to a stop just for Mama, my sister and me. The conductor always stood at the top of the steel boarding steps like some uniformed captain of a sea-going vessel. He would hold out a hand to help Mama, but I would half crawl, half jump up those steps, intent on proving I could climb on board without assistance. If anyone ever asked me what I wanted to be when I grew up, I answered without hesitation – a train conductor.

I used to watch the conductor with eyes that hungered for heroes. He was as agile as a spider on a web and as confident as an army general at the head of a parade. While women and children grabbed seats or leather straps to steady themselves in the lurching car, the calm conductor walked the aisle of the pitching rail-car with legs immune to the swaying motion. He kept both hands free to punch tickets and ring fares while his feet seemed attached to the floor with separate springs. How could he remain so casual? It was a mystery. His image was an inspiration, dressed in a smart, black uniform with gleaming brass buttons and a visored cap cocked at a rakish angle with the word "conductor" spelled out in brass letters across the front. He had a silver change maker hooked to his belt and could calculate twenty five cents out of a dollar faster than I could say the words. The letters "P - E - R - Y" on his lapels meant something, but I didn't know what. Mama explained that they stood for, "Pacific Electric Railway."

The power and knowledge of this "King of the Rails" was

uncanny. Through a series of mysterious signals, he told the motorman when to stop, when to start and when to slow down. He knew by heart every stop along the way and had developed a resonant voice that made "Azusa" and "Cucamonga" sound like "The Casbah" and "Shangri-la." He could help a faltering passenger into the car, call out a destination and wave to a switchman all at the same time. His authority and control were total. The conductor's job was more than an occupation; it was high adventure.

The long ride out to Angelus Temple – Aimee's place – might have seemed tedious and boring to some, but it was the most exciting part of the day for me. The religion sessions that followed were the tiresome times. Mama may have thought that I was memorizing the books of the Bible while we were sitting there listening to Aimee, but actually I was trying to memorize all of the stops between Los Angeles and the little Midwick station where we lived. I figured that if I started learning them now, maybe I could call them all out by the time I was old enough to be a conductor.

While we were at Aimee's temple, they gave Mama an "anointed handkerchief." This was a small piece of white cloth, about the size of a square of toilet paper, with a splotch of olive oil in the middle. It wasn't nearly big enough to blow your nose on, so I didn't know why they called it a handkerchief, and I didn't know what the oil was for either. A magic potion of some sort, I supposed. The cloth seemed to be a souvenir – like a shell from the seashore – to show that you had been there. For Mama, it was much more than that. She held it to my back like it was a holy poultice with magic power that would create a backbone where none was.

The trip back home was even more exciting than the trip to the temple. We had to catch the last train out for the night. If we missed it, we would be stuck in downtown L.A. until the morning. That never happened. We always made it to the main terminal on time and Mama always saved out enough money for car fare – Aimee got the rest.

At night, the conductor was even more awesome. He had the eyes of a cat, peering into the black night and calling out each station along the way. If anything, he was more poised than in the daylight. He could lean against an empty seat, punch tickets, make change and whistle "Stormy Weather" without missing a beat.

One night, on our way back home, the conductor must have seen me staring at him, because he winked and then took a step closer. I felt something in my hand. It was a penny, shiny and new, still warm from his own hand. At that moment, I suffered from an agonizing mixture of pleasure and embarrassment. Just to be noticed by the conductor would have been quite enough, but to receive a gift was something like divine ordination. Mama prompted me to say "thank you," while I clutched the penny in my fist as though it might turn to mercury and vanish into thin air.

All too quickly, the ride on the crimson tram ended and Mama took my hand as I jumped off the bottom step of the trolley. My sister, Mildred, followed along behind. Mama and Mildred waited while I watched the swaying, red lights disappear into the Southern California night.

The next day, I walked down to Midwick station by myself. I wasn't supposed to do that without asking, but I had learned that sometimes, when you wanted to do something badly enough, it didn't pay to ask.

After checking to see that there was no one waiting for the train, I took the penny out of my pocket and placed it carefully on the rail. I knew that I wasn't supposed to do that. Papa had given me stern warnings and explained all the dangers of putting things on train tracks. Train wrecks had been caused by putting things on railroad tracks – even small objects. The train could be derailed – turn over – people could be killed –

we could all be sued and go to jail. But I didn't see how a little old penny could do all that. Mama only had told me that God was always watching me, but I didn't think that God would mind that much.

An hour or so probably passed, but it seemed like two, as I peered down the tracks seeking the first sign of the approaching trolley. The fear of being discovered did not ease my impatience. At last, I heard the familiar whistle and the crossing signal began its back-and-forth hula. I could see the square, red trolley loom larger as it bore down on the crossing. I stood well back from the track so that it would not stop for me and also so I could get a running start in case Papa had been right about causing a train wreck.

The giant, steel car flashed past in a red blur and I saw the conductor standing in the rear doorway, feet apart, hand raised in a wave. I waved back frantically, dancing a jig of delight. When the dust had cleared, I ran to the rail to retrieve my penny. There it was, thin as an egg shell and shiny as a mirror. The oblong image of Lincoln was still visible, only now he seemed to be smiling.

Papa came home that night. Mama didn't ask where he had been and Papa didn't ask where she had been, either. After some days of silence, the harsh words and raised voices began again. I seldom understood what was being said, because they talked about things from the past that happened before I was born, people I didn't know and places I'd never been.

Once, after there had been a lot of shouting, I found Mama in the pantry, surrounded by shelves loaded with cans of evaporated milk and boxes of rolled oats, with her "anointed handkerchief" spread out on her lap, just sitting there with her eyes closed.

"What are you doing, Mama?" I asked.

"Oh, just thinking about heaven, I guess," she said.

Thinking about heaven didn't mean much to me at the

time. I had trouble seeing streets paved with gold rather than asphalt, and I couldn't imagine big pearls for gates. But I thought I knew what Mama was doing.

Sometimes when Papa got mad and the voices got too loud for me, I would go out behind the wood pile in the backyard, pull out the flattened penney from my pocket and feel the smooth, oblong surface. Holding it there in my hand, I could hear the "clickety-clack" of the steel wheels on the rails while I walked the aisle of the "Big Red Car," in my black uniform, calling out, "El Monte, Azusa" and "Cucamonga."

CHAPTER 9

¡CANTAME UNA CANCIÓN, AMIGO!

*"Bitter poverty has no harder pang
than that it makes men ridiculous."*

-Juvenal

"You've got to quit scuffing the toes of your shoes," Mama said. I was cutting out inserts from the cardboard separators found in Shredded Wheat boxes in order to put them inside my shoes.

"I don't see why. The soles wear out first anyway, no matter how much I scuff the toes." I stuck my finger through the large hole of my right shoe and wiggled it back and forth.

"Don't do that," Mama said. "It makes the hole bigger."

That was all right by me. I hated the high-top leather shoes I had to wear. I wanted low-cut shoes like all the other kids had, but Papa said that high-top shoes kept my ankles straight. The sooner my shoes wore out the better. Maybe I would get to go barefooted for awhile.

The seriousness of the great depression had not hit me yet. I thought it might be nice to do without shoes. Papa had a job teaching at Roosevelt High School in Los Angeles while everyone else seemed to be out of work. I knew that other people were hungry and couldn't buy clothes, but not us. We were rich by comparison. So why go to all the trouble of cutting out cardboard insoles to make my shoes last longer? It seemed to have something to do with patriotism, whatever that was. If you loved your country, you saved string, plastered tinfoil together into a large, silver ball and cut out cardboard insoles for your shoes.

I was only four years old when the stock market crashed. I wasn't sure exactly what that meant, but it sounded like some big market in New York fell down to the ground. Had there been an earthquake? In California, we knew all about earthquakes. Anyway, it made everybody poor and Papa said that some people had lost so much that they jumped out of high buildings and died. That was something I couldn't imagine – jumping out of a high building just because you were poor. If I were poor, I'd eat walnuts off our tree three times a day, but I sure wouldn't jump off a building.

I was not quite eight years old when President Roosevelt closed all the banks and Congress passed the National Recovery Act. I didn't know what that was all about either, but windows and automobiles up and down our block had N.R.A. stickers in various sizes. Papa said it was to show that you were behind the president and wanted the depression to end. I had N.R.A. stickers all over my tricycle – I wanted a new pair of shoes.

The way I knew that we were in a depression was by the number of "bums" that came to our door for food. That's what Papa called them, so that's what I called them. Papa said they rode the freight cars and slept outside – they didn't have homes. They were usually dirty, scruffy looking and had their blankets tied with a belt and slung over their shoulders. They always came to the back door – never to the front – and asked Mama if she could spare a little something to eat. If Papa was home, he made them work for their meal, but Mama gave them something whether they worked or not.

"Why don't you invite him in?" I asked Mama, when she

had served one man a plate of corned beef hash out on the back steps by the cellar.

"Because we don't really know him," she said, "and it isn't safe to invite a stranger into the house. He might turn out to be a thief and rob you. A good, hot meal has the same vitamins whether you're inside or out."

From then on, I imagined that every "bum" had a knife or a gun hidden in his bed-roll. I didn't like the idea of having to ask for food, but other than that, being a bum sounded like an exciting life – almost like the pirates in the olden days. I had pictures of pirates on bubble-gum cards which I stashed away in a White Owl cigar box, along with extra N.R.A. stickers and various other treasures.

Word got around that there was food at our house, because more and more bums came to the door. I wondered if they marked our house in some way so that other bums would know where there was a free meal. They weren't all dirty looking, though. One man said he used to be a bookkeeper at a bank and needed money for food for his family. Papa put him to work chopping weeds in the backyard. We always had plenty of weeds to chop. He worked until noon and then stopped to eat. He asked Mama for some bandages for his hands because he had worked up several bad blisters. After Mama put salve on the blisters and tied strips of ripped-up sheets around his hands, he went out and worked all afternoon and again the next day.

Not everyone worked the way Papa told them to. Our house sat on two oversized lots with several fig trees, plum trees, a huge walnut tree and many shrubs – and lots of tall weeds. It was easy to hide out, if you wanted to. One day, one of the men that Papa sent out to chop weeds lay down in back of the wood pile and went to sleep. When Papa discovered him, he chased him over the fence with a hoe. That man didn't eat at our house that day and he never came back. I thought maybe he became a pirate and ran away to sea. That's what I would have done.

The scene that stands out most vividly in my memory is of the Mexican boy that came knocking at our front door one early summer evening. I say "Mexican" because that's what everyone called Spanish-speaking people in those days. I can't ever remember using the term "Hispanic" or "Mexican American" or "Latino." It didn't seem to matter that people might be born in America of Cuban or Puerto Rican parents; they were still "Mexicans." The impression I got was that Mexicans were somewhat American, but not completely. They had a skin darker than mine – although I usually had a pretty good tan – and they spoke with a distinct accent. "Mexican" meant that they really belonged somewhere else, even though they were here.

Papa answered the door that night and heard the Mexican boy's request. "May I sing for you, Señor?" he asked. "My father, he is out of work and my brothers and sisters, they have nothing to eat. I will sing for pennies. May I come into your house and sing for you? I dance, too, a little."

I was surprised when Papa said, "Si, amigo!" and opened the door. I was surprised, first of all, because we had company that night and Papa didn't like his social engagements interrupted. I was surprised, too, because Papa never would allow strangers into the house. Maybe it was because this stranger was so young. Maybe it was because Papa always welcomed the opportunity to show off his mastery of the Spanish language. Maybe it was because there was something about the boy's shabby appearance that bothered Papa. He didn't part with money easily. There had to be some tangible benefit in return – hoeing weeds, stacking firewood or washing windows. But singing? Never.

The Mexican boy entered the house and walked across the living room to stand by the Victrola. If he was nervous, his hands did not show it. They hung loosely at his side. If he was experiencing shame, he kept it hidden behind large, ebony eyes. I judged him to be about as old as my sister – maybe eleven or twelve – about three or four years older than I. He wore no shirt or shoes and his skin reminded me of tan velvet. The pants he wore had gaping holes at the knees like jagged, open mouths. Didn't he have a mother? Didn't she know how to sew on patches?

Perhaps what impressed me most was that he did not smile. It was as though his body was present with us, but his mind was in some far distant, more comfortable place. "I will sing for you, amigos," he said. "My first number will be, 'La Cucaracha.'"

I could not understand the words of the song, but I knew it was in Spanish – something about a cockroach. Papa nodded his head in time to the tune and smiled his approval. The Mexican boy did not look at me – or at anyone seated in front of him. His dark eyes looked over our heads – out the window – as though he were singing to a crowd in some large, distant auditorium.

When he finished the first verse, Papa clapped enthusiastically, and our company followed his example. Without a break, the boy resumed his singing and shuffled his bare feet on the hardwood floor in a silent sort of tap-dance. It reminded me of the loose jointed, wooden, Negro doll that I had, which was glued to the end of a stick. When I jiggled the stick, the doll danced in time to whatever tune I might sing. Negroes like to dance, Papa told me. They have a natural rhythm in their blood. I thought it must be nice to be so happy with life that you danced all the time. Mexicans must be like that, I was thinking. Here was this dusty-skinned boy dancing in rags and bare feet. But was he happy? He didn't seem happy to me. There was no enthusiasm in his shuffling feet and no smile on his face. Did he pretend to be a happy dancer, like I pretended to be a cowboy sometimes? Did he sing about cockroaches because he had so many in his kitchen, or did he sing only for the pennies?

The Mexican boy finished his dance and threw his arms into the air like two exclamation points. "Bravo!" Papa said. "¡Bueno! ¡Bueno!" The boy's mouth stretched into a grin like a rubber-band and quickly snapped back again. The small audience in our living room applauded and Papa threw him a nickel.

The boy caught it in mid-air. "¡Gracias, amigo!" he said. Papa threw him another nickel. It rolled under the curved legs of the Victrola and the boy quickly scrambled for it. Two nickels. I was surprised at Papa's generosity. Our visiting guests didn't throw any money at the boy. Two nickels would buy two loaves of bread or pay my way to a Saturday matinee. I thought maybe I could memorize the Spanish words to "La Cucaracha," if Papa would give me a nickel every time I sang it. But I didn't think he would do that.

Maybe I could go door to door like the Mexican boy. Maybe I could be a great entertainer and get rich. But the Mexican boy certainly wasn't rich, and there was something of a sad disgrace in his large, dark eyes. Would I stand before a group of total strangers and shuffle my bare feet on the hardwood floor for their amusement? Would I sing about cockroaches for a nickel – even fifty cents?

"¡Gracias, amigos!" The boy bowed from the waist and headed for the door. The room full of people waved goodbye.

"Just a minute," I whispered to him. I raced back to the closet in the laundry room where I had my treasures hidden. I reached for the White Owl cigar box, half filled with marbles, bottle caps and pirate cards, and pulled out an N.R.A. sticker. I ran back to the front door and handed it to him.

"Here," I said. "It's for you. Put it on your window. President Roosevelt will end the depression and you can get some shoes."

The Mexican boy looked at it and twisted his lips into a half smile. He stuffed the sticker into his pocket and said, "Gracias."

The next day, Mama gave me two more pieces of cardboard from a Shredded Wheat box. "These will make good insoles for your shoes," she said.

"I know, Mama." I took off my shoe, placed it on the cardboard and carefully traced around the sole with a pencil.

CHAPTER 10

PROPHECIES

"A hopeful disposition is not the sole
qualification to be a prophet."

-Winston Churchill

You couldn't be a Gypsy until after dark, at least that's what my sister, Mildred, said. I had never met a Gypsy, but Mildred said a real Gypsy could read fortunes and tell the future. That's pretty heady stuff for an eight year old. She dressed up like one so that I would know a Gypsy if I ever met one on the street – red and gold silk shawl with fringe around the edges, a purple scarf on her head and tons and tons of beads and rings and heavy rouge. Some Gypsies had crystal balls that they could look into to see the future, but she didn't have one. Instead, she opened up your hand and saw all kinds of things from the criss-cross lines that ran from your fingers to your wrist.

Mildred was practicing for the school carnival where she was going to run the fortune-teller booth. At first she tried an upside down mixing bowl for a crystal ball, but it just didn't look real enough, so she decided to use a candle planted in the middle of a card table and read palms instead of a crystal ball. The candle made eerie, dancing shadows on the blankets she had strung up on wires. I could see why you couldn't be a real

Gypsy until after dark.

I didn't really believe that my very own sister could tell your fortune, but I believed that some people could. My brother, Raymond, said it was all hokum, but what did he know? He was in college and college made you doubt everything. That's what Mama said, and so I decided I wasn't ever going to college. What would life be without spirits, ghosts and fortune tellers? Besides, the future was sometimes revealed to members of our own family. If my sister got older and wiser, maybe even she could tell what was going to happen before it actually happened.

My Grandmother, Elvina Peet Rees, could foretell the future. She had done it. Maybe not more than once, but if you're a fortune teller, you only need one convincing demonstration to convince the world that you can do it. It's sort of like a baseball player that strikes out twelve times in a row, but if he hits a game-winning home run, that's all anyone remembers. Grandma's "home run" was rehearsed for years at family gatherings or any time anyone would listen.

Grandma was old and shriveled, but very wise. She could also do astounding physical tricks like making her teeth fall from the roof of her mouth at will. Try as I might, I could never do that. It was no surprise to me, then, to learn of her uncanny ability to read tea leaves. Sometimes she would show me the bottom of her teacup, bestrewn with wet tea leaves like some abstract art, and explain the strange and wonderful things that she saw – faces and ships, animals and castles, insects and flying machines. They were all there, if you just knew how to see them and interpret what you saw. Reading tea leaves was clearly a science open only to a few – like Gypsies and Grandma.

Her status as family oracle was confirmed one December in 1925 as Papa, my Uncle Clayton and other family members were contemplating attending the Rose Parade in Pasadena on

New Years Day. There was no television and black and white newsreels didn't begin to capture the drama and excitement of actually being there, so even though it would demand getting up before dawn, packing lunches and fighting the tourist traffic, it seemed like it would all be worth the effort. That is until Grandma spoke up.

"No," she said with the stern tones of the matriarch that she was. "You must not go to the parade. Not this year."

"Why? What on earth do you mean? What in the world makes you say that?" These and a dozen other objections murmured up from the rest of the family. She had everybody's attention.

"Because I saw something terrible last night in the tea leaves," she said with authority.

"Tea leaves?" The wonderment was in unison.

"Certainly, Mama, you're not going to let superstition ruin a grand parade." It was Papa speaking.

"I know what I saw," Grandma said. "It was plain as day. I saw long planks piled on top of each other like jackstraws. Boards dropped in great heaps and hands – hands reaching up – voices crying for help."

"You heard voices in the tea leaves?" Papa asked, his lips curling at the corners.

"The bleachers are going to collapse," she said. "I don't know where or how along the parade route, but I know what I know. If you go, someone will be hurt – maybe even killed. I'm telling you, don't go. If you do, you can't say I didn't warn you."

Perhaps it was a slight surrender to superstition on Papa's part, or maybe just a succumbing to his mother's wishes, but the family did not attend the Rose Parade that year, January 1, 1926, and it's a good thing that they didn't.

On January 2, the headlines screamed, "Two Dead: 100 of 200 Injured Treated After Pasadena Tragedy." An Associated

Press report stated, "Pasadena, with its hundreds of thousands of guests for the thirty seventh annual Tournament of Roses pageant, was thrown from a scene of joyous enthusiasm into a turbulent tragedy when a grandstand seating 350 men, women and children collapsed as the floral parade was passing and 135 more women and children were injured and taken to hospitals while about 100 others were given first aid treatment."

A man seated in the 27th row gave this account: "I felt a quiver of the stands and saw it slowly giving way and sliding toward the right hand corner. . . Then the whole stand groaned under its weight of humanity and fell with a crash. The rows of people who a moment before sat watching the passing of the parade were thrown into a mess of broken timber and cracking boards."

It happened just as Grandma said it would. Was she psychic? I don't know, but Papa went out and bought her another pound of tea.

Papa was a scientist, or at least he considered himself to be. He had no time for astrologers, soothsayers or things superstitious. So why did he stop in at the mind reading booth down on Main Street in Los Angeles? Who can explain the small contradictions that co-habit the mind? Perhaps it was a strong desire to confirm the wisdom of his recent investment.

Papa had just returned from closing a business deal in Imperial Valley, California. So taken was he by the alchemy of water, soil and California sunshine that he succumbed to the sales pitch of a California developer who convinced him that grapefruit would be the yellow gold rush of the future. "Yessiree! The yellow juice of this luscious fruit will turn to rivers of gold flowing into the coffers of the Rees family." Papa liked grapefruit. Why shouldn't everybody? He was sure that the developer was right – that his shrewd ability to sniff out ground-floor opportunities would one day make him another

Rockefeller or Charles Crocker. Convinced of his own ability as an entrepreneur, he invested thousands of his hard earned dollars in acres of grapefruit groves. To record for posterity his wise decision, he posed for pictures beside one of the trees, holding several large grapefruit in his arms. He slipped the photographic plates into his brown, leather valise and strapped it shut.

Hours later, he arrived in Los Angeles and found his way to the mind reader. To my knowledge, no one ever asked Papa why he detoured down Main Street, certainly not the upscale part of town. And no one ever asked him to explain why he would go into such augury or how he found the place. The event that followed was so remarkable and authentic that to question how he happened to be there seemed almost irreverent.

According to Papa, the diviner closed her eyes, splayed her hands out on the table and told him that she had a vision of his standing by a tree of some sort. "Yes, yes, it is a tree," she said, as though trying to see through a mist. "It is not a large tree, but it is loaded with some kind of fruit. What is the color? Oh yes. Now I see. It is large and yellow. A kind of large, yellow fruit." All this the woman said without ever looking into his valise or discussing his business venture with him beforehand. If ever there was an endorsement of his investment, this was it, Papa said. It was tantamount to divine approval. It would go down in the family archives as proof positive of the veracity of clairvoyance.

It seemed to me that just about everybody in our family was prescient, or at least leaned in that direction. My Uncle Clayton added certainty to my conclusion. He predicted a future tragedy in his life with uncanny accuracy.

Uncle Clayton was Papa's older brother and was the only living brother he had. Two other brothers had passed away before I was born. Uncle Clayton endeared himself to me early on. He was always good for a giggle and was so far out of sync with the rest of the family that the resulting friction was always fun to watch. The stiff patch of bristles over his upper lip danced up and down as he talked. He was the only member of the family defiant enough to grow facial hair. His deep set brown eyes held a twinkle that told you he was a born tease. He was outrageously irreligious, which was a constant concern and annoyance to my staunch Methodist Aunt Mildred and Grandma Elvina.

Aunt Addie, Clayton's wife, was swallowed up in the shadow of her eccentric husband. The love and devotion between them was obvious, but Addie's personality was beige in comparison to Clayton's. She was, however, a balance to his outspoken nature and unpredictable behavior. Addie, like cream in strong coffee, made Clayton at least tolerable in family gatherings.

Uncle Clayton's fame as a predictor was his constant reference to the eventuality of an automobile accident.

"Oh yes. I'm going to get mine," he used to say. "It's just in the cards. I'm going to get mine."

"Now, Clayton," an agitated Aunt Mildred used to answer, "Don't talk that way. You're always so negative. When you keep talking like that, you're just setting yourself up for bad things to happen."

"Talking about it doesn't affect it one way or another," Clayton used to say. "It's a matter of statistics – the law of averages. I'm just talking scientific fact. As much as I drive and as crazy as the drivers are here in L.A., I'm bound to get mine sooner or later."

"That's just nonsense," Aunt Mildred shouted. She had to shout because Uncle Clayton was almost totally deaf. He had one of the latest hearing aids, a bulky device that ran from his ear to his waistband where it hooked into a battery pack, but the electrical wonder did more squealing than amplifying.

"If you flip a coin, Mildred, that coin may turn up heads three times – four times – maybe even ten times, but eventually it's going to land tails. It's bound to. The law of averages always works. It's a scientific fact, Mildred.."

Aunt Mildred threw up her hands and walked out of the room. That's the way their arguments usually ended. She didn't like to argue and Uncle Clayton didn't like to lose. Besides, it seemed to me, science was always on his side.

I wasn't there when his prophecy came true. It was not talked about much. Tragedies never were talked about in our family. My knowledge of it came from word clusters gleaned from whispered conversations. The street names are lost in the recesses of concealed memory as are the circumstances of the accident. The part that is certain is that Clayton regained consciousness underneath the car with hot water from the radiator dripping onto his head. Aunt Addie lay dead.

The horror of that tragedy was the first death that I can remember in our family. The details were kept from me. My ears, it was decided, were too young to hear the particulars. My Uncle Clayton was never quite the same after the accident. He suffered from guilt for the rest of his life. "It should have been me," he said. "It should have been me."

My sister's role as a Gypsy never produced any startling revelations, but to my mind, many of the members of my family were virtual soothsayers. With uncanny accuracy, their predictions came true. My Grandmother, my Father and my Uncle – they all had the Rees fortuneteller gene. It ran in the family.

CHAPTER 11

UNDER THE BLACK CLOTH

All the world's a stage,
And all the men and women merely players;

-William Shakespeare

A casual look at our old photo album gives the impression of a thoroughly normal family. The pictures are of a middle class family unit enjoying birthdays, camping trips, horseback rides, that sort of thing. If you looked closer, you would see than no one ever smiled in these pictures, except maybe my Uncle Clayton. Uncle Clayton smoked cigars, drank whiskey, wore crazy hats and clowned around too much to suit the rest of the family. Perhaps that's why he wasn't included in many of the pictures. It was also why I was drawn to him. He was fun.

Nobody smiled for the camera for two reasons: First, everybody knew there would be an explosion. If it was an indoor shot, Papa used flash powder to light up the room. It paralyzed us with fright. He placed the powder on a small, rectangular platform which he held high above his head and ignited with an electric spark. When it exploded, it gave off a brilliant flash, made a lot of smoke and sounded like the firing of a cannon to my young ears. Papa assured us that there was no danger, but I didn't believe him. I thought it was dynamite that he used and I also believed that it was the powder blast that drew him into photography in the first place – it scared the blueberries out of everybody. I knew that someday he'd shoot our pictures and we would see nothing but burnt flesh and charred bones in the prints.

The second reason that nobody smiled was that nobody was happy. The somber faces were the only honest images in the photos, everything else was pure fantasy. Papa loved to make up his own private fairy tales and then illustrate them with pictures of the family.

The photograph of the grapefruit trees is a good example: row upon row of trees all coming together at some point on the horizon in Imperial Valley with Papa standing in the foreground, arms loaded with big, yellow grapefruit. Papa owned most of those trees, as was previously pointed out. However, Papa almost lost his underwear in the deal. I heard Mama and Papa fighting about that lots of times. The investment which was supposed to produce yellow gold turned out to be nothing but sour juice and bitter rinds.

There were lots of other photographs. The camping pictures used to gall me the most – the whole family sitting in front of the huge army tent, blackened pots and pans near the fire along with a pile of freshly chopped wood. It was all hype. Like a mini-movie set, it was staged in our own backyard just for the purpose of the picture. Papa never took us camping a day in our lives. He went camping quite often – staying out for a month or more – but we were never invited along. Sometimes I felt like we lived on the sound stage of a Hollywood movie studio.

Like all the rest, the picture of me perched on the saddle of a horse was nothing but a photo op. I was embarrassed by it, but it did no good to complain. Papa enlarged it, tinted it and hung it on the wall in the living room anyway. The cowboy hat on my head was two sizes too big and slid down to my ears. I looked like a lizard peeking out from under a rock. I wore chaps, too, but like the hat, they were a couple of sizes too large. There I was on top of that horse, grim faced, scared and miserable. The horse shared my mood. You could see it on his face. It was my first and last equestrian experience. The whole "ride" lasted just long enough to get the picture and I never went near a stable or a paddock again.

Our whole house was full of "props." There was the big kettle that hung over the fire in the fireplace – we never cooked in it. The picture of the elaborate electric train in the backyard – we never actually ran it out there. As a matter of fact, it was Papa's train. He ran it – we watched. The big bowl of popcorn in front of the fire – we never popped it there or ate it there. The big jack-o-lantern – I never carved it. Papa carved it for the picture.

Pictures taken on my birthdays were the most contrived and irritating of all. After I was diagnosed as having a tubercular spine, the doctors put all sugar on the "no-no" list. I was not to have any sugar – ever. But how do you bake a birthday cake without sugar? Mama found a way. On every one of my birthdays, she took a small kitchen basin, turned it upside down, slathered it with icing and put candles on top. Voila! Instant birthday cake. Papa got out the camera and shot the pictures. They were great. Festive, familiar, fitting – and fake. I never tasted a piece of the cake because there wasn't any.

For reasons I could not understand at the time, when Papa took a picture, he draped a black cloth over the back part of the camera and then stuck his head under the cloth. It made photography mysterious to me. One day I asked him about it and he let me climb under the black cloth with him. To my amazement, there was the world – upside down. I couldn't believe my eyes. Wherever he aimed the camera, the Christmas tree, the fireplace or the cat sleeping on the sofa, the image was clear as crystal, but upside down on the glass screen. Papa tried to explain what happens when light passes through a lens, but I couldn't comprehend it at the time. What was very plain to me, though, was that I was living in two worlds – the one in front of the camera and the other under the black cloth.

My Uncle Clayton knew all about the two worlds of our family. He could see the difference between what was happening in the album pictures and what was happening in real life. To look at the pictures, for example, you would think that Papa had the best of relationships with his children. There was my older brother, Raymond, playing checkers with Papa, or sitting behind the steering wheel of the car, or sitting in front of the Christmas tree with the rest of the family. But Uncle Clayton knew that Papa and Raymond had a cat-mouse relationship. The day would come when Papa would call my brother Raymond "nothing but a bum" and would forbid him to enter the house. Before Raymond finished high school, Papa would disown him and demand that no one in our family have contact with him or help him in any way. Uncle Clayton could see that day coming and, being Papa's older brother, decided that he would try to head it off.

One day Uncle Clayton drove all the way over to our house from Southgate to Alhambra to have a heart-to-heart talk with Papa. Uncle Clayton lowered his lean form down onto the back step beside Papa and lit one of his ever present cigars. As the oldest male member of the Rees clan, he enjoyed a certain clout that none of the rest of us had. After a few springboard sentences about politics, automobiles and investments, Clayton took a few long draws on his cigar and began.

"Harry," he said, "I think maybe you could be more of a dad to Raymond."

Papa never wanted advice from anyone, least of all his older brother. "What are you talking about?" he asked. "No one in this world provides better for his children than I do."

"That's not what I mean, Harry."

"Then what do you mean?"

"I mean you ought to be a pal to him, for gosh sakes. Take him fishing. Put your arm around him. Tousle his hair. Josh with him." Clayton slid his thumbs up and down the inside of his suspenders, trying to make his point. "You put food on the table, sure, but there's a lot more to being a dad than that. I think Raymond respects you all right – maybe even fears you – but you want more than that, don't you?"

Papa scowled and gyrated his shoulder, the way he did when he was agitated. "Why? Has Raymond been complaining to you?"

"No, no, no. He would never do that."

"Well, I should hope not. All my children have it pretty damn good."

"Look, Harry," Clayton continued, "it's nice to have three squares a day and a roof over your head, but that doesn't make a dad. Raymond needs someone to believe in him – someone to be proud of him – someone to love him. He wants a 'regular fella' for a dad. Can't you be that for him?"

To someone like Papa, who considered himself to be an expert in all things, even family relationships, correction never comes easily. Papa sat opening and closing his fingers around the fist of his left hand. He was trying to digest what his brother was saying – trying to make some kind of sense out of it – trying to mesh it with his own understanding of fatherhood. Suddenly, he got to his feet with a look of proud determination. He would prove to Clayton – and the world – that he was a "regular fella."

One day there was a cloud of dust and a flurry of activity out behind the garage. With Papa, you never asked what was going on, you just stood by and watched it happen. It was obvious that Papa was building again. There was a cement mixer, lumber, bricks, shingles – it was a major project. After several weeks, the job was completed – a gymnasium the likes of which the City of Alhambra had never seen. Probably only the high school had a bigger or better equipped gym. Papa's gym had a trapeze, parallel bars, an acting bar, Indian clubs, dumbbells and, in addition, a full stage with dressing rooms and portable scenery. It was magnificent – the talk of the town.

"What do you think of it, Clayton?" Papa asked, after our newest property improvement had been in place for awhile.

"Impressive," Uncle Clayton said, lighting up a cigar.

"I guess no one can say I'm not a Dad to my children," Papa said. Uncle Clayton sighed, shook his head and walked away.

One Sunday afternoon, Papa carried his camera and tripod out to the new gym and set it up facing the stage. He arranged the scenery, put a few props on the platform, stepped behind the camera, and put his head under the black cloth. The view on the glass plate was upside down, but Papa couldn't tell the difference.

CHAPTER 12

FORBIDDEN FRUIT

"The only way to get rid of a temptation is to yield to it."

-Oscar Wilde

Even as a youngster, I found it hard to believe that a snake could talk and I didn't see what was so bad about eating fruit from some old tree in a garden called "Eden." In fact, not much about the story in the third chapter of Genesis made any sense to me, but I did understand the meaning of temptation, and Mama told me that was what the Genesis story was all about. It was evident, in my eight-year-old world, that life was full of traps set out by the Devil. Take the street that I lived on, for example.

The main thoroughfare of Atlantic Boulevard, running from Pasadena to Long Beach, ran right in front of our house. The traffic was heavy most of the time. Mildred and I used to invent games to play involving the traffic. One such game was to count the number of Fords, Chevys and Plymouths that passed our house within a certain time span. Pretty dull stuff, but what else was there to do in Alhambra on a summer afternoon? During one game, Mildred got bored and left me to do my own counting. Before long, the passing cars appeared not just as Fords, Chevys and Plymouths, but as enticing, moving targets, beckoning for a kid to try his skills as a marksman.

To test my aim, I needed missiles, first of all. There were plenty of those around. Papa had a pile of stones and gravel in the backyard, ever-ready to mix concrete for one of his building projects. Here was an endless supply of ammunition. I gathered stones from the gravel pile as carefully as David, the shepherd boy, chose the weapons to slay Goliath. The stones were round, smooth and about the size of golf balls.

The nearest traffic light was way up on Valley Boulevard, many blocks away, so all of the cars were whizzing by at thirty five miles an hour or better, by the time they reached our house. These were challenging targets for any budding Cy Young.

I wound up and let fly with a stone. It bounded harmlessly on the pavement and skipped to the gutter across the boulevard. I missed. I threw another and missed again. I missed so many times that I used up the entire pile of rocks and had to go for more. I was a terrible shot, but I seemed to be improving slightly with every throw. The stones were definitely getting closer to their marks and I was encouraged.

The thought crossed my mind a time or two that maybe I shouldn't be doing what I was doing, but what possible harm was there in it? Even if I accidentally hit something, it wouldn't do more than put a tiny, little dent in a car or perhaps flake off a small chip of paint, and who would care about that? Developing my aim was serious and important. I might be a baseball star someday and besides, this was a lot more fun than counting cars.

I was not given to math or physics at that young age, but eventually I reasoned that if I threw the stone slightly ahead of the target, the passing auto and the hurled rock would meet at the same place in space and time. I tried it.

"THUNK!" It worked! It worked! At last I hit a car broadside, a four door sedan heading south toward Long Beach. It must have been going forty, at least. I raised my arms and danced a small victory dance.

To my surprise and horror, the car slammed on its brakes, coming to a screeching halt in front of the Hooper's house, two doors down from us. The driver, red faced and puffing, marched toward me with the rage of a bleeding bull. I headed up the driveway to the backyard with the man hard on my heels. Our backyard was a maze of small buildings, trees, weeds and dark places to hide. I knew that he would never find me, once I made it to the woodpile. The scrap lumber Papa saved for the fireplace was piled as high and deep as a small building. I dove behind it and, from the shadows, planned my next route of escape. The man did not continue to follow me, but instead stopped at our back door to talk to Mama. It was then that I knew I was in serious trouble.

Mama called my name, but I did not answer. She called again and included my middle name. How I hated that middle name "Elton." Whenever it was included in a call, it was a summons that could not be ignored. It was as though my full name had been published on an arrest warrant. Not to answer when my middle name was called was tantamount to contempt of court. Like a criminal walking to the gallows, I jammed my hands into the pockets of my overalls and shuffled toward the back door. Seeing that justice was about to be administered, the driver of the car turned and marched back down our driveway with the air of a Federal Marshall.

Mama didn't spank me, although I'm sure that is what the man expected and wanted, but Mama was not the violent sort. She always had more constructive means of punishment. After explaining to me in stern words the dangers of throwing rocks at passing cars, she set me to work beating dirt out of the living room rug, which was hung over a line in the backyard. I would have preferred a spanking. With each swat of the wire rug beater and each cloud of choking dust, I learned about temptation and sin and sin's rewards, although it did not seem to me that the punishment ever fit the crime. How could an hour's labor in the hot sun compare to a teeny-weeny dent in a car door? Where was justice? Sin had a strange pay scale.

I discovered early that some temptations crept up on you when you least expected them. All of a sudden there they were, like stumbling into quicksand. One summer night, long after the sun had set, I was walking down our long driveway toward the street in front of our house. Mrs. Doyle had her window shade up, giving a clear view into her kitchen. There she was, the widow Doyle, standing in front of the kitchen sink washing out her corset. Ordinarily, I would have walked right by, but not this time. She was standing there at the sink clad only in her bloomers. The only naked breasts I had ever seen were in the National Geographic magazine. I stood transfixed. How could I move? I knew that staring through someone's window at night to take in some forbidden scene was wrong. People who did that, Papa said, were "peeping Toms." If anyone got caught doing that, he could be put in jail – that is if the people who caught him didn't beat him to death first. It was an unspeakable sin.

The pulsating roar in my ears was louder than a California hail storm. She turned her back to me to hang up her corset to dry and then returned to the sink again to empty the wash water. With every movement of her body, those large, pendulous breasts waved to and fro like palm trees in a breeze. I was spellbound, drawn irresistibly to the window and yet repelled by the enormity of my wickedness.

Suddenly she moved toward the window, perhaps to pull down the shade. I didn't stay to find out. The prurient spell was broken and I ran as fast as I could around the front corner of the house, through the door and into the living room. I stood for a moment just inside, struggling to catch my breath and flee the pursuing Devil.

"What's wrong?" Mildred asked.

"Wrong?" My heart was pounding like our old washing machine with a full load of clothes. "Who said anything was wrong?"

"You're all out of breath."

"I know," I said. "I just ran around the house. Nothing's wrong."

I marched to my bed out on the back sleeping porch, but I could feel my sister's suspicious glare glued to my back. Flopping down hard on the bed, I buried my head in the pillow and prayed.

"Oh God, oh God, oh God! You gotta forgive me!"

My sin was right up there in rank with John Dillinger and Pretty Boy Floyd. Murder and bank robbery paled in comparison. I had looked at a woman's naked bosom. I had probably committed adultery. Maybe even worse. I was going to hell for sure, but I decided then and there to make my confession only to God. I hoped that He might forgive me, but I knew that Papa wouldn't, I didn't think that Mama would, and I was dead sure that my sister and brother would never speak to me again, if they ever found out. I thought of going to the widow Doyle to apologize, but I didn't want to embarrass her, and besides, she would probably turn me into the police and I would spend the rest of my life in jail.

For many days afterward, I thought about my unwitting act of voyeurism and determined that some temptations are too overpowering to resist and some sins too evil to confess.

I had a lot of trouble trying to keep straight what was right and wrong. I knew it was wrong to look through the widow Doyle's window. That was obvious. Other things were less sure. Some things that grown-ups said were sinful didn't seem so bad at all. Sometimes right seemed wrong and wrong seemed right. The whole ethical world was upside down at times.

Mama used to read to me from the Bible where it said,

"Vengeance is mine. I will repay, saith the Lord." She explained to me that we were not supposed to get even with people that had wronged us. Let the Lord take care of it, she used to say. We were to forgive; God was to pass out the punishment. That didn't always seem right to me. Sometimes God was a long time in handing out penalties. Sometimes He didn't even do it at all. How could anyone call that fair?

When I was about ten years old, something that offended my sense of justice was the way kids teased me about the brace I was compelled to wear. It was a funny looking affair that laced up in front like a giant shoe and was made out of stiff, pink fabric with little fleur-de-lis all over it. Then there were two steel rods running up the back that arched over the shoulders and were covered with leather. They looked like ram's horns. It wouldn't have been quite so bad had I been able to keep my shirt on, but the doctors said I must get "plenty of sunshine," so I had to wear this medical monstrosity outdoors with nothing on but short pants.

Marvin was a new kid who moved in about two blocks from us. The first time he saw that brace, I thought he would choke to death laughing. "What are you wearing, your mother's corset?" he yelled.

"Shut up, bean brain," I said. I hated Marvin. I hated everything about him. The other kids seemed to like him, but I wished that he'd go back to what ever rock he crawled out from.

"Yoo-hoo!" he shouted in a high pitched voice, "you in the pink corset. Can I hold your hand?"

"How'd you like a punch in the nose, Marvin?" I screeched. I hoped he wouldn't take me up on it, because he was bigger than I was.

"Oooh, no!" he said. "I never fight with girls in pink corsets!"

Why didn't the Lord strike him dead right there? Then I

might have gone along with the "Vengeance is mine" thing. But no. He stood there swinging his hips and raising his legs in little kicks like a chorus girl. What could I do? I could run into the house, but that would be letting this creep get the best of me. Besides, Mama would just send me outside again and tell me "not to pay any attention." I could exchange insults, but then he'd probably beat me up. I could get one of my friends to punch in his face, but at this point, it didn't seem like I had any friends.

Where was God when you needed Him? I could feel the tears rising like an ocean swell. "Don't let me cry, God," I prayed. "If you're not going to strike him dead, at least don't let me cry."

Marvin left after while, bored with his own taunting, leaving me to regain my wounded dignity and curse my girlish looking brace. I told myself that I didn't care what the Bible said, I was going to bide my time and get even with Marvin if it was the last thing I did. I would wait and then I would pay him back double.

Our backyard, consisting of two large lots, had plenty of room to build on and Papa was a builder. First there was the double garage he had built with another half-story on top and a tool shed at the back plus a storage room. Then there was the gymnasium, as big as some houses, my sister's "playhouse," containing two large rooms big enough for any adult to move around in comfortably, a bird aviary and a "sun-house." The "sun-house" needs some explaining.

The orthopedic doctors who treated me insisted that I needed sunshine – lots and lots of sunshine. I needed the vitamin D, and all that. I should take sun baths, they said, without any clothes on for at least an hour a day – longer if possible. It was the "without any clothes on" that gave Papa an excuse to build another building. I was, after all, getting a bit too old to run around naked in the backyard, so it was best to build a special enclosure the "sun-house." This would be no ordinary "house," however. Papa never did anything in an ordinary way. This structure would be the size of a small bedroom, large enough to accommodate more than one person at a time, and would have a wide, open exposure aimed toward the Southern California sky. It would look like a cube with the corner sliced off at an angle. In case of rain, a heavy canvass could be rolled down over the opening to make it waterproof.

This might have been enough for most people, but not for Papa. How would one compensate for the movement of the sun across the sky? How could this "sun-house" be used any hour of the day? Simple. Mount it on an axle so that even a child could turn the building a full 360 degrees. It worked fine.

Privacy was ensured by a hook and eye which could be latched from the inside. There was another small problem. How do you keep a less-than-willing youngster inside the contraption for a full hour? This was easily solved by putting another lock on the door which could be hooked from the outside. With the addition of a wooden walkway leading up to it, the "sun-house" was complete.

A day after the teasing incident, Marvin came back again, this time more inclined to play than to taunt. I was still sporting the hated corset, but I guess the novelty of it had worn off for Marvin.

"Hi," he said, as though he had quite forgotten about the day before.

"Hi," I replied, continuing my building of a make believe dam in Papa's sandpile.

"Wanna play?" Marvin asked.

"Maybe."

"You've got a swell backyard."

"Yeah."

"What's that over there?" I looked up only long enough to see that he was pointing to the sun-house.

"That? That's the sun-house," I said, speaking as though every well equipped backyard must surely have one.

He looked curiously at the yellow clapboard structure. My pulse quickened as I remembered yesterday's encounter. God had not done anything about it. Heaven's justice was nowhere to be found. Wasn't it time for a small bit of retribution? Would just a little bit of vengeance be so bad?

"What's inside?" Marvin asked.

"Nothin'," I said. "Just a cot. Here, I'll show you."

I jumped up and led the way, stepping confidently onto the wooden walkway and marching toward the sun-house, Marvin at my heels. I pushed open the door, showing only the bare interior, save for the cot in the middle.

"Go on in," I said, as though I meant to follow. Marvin was about to step through the doorway when I gave him a shove that sent him sprawling across the floor. Quickly, I slammed the door shut and locked it from the outside.

"Hey! Whatcha doin'?" Marvin shouted.

With all my strength, I began pushing at the corner of the sun-house and it obediently began to move in a counter-clockwise direction.

"Hey, what's happening?" Marvin whined.

I kept pushing as fast as my legs could pump up and down. The sun-house picked up momentum like a playground merry-go-round.

"Let me out of here! Help! Help!" I could hear poor Marvin wailing at the top of his lungs. He tried to stand up, but I could hear him fall with a thud as the floor spun under him.

"I think the world's coming to an end, Marvin! The earth is moving and shaking and we're all gonna die!"

"Aaaaaaaaaaah!" Marvin was screaming now and banging on the walls. I was feeling a special kind of glee and energy I didn't know I possessed as I kept spinning the sun-house in ever faster circles.

"It's over, Marvin! It's all over for you! The buildings are falling down all around and the sun-house is twisting off its foundation! Can you feel it, Marvin? Can you feel it?"

"Aaaaaaaaaaah!" came the reply.

"Bye, bye, Marvin! I can't help you, Marvin!"

I had never heard such screeching from a kid in all my life. He was hitting the inside of the sun-house until I thought he might knock loose some of the siding.

No telling how long I might have continued, but I was getting out of breath, so I let the sun-house slow down until I could stop it so that the door opened onto the boardwalk. Grinning, I unlocked the door and opened it. Marvin, still wailing, staggered out and collapsed, got up again and then ran in a zig-zag pattern toward home.

Marvin didn't come over again for a long time. We finally "made up," and he never teased me about anything again.

Mama still read that Bible verse to me, "Vengeance is mine, saith the Lord." I listened and I believed most of the time. But getting even was kind of nice, too. Anyway, maybe it wasn't such a terrible sin to help God out a little when He got too busy to handle routine justice for Himself.

CHAPTER 13

BULLETS OF SOAP

"I heard the bullets whistle, and believe me,
there is something charming in the sound."

-George Washington

Like many Americans, Papa had a love affair with his gun. The gun was a Colt .38, as I remember. He kept it cleaned, oiled, polished and loaded. I believe he considered his life an anachronism. He would have much preferred the Old West where the gun was the law of the land and real men settled their disputes with bullets. I have no way of discerning his fantasies, but judging from his pride in his weapon and the way he displayed it at every opportunity, he must have entertained secret images of show-down duels at high noon.

I never touched the gun, although I had lots of opportunity. I knew where it was. He kept it under his pillow in case burglars tried to break into the house. I used to secretly wish that a burglar would actually try to climb through the window so that I could watch Papa mow him down with a hail of bullets just like Edward G. Robinson and James Cagney did it in the movies. I would watch from under the bed at a safe distance.

I could never figure out how he could rest his head comfortably on the pillow with a hardened steel revolver putting a lump where feathers ought to be. I didn't know anything about safety catches, but used to wonder what might happen if the thing went off in the middle of the night. That would produce one kicker of a headache to say nothing of what it would do to the pillowcase.

I actually saw him fire the gun only once. He took me out in the backyard, set up a piece of four inch thick board and demonstrated what a bullet from a .38 would do. I was impressed. That revolver had the kick of a mule and the sound of a cannon. My ears rang for a week. Today, you would be arrested for firing a gun in your backyard, but in 1936, people probably just shrugged and said, "Old man Rees is at it again."

One day, when I was about eleven years old, I found him carving small bits and pieces from a yellow bar of Fels Naptha Soap. "What are you doing, Papa?" I asked.

"I'm making soap bullets for my Colt," he answered.

It was late October, and they were having an all-school Halloween party at Roosevelt High School in Los Angeles where he taught. He was going to dress up as a cowboy, he explained, and fire soap bullets into the ceiling. In today's world, he would be fired on the spot, arrested and put in jail. But back then, it was clever, funny and scared the liver out of students and faculty alike.

"Could you kill someone with soap bullets?" I asked.

"I suppose you could," he said, "if you hit them in just the right place, but it's not very likely. Sure would leave a nice, clean wound though." Then he laughed at his own joke. "You needn't worry. I'll only aim the gun toward the ceiling."

But I did worry. Not about the soap bullets, but about that gun. Papa had an explosive temper. Most of the neighbors had seen his temper in action and worried about that gun too. Ever since the altercation with Mr. Hooper, two doors down, when he saw Papa waving his gun around and threatening to kill himself or Mama, Mr. Hooper kept his distance. Papa was not real popular with the neighbors.

Papa's temper exploded most often, however, within his own family. Like the cycle of the tides, Papa yelled at Mama mostly on the weekends when he was home from school. Then, during the week, they would not speak to each other, only to have the shouting resume again on Saturday and Sunday. It was a routine I hated and feared, but was unable to do anything about.

One Saturday morning, the air was shattered by the usual eruption of loud words and threats. Mama had retreated to the front bedroom where Mildred usually slept, although on that day she was not home. Papa followed her there, shaking the house with his hostile footsteps.

"No one else would put up with what I do," he yelled. "Anyone else would have walked out a long time ago."

"Then go ahead and leave us." Mama was crying hysterically. "It's what you've wanted all along, isn't it? If you don't love us, then go ahead and leave us alone."

"You'd like that, wouldn't you? You'd give anything just to get rid of me." Papa moved closer to Mama and was shouting into her face. "Well, it's not that simple, although God knows I wish it was."

My insides were wrenching to see Mama cowering the way she was. I wanted to throw up. Maybe if my brother had been there – maybe if my sister had been there – but there was no one to defend her. I had never stood up to Papa, although I had wanted to several times. My mouth went dry and I couldn't control my shaking.

"Stop it, Papa." I moved over in front of Mama and spread my arms out wide. "You stop it, Papa, or else."

For just an instant, Papa seemed surprised, but his surprised quickly turned to amusement. He laughed a quiet kind of laugh, the way one might chuckle at a pathetic little kitten bristling to a Great Dane.

"Or else what?" Papa asked, calling my bluff.

I was crying, trembling and gasping for air. "Or else I'll shoot you!"

Mama gripped me hard and pulled me away. Papa just put his hands on his hips, smiled, shook his head and walked away.

Mama knelt down in front of me and looked at me with tears streaming down her cheeks. "What a terrible thing to say!" Then she pulled me to herself and held me close while I buried my head into her neck and shoulder and sobbed.

"I understand what you were trying to do," Mama said, "but you have to remember that he is your father. You may not like the way he acts sometimes, but you must never threaten to shoot him. You must apologize straight away."

Apologize? How could I apologize? Why shouldn't he apologize? Everything in the grown-up world seemed strange backward.

"To kill someone," Mama said, "is a terrible, terrible sin."

"But I didn't want to kill him, Mama," I said. "I wouldn't shoot him with real bullets, just bullets of soap. They don't kill you. They just leave nice, clean wounds."

CHAPTER 14

THE BLEEDING MOON

---

*"When he opened the sixth seal, I looked, and behold,
there was a great earthquake, and the sun became
black as sackcloth, the full moon became like blood,
and the stars of the sky fell to the earth as the fig
tree sheds its winter fruit when shaken by a gale; the
sky vanished like a scroll that is rolled up, and every
mountain and island was removed from its place."*

-Revelation 6:12-14

"My dear brothers and sisters out in radio land, the end of time is near. We see the signs all about us. The sixth seal is about to be opened. You will look to the sky and see a bloody moon and a vanishing sky." The radio evangelist was raising his trembling voice and striking fear into the hearts of his audience, and most especially my own. I was only eleven at the time, but paused in my review of the pirate cards I was collecting to note the urgency of his message. There was so much in the Bible that I didn't understand. Why did God make it all such a puzzle? Mama didn't understand it either and Papa scoffed at the whole business, but these radio evangelists that Mama listened to seemed to be able to figure out everything.

There were strange images in the sacred pages that only

the specially anointed could discern; esoteric prophecies that told about climactic battles and the destruction of the earth.

These were mostly recorded in the book of Daniel and the book of Revelation. I couldn't put together all they were saying about a huge statue with a head of gold and feet of clay. I didn't understand why the "mark of the beast" was 666 instead of 444 or 999. Heaven knows I couldn't decipher the meaning of the four colored horses that came thundering out of the last book of the Bible. All I knew was that the end of time was mighty close and all who hadn't been "born again" would be cast into the bottomless pit forever. "Forever" seemed like such a long, long time and the possibilities for sin were so numerous that it was almost impossible to stumble through a day without committing some sin or other that would throw you into the pit.

Mama never seemed to question any of it. I suppose she considered herself to be pretty much out of the "sin loop" anyway and if not, then the bottomless pit couldn't be much worse than what she had to put up with on a daily basis. Papa's God was a "no show" and Mama's God was in a constant snit about something, ready to squash you like a mealybug. Maybe it was the constant bombardment from the radio evangelists or maybe it was just the vacuity of Papa's religion, but for whatever reason, Mama's God seemed more believable to me than Papa's, so guilt came with the package and was an ever present part of my psyche. Even playtime took place under a cloud of anticipated doom.

One of my favorite adventures, whenever I could save up the necessary cash, was going down to the local ball diamond to watch the minor league commercial baseball teams square off. The players were only in their late teens or early twenties, but they were dazzling gladiators to my young eyes. Bedecked in uniforms advertizing Mallory's Gas Station or Crawford's Market or the El Rey Theater, they were the epitome of all to which I aspired. Nothing could match the exhilaration of a night game in late summer. The fact that it was vaguely sinful only enhanced the excitement.

It was just such a summer evening that lured me to the baseball field. I had enough money saved up for the game and even enough for an ice cream bar as well. Papa was away at some meeting, but he was not interested in sports anyway. Mama was home, but never went to ball games. Raymond didn't live at home anymore and Mildred was out on a date, so I went to the ball park alone. The night was beautiful – cool and clear with a moon as round and plump as a ripe canta-loupe. I put off buying my ice cream bar until the fifth inning. I wanted to savor its smooth, chocolate flavor throughout the rest of the game. Having made my purchase, I settled back into the bleachers to soak up the atmosphere and watch my favorite team perform.

It was only by chance that I looked upward to glance at the moon. But what was happening to it? It was not the bright, shining orb I had seen before. Now it seemed sickly, pale, fading from view. I looked at the rest of the crowd. No one had noticed. They were all intent on the game. But why would they notice? They had not been warned of the ominous portents in the sky the way I had been. The end of the age was to come as a "thief in the night." This sinful crowd would never know its fate until it was too late. I looked again. All of a sudden, there was no moon. It had evaporated altogether.

In meteorological terms, the phenomenon could easily be explained. A subtle fog was creeping in from the coast. This, combined with the bright lights on the ball field, slowly and quietly obscured the brightness of the moon until it seemed to disappear from the sky as if by magic. But I was not open to natural weather explanations at the moment – I was awed by the supernatural. I was thinking about it, expecting it and dreading the end of the world. Was this the final destruction of all things?

I struggled to unscramble the harbingers of doom. The heavens would vanish. Was this what was happening? And the moon would turn to blood. Or was it the sun that would turn to blood? The stars would fall, that was for sure. Had they already fallen? They sure as heck weren't up there anymore. Maybe they had all fallen onto Africa or went hissing down into the Pacific Ocean. Where was this beautiful sky I had seen? It had been there just moments before. Now it was gone. Where were the four horsemen of Revelation? They would probably appear at any moment. There was no time now to sort out all of the prophecies. I should have listened more carefully. I should have studied them more intensely. I should have repented, too, long ago. Was it too late? Maybe not. One thing for sure, this was the beginning of the end of the age and I wasn't ready. These stupid people watching the game didn't know it, but I knew it. They would all be cast into the bottomless pit before the sixth inning, but I must get out of there fast. I didn't want to be caught at a godless baseball game when the end came.

Ice cream bar in hand, I raced the mile or so toward home. Once I left the ballpark, the shouting of the crowd and the noise of the game ceased. There was an awful stillness that made the pounding of my heart the more pronounced. I looked at the sky again. Still no moon, no stars, no anything. Soon blood would be dripping through the empty sky. I knew it. I increased my speed, gasping for breath. I must get home. I must get away from the Sodom and Gomorrah of the ball game. I ran harder, my stomach twisting into a pretzel. Faster. Faster. I must run faster. The four horsemen of Revelation were breathing hot air down my neck. After a marathon of running, at last I stumbled, breathless, into our own backyard.

Because of Papa's penchant for building, our backyard always looked like the staging area for a construction company – a pile of gravel here, a stack of bricks there, a mound of sand over yonder. In the middle of all the left over building materials, a twelve by twelve beam was held off the ground by a couple of slabs of concrete. The beam itself must have been twelve feet long. Its intended use had long been forgotten, but the neighborhood kids and I used it as a main prop for our fantasies. One day it would be a pirate's gang plank, the next day it would be a monstrous howitzer and the next a bar in a Dodge City saloon where cowboys could down their whiskey straight from the bottle. But tonight – tonight it would be an altar where a worthless sinner could cry out his repentance. I sunk to my knees in the soft earth and sobbed.

"Please, God, save me from the bottomless pit!" I wailed. I cried out my confession of sins, real and imagined; the little white lies, that now didn't seem white at all, the times I had complained to and about my parents, the spats I had with my sister and the times I stole apricots from the neighbor's tree. Yes, yes, yes, all those horrendous sins stood out in accusatory witness damning me to hell. I was a goner.

I had heard the evangelists talk about a rapture as well. All the true believers would be whisked away into heaven while the devil would be let loose to torture and afflict the poor suckers that were left behind. Is that what was happening now?

"Oh God," I cried, "take me with you. Don't leave me here behind."

I jumped up from my would-be altar and ran inside. "Mama. Mama!" Where was Mama? I checked every room in the house. She was not in the kitchen. She was not in the bathroom. She was not in bed. She had been raptured away. That was the only explanation. She was gone, gone, gone. My sister, Mildred, was gone too, but she was on a date. Or was she? Had she been raptured too?

I ran to my own bed, covered my head with a pillow to muffle my cries. There was no choice now but to prepare for

95

"the great tribulation" the evangelists were always talking about. I would have a giant 666 stamped into my forehead and be badgered by the devil for a thousand years. I had run until exhaustion took over and cried until I went to sleep. I don't remember what time that was.

In the morning, the sun streamed in through the windows of the back sleeping porch. I heard the familiar rattle of dishes from the kitchen and the singing of mocking birds in the yard. I jumped out of bed and ran to the kitchen.

"Where were you, Mama?" I asked. "I mean, last night. No one was home."

"Oh, I just stepped over to Mrs. Doyle's for a minute. I wasn't gone long. You must have come in when I was over there. I didn't think you would be home so soon from the game."

"Oh," I said.

"I checked on you when I came in. You were already asleep."

"Where's Mildred?"

"She's still asleep. She got in quite late. Are you hungry?"

"Not really," I said. "I think I'll go out back."

I turned to go out the back door.

"Did you enjoy the game?" Mama called after me.

"Yeah, it was okay."

The screen door slammed shut after me. So the rapture hadn't taken place. I wasn't left behind, the sun was up and shining and the moon didn't have a nosebleed. I shuffled out to the long, multi-purpose beam in the backyard. There in the middle was a sticky puddle of melted chocolate and vanilla. Just below, were two knee imprints in the sand and scattered all around were curious circles that looked to me like the impressions of horses' hooves.

CHAPTER 15

BANNED ON ARBUTUS STREET

"I never travel without my diary. One should always have something sensational to read in the train."

-Oscar Wilde

The book had a bright red cover with the title printed in gold letters on the spine. It stood with equal stature next to a copy of Beowulf and Chaucer on my Aunt Mildred's polished end table.

"What's that about?" I asked my Aunt.

"That book?" She looked away when she answered me, as though straightening the picture on the wall was much more important than the red book. "Oh, that's just somebody's old diary."

"Can I read it?"

"May I read it," she corrected. My Aunt Mildred was an English teacher at Huntington Park High School, and she never let the improper use of a word slip by unnoticed. "'Can' means are you able. 'May' means do you have permission."

"Okay, then may I read it?"

"Well, I don't think you'd be interested," she said. "It was written a long time ago and some of the English words have changed so that you wouldn't understand them."

She tugged at the cuffs of her blouse. It was the first time I had seen Aunt Mildred discourage me from reading anything. This definitely must be a heart-pounder.

I picked up the book and read the spine. "The Diary of Samuel Pep-Pep-Pepees."

She took it out of my hand and put it back on the table. "Samuel Peeps," she said. "Pepys is pronounced 'Peeps.'"

"Okay, 'Peeps' then. Why can't I read it?"

"You wouldn't understand it."

"Yes I would. I'm eleven."

"Mr. Pepys used French words sometimes. He even wrote in his own special code. It's difficult to read. You would be bored," she said.

Something strange was going on here. My Aunt Mildred was always eager to have me read. She was the one who introduced me to "Tom Sawyer" and "Treasure Island." One of my favorites was "Black Beauty." Even the horrors of Edgar Allen Poe were not to be avoided. So what could be so bad about this Pepys guy? Did he swear a lot? My Aunt Mildred was dead set against swearing. She didn't even approve of "gosh-darn." Did Pepys do nasty things? How could anything he did be worse than some of the pictures in the National Geographic? Aunt Mildred had no objection to my reading its pages, even though there was an occasional picture of a jungle tribe with shirtless women.

"Why did he write in code?" I asked.

"Probably because he didn't want people to understand what he wrote," my Aunt said.

"Then why did he write it in the first place?"

"Diaries are private. Sometimes people write thing in diaries that are personal. Nobody else should ever read them."

"Then how come you have a copy of his diary?" I asked.

She walked over to the dining room door and called out to the kitchen. "Bland. Bland, come out here and take the parakeet out of its cage."

My Uncle Bland had a pet parakeet that he had taught to dance when he took it out of its cage. I used to like to watch him do that – my Uncle shuffling his feet while the small, green bird fluttered its wings and made its spindly legs move up and down on the floor.

Most of the time, my Aunt wasn't too keen on having the bird out of its cage because it pooped on the rug, but it was obvious now that she was looking for diversionary action to draw my attention away from Mr. Pepys.

Uncle Bland came out of the kitchen wiping his hands on the white apron that was tied around his middle. Aunt Mildred quickly disappeared into her bedroom.

"Want to see the bird dance?" my Uncle asked.

"Yeah, sure," I said without enthusiasm. I stared at the dancing bird, but my mind was still on Pepy's Diary. Aunt Mildred seriously underestimated my determination to mine the book for whatever forbidden sentences might be lurking there. For the rest of the day, I stalked that book like a cat might circle the parakeet.

Every time that we went to Arbutus Street for Sunday dinner, the whole family wandered out to the backyard to "ooh" and "ahh" over Grandma's roses. It was a firmly established ritual. Papa and Uncle Bland would sit in the green Adirondack chairs and discuss the virtues of Franklin Delano Roosevelt while Mama, Grandma and the two Mildreds bent down to smell every rose in the garden and talk about my sister's high school English class. Since Raymond was away, this left me to find my own amusement.

I edged my way from the yard toward the back corner of the house with the stealth of a praying mantis, glancing over my shoulder to be sure that all were occupied with the usual grown-up palaver. Once clear of the corner, I raced down the grassy strip that ran through the center of Aunt Mildred's driveway, making sure that my high-top leather shoes made no noise. Quietly, I slipped through the front door of the house and crept over to the end table. But where was the red book? It was gone. Aunt Mildred had taken it away. What had she done with Mr. Pepy's diary?

I scanned the room with my eyes like a burglar hunting for the family silverware. Not on the end table not on the coffee table not on the dictionary stand. I reached down between the cushions on the davenport, thinking that perhaps she had stuffed it there in haste. There was nothing.

I checked the magazine rack, Uncle Bland's pipe stand, Grandma's knitting basket – Aha! The mantel. There, on the mantelpiece over the fireplace lay the red book, filled with the forbidden, chock full of wickedness. The house was as still as a graveyard under fresh snow except for the ticking of the Seth Thomas clock and the pounding of my own heart. I was alone – wonderfully alone to explore the lurid sins of Mr. Pepys.

The first few pages were unrewarding – words about his family and living quarters – references to the King and Parliament. All of it seemed to be written in old English – like the Bible.

"Blessed be God, at the end of the last year I was in very good health, without any sense of my old pain, but upon taking cold. I lived in Axe Yard, having my wife, and servant Jane, and no more in family than us three."

Not much excitement there. My trembling fingers flew at random through the pages, hunting for the nasty, hidden words. Where were they? The clock tic-tocked like a Puritan preacher clucking his tongue at my feverish search. Suddenly the clock chimed the hour. I nearly dropped the book. I stood still for a moment to listen for the slam of the back door, but all was quiet again, so I resumed combing through the dull days of Mr. Pepys.

Hello. What's this? A certain Mr. Herbert came into a bar

and found Mr. Pepys "tumbling of la little fille." What does "tumbling" mean? And what is "la little fille?" And a few pages farther on, here is a "Betty" whom he tries to get alone for some "tousing and tumbling." Is that like kissing? Necking? What does it mean? And here is another mysterious sentence about the same Betty. "I animais her de toute my corazon."

What does that mean? Is it French? I must find out. "I" and "her" and "my" are the only words I understand in that sentence. Wow! Mr. Pepys really knew how to write a diary.

"What are you up to in there?" I swivelled on my heels to face Aunt Mildred. My face was as red as the book in my hand.

"I – I – the book – I thought – I mean, I was trying to read it. It's kind of difficult."

"I thought you might have some trouble with it," she said, as she took the book from my hands with a firmness that brooked for no argument. "Mr. Pepys didn't write in clear English."

"What does 'tumble' mean?" I asked.

"Usually it means to fall. Like, 'The book tumbled off the table.'"

"Oh," I said. "Mr. Pepys must have fallen off something with a girl named Betty."

Aunt Mildred didn't so much as raise an eyebrow. "Mr. Pepys wrote in the seventeenth century nearly three hundred years ago. Some words change their meaning."

"How about 'a-nee-maze,' or something like that?" I asked. "Mr. Pepys 'a-nee-mazed' this same girl."

"The word is 'animais,'" Aunt Mildred said. "It's a French word."

"Well, what's it mean?"

"What are you studying in school?" Aunt Mildred would have made a good spy. You could never get out of her any more information than she wanted to give. Even if the Germans or Chinese tortured her, she'd never give in. She'd always answer a question with another question.

"I dunno," I said. "Long division, geography, stuff like that."

"The nice young lady who comes to your house to teach you – isn't she giving you English lessons?"

She was referring to the home-school teacher who came to my house because the doctors said I was too "fragile" to go to public school.

"Oh, yeah. Sure. She teaches me English," I said.

"Well what's a prepositional phrase? Do you know?"

I looked at her with a blank stare. "I don't think so."

"Can you even define a preposition?"

"Uh, no."

"So I think you had better study English words before you worry about French."

I could tell by the way she tightened her lips that now she was not only upset about my reading Mr. Pepy's diary, but also considered foreign words an attack on her profession, her education, and her native tongue.

"Papa teaches me Spanish words sometimes," I said. Hiding behind Papa always seemed to be a pretty good defense in any situation.

"Now look here," she said. "English is what we read, English is what we write, and English is what we speak. Can you diagram a sentence in English?"

The conversation was part lecture and part scolding. "I'm not very good at it," I confessed.

"Well then, I'll help you until you get good at it," she said. "In the meantime, I think you had better master English before you waste time on French, Spanish, or any other language. I don't care what your Papa says, you're not really educated until you've learned your own language. After that, there will be plenty of time to learn foreign words."

With that, she turned and marched out of the room, taking Mr. Pepy's diary with her. Now I would probably never learn what he'd done to Betty. I looked at the parakeet in the cage. It squawked and I could swear it was grinning at me.

When we got home from our visit to Aunt Mildred's, my interest in diaries, thanks to Mr. Pepys, was fanned into flames. The daily entries into the private diaries of individuals were more than accounts of routine activities, they were windows into the soul.

"Let me read your diary," I said to my sister, Mildred. I knew that she kept one. I had seen it. It was bound by a small strap with a gold lock. Anything with a lock on it held enormous interest for me. Now here was a chance to find out what she really thought – who she liked – who she hated – what she did when she was out of the house. Had she ever "tumbled?" Did any boy "a--nee--maze" her?

"Let you read my diary?" Mildred asked. "Do you think I'm crazy?"

"C'mon," I pleaded. "I'll give you ten cents."

"You don't even have ten cents."

"Not now, maybe, but I will by the end of the month, when I sell all my Saturday Evening Posts."

"Hah!" she said. "Ten whole cents. I wouldn't let you read my diary for ten whole dollars."

"I could read it for nothin', you know, if I really wanted to," I said with a shrug of my shoulders.

"You could not. It's locked."

"I could pry it open. That's easy."

"Try it," she said. "You'd be dead on the spot before you could read it."

Reading Mildred's diary would be even better than reading Mr. Pepy's. I could learn a lot about stuff that men and women did by reading Pepy's diary, but I could learn about what my very own sister did by reading her diary. That would be a lot more exciting and would give me an unmatched sense of power.

Hunt as I would, I could never find my sister's diary after that. I would never know if she had toused or tumbled or if she knew any French words.

But if I couldn't read someone's diary, then I would write my own. I might not be able to crack somebody else's code, but I could invent one of my own that nobody could decipher. It was a wonderful game, this diary business teasing others with secret writings they couldn't understand. It was a coming of age. It was being grown up enough to have powerful urges and emotions and give those wild feelings and events the permanence of symbols on a printed page. I set about my new found task with a kind of inner smile that I had never experienced before. Codes were simple to invent – hard to decipher. My Ovaltine Little Orphan Annie Decoder Pin had taught me that. I gave each letter of the alphabet an assigned number. I was used to it, so it didn't take long to do. *"This afternoon I played spin the 4-17-22-22-14-7 with Joan and Marietta and Theron. Joan and Marietta both 13-11-21-21-7-6 me, but Joan 13-11-21-21-7-6 the best!"*

There. Maybe someday my diary would have a red cover with gold printing on the spine and rest on someone's end table along with Beowulf and Chaucer.

CHAPTER 16

DROP ME OFF AT THE CORNER

I remember, I remember
The house where I was born,
The little window where the sun
Came peeping in at morn.

-Thomas Hood

Our house had a reputation in the neighborhood, almost like a person can have a reputation. People talked about it, gawked at it and pointed to it. Lots of houses are like that – haunted houses – crazy houses – houses of ill fame. Our house was none of those things, but there was enough that went on to make me wish that I lived somewhere else. At the age of twelve, I was painfully conscious of this neighborhood attention.

The house wasn't bad looking for the late 1930's. It was a yellow and brown, wood-siding structure with two Romanesque columns supporting the front porch roof. Papa had built it himself and it was the house where I was born. The house wasn't the problem. It was Papa. Everything that Papa did in and about the house was so grandiose, conspicuous and even bizarre. It all made people wink and smile and refer to our house as "that house."

There was our lawn, for example. Mowing the lawn was a

fairly routine task at most houses, but not ours. Papa was an electrical engineer, remember. This meant that pushing an ordinary lawn mower would be beneath his training and skill. The fact that there were no power lawn mowers around in the late 30's and early 40's did not deter him. He made one – electric, of course. The electric motor mounted on the specially welded frame had enough horse power to pull a bus. Our front lawn covered two whole lots, so the electric cord to the mower had to be well over a hundred feet long

Mowing the front lawn became more than a curiosity in our neighborhood – it was an event. Our house sat prominently in the middle of the block on South Atlantic Boulevard. The traffic was always heavy. It served as an excellent showplace for Papa's inventive genius. Automobiles slowed to a crawl, brakes screeched and necks craned as Papa marched to and fro like a drum major, whipping the electric cord in arcs and circles lasso style. He loved it. I felt like a ringmaster at a Barnum and Bailey Circus.

One thing Papa's machine did not do was edge the lawn. For some unknown reason, he overlooked this task as being irrelevant to the main attraction. As a result, our lawn always had a tall fringe around the perimeter. At times, it resembled a hedge. Sometimes when Papa was away, I would sneak out with whatever clippers I could find and lop off the top few inches.

There were other features of the front yard that attracted attention as well – the long row of lantana bushes that never was trimmed, the scraggly red berry tree that never saw the pruning shears and the large "No Peddlers or Solicitors" sign that looked more like a huge quarantine placard than a simple warning. This was just the outside, but what about the inside?

Well, there was the pool table. Ours was the only house in the city – maybe the whole State of California, with a pool table in the front room. This was not a child's carom set, but a

106

full size, regulation pool table with heavy slate an inch thick and an expanse of green felt that resembled a football field. No other room in the house was big enough to accommodate it, so it was placed in the living room. It was impossible to walk around it without turning sideways. I cringed as I looked at the expressions on faces as people entered our living room for the first time – shock, wonder, amazement, amusement – it was all there. The pool table was, shall we say, a "conversation piece." Papa liked that.

The first question out of any sane person's mouth was, "Who's the pool shark?" Certainly only a world class pool player would sacrifice his living room to a pool table. Who, then? Mama? No, she did not play pool. Neither did my brother or sister play pool. I did not play pool. Not even Papa played pool. The fact of the matter is that no one in our family played pool. Even distant aunts, uncles or cousins did not know a cue ball from a bowling ball.

The next logical question would be, "Why?" If no one played pool, why was there a pool table in the front room? It was a bargain that was the reason. That always sounded reasonable, somehow, coming from Papa's lips. Some movie star in Beverly Hills was breaking up house keeping. Papa went to the auction and picked up this two thousand pound, room sized pool table for a song. The fact that it was inconvenient, bulky, unused and ugly seemed to have no bearing on the fact that Papa had maneuvered a shrewd business deal. He never seemed to see the smirks and grimaces on the faces of others, or else he thought they were chuckling because of his sharp trading ability. Papa was in paradise. I was in pain.

Another source of mental anguish for me was Papa's ongoing root beer bottling venture. It might have been only an aphorism springing from the great depression, but the rule at our house was, "never buy at a store what you can make yourself." Root beer fell into that category. Papa got the extract, yeast, bottles and caps and went into the production of root beer as though we were the sole suppliers for the whole city of Alhambra. After the brew was bottled and capped, Papa stored the finished product in our cellar on racks. This was the closest thing to a wine cellar that we ever had.

All would have gone well, I suppose, except for the fact that Papa couldn't halt the fermenting process. The result was a frequent, unpredictable and violent explosion in our cellar.

One of the most embarrassing moments occurred during a visit from a committee of deacons from the Pentecostal church close by. After expressing their concern for Mama's health and preparing to lift "our burdens to the throne of grace in prayer," an ear splitting carronade fired from somewhere deep in the bowels of our house, followed by the sound of falling shards of glass and a hissing, fizzing noise. I watched Mama's sallow face metamorphose to the color of tomato sauce. She twisted the corner of her apron with her fingers and tried to explain the savage blast as just a small side effect from Papa's hobby. They attempted smiles of understanding, but they never paid a return visit. And did Papa quit making root beer? Never. He continued fine tuning his recipe, even though he routinely lost fifty percent of every batch to the dark confines of the cellar through bursting bottles.

For me, the most dreaded season of the year was Christmas. While other kids my age looked forward to Christmas Eve with enthusiasm rivaled only by finding a pot of gold at rainbow's end, I wanted nothing more than to leave the country or at least hide under the wood pile until Christmas was over. It wasn't our Christmas tree that bothered me so much, although Papa always cinched it tight with enough silver tinsel to keep it secure in a hurricane. Nor was it the cheap, but practical, presents heaped under that trussed up tree –a bar of Fels Naptha Soap, a toothbrush, or a pot scrubber each wrapped individually as if it were the Hope diamond.

No, I could live with all that. What turned me to jelly again was Papa's electronic genius. He was anything but a religious man and he certainly did not embrace religious music, but somehow the carols of the season gave him another opportunity to display his expertise with things electrical.

Each Christmas Eve, Papa hooked up our phonograph to the largest and most powerful loudspeakers this side of the Mississippi, placed them on either side of our front porch and blasted the whole city of Alhambra with Ernestine Schumann-Heink singing "O Holy Night" and "Silent Night." For those who lived within a radius of two miles, the night was neither "holy" nor "silent." No one dared speak to Papa about the holy noise. They all knew he owned a pistol and would challenge any attempt to infringe upon his freedom of expression. Thus we promoted "peace on earth" once a year and demonstrated in decibels the proper way to observe the season. On Christmas day, I stayed indoors.

In the 1930's, the word "phobia" was unfamiliar to me, as were the words "consternation" and "chagrin." One can have feelings, however, without being able to define them. I do remember this. When a helpful friend or stranger would give me a lift home, I would always say, "just drop me off at the corner – that's close enough."

CHAPTER 17

MONEY OF MY OWN

"It is one thing to have a right
to the possession of money, and
another to have a right to use
money as one pleases."

-Pope Leo XIII
(Gioacchino Pecci)

"Saturday Evening Post, Mister?"

The man walked on by as though I were nothing but a painted fire plug stationed on the sidewalk. He had money. I could hear it jingling in his pocket, but it would go for other things, a cigar maybe, or a bottle of Nehi soda.

I hadn't sold a single magazine all afternoon and probably wouldn't. My expectations weren't high because it had been three days since the new weekly issue came out and every day that passed meant I was less likely to make a sale. I learned that bit of sad reality from almost a year's experience, so if I sold one today, it would be a miracle.

The canvas bag slung over my shoulder was getting heavier by the minute. It weighed about fifteen pounds, but it felt like fifty. It was worse on the first of the month, though. That's when the Ladies Home Journal came out and also the Country Gentleman. Those were the monthly magazines and were as heavy as sandbags. I made more money when I sold them, but they were harder to get rid of. The Saturday Evening Post sold for a nickel, and I got to keep a penny of it. The Journal and the Gentleman each sold for a dime, but I made two cents off each one.

There were more rewards for selling the Saturday Evening Post than just money. The publisher gave you "greenies" and "brownies" too. A "greenie" was a coupon printed in green. When you sold five "Posts," you got a "greenie." When you earned five "greenies," you could exchange it for a "brownie," a coupon printed in brown. With "brownies," there was no limit to the number of prizes you could get, flashlights, pocket knives, baseball caps – even bicycles. Of course, you had to have several hundred "brownies" to get a bicycle. Still, the distributor always gave me pictures of kids in New York or Chicago who had won bicycles. These were supposed to inspire me to spend more hours selling magazines.

I used to stand in front of Crawford's Market, the busiest place in town, but while people had money for everything else, almost no one ever wanted a magazine. I wished I had something else to sell, gum or Cracker Jacks or matches – something that moved faster and didn't weigh so much. I once watched an organ-grinder with a pet monkey. It seemed such an easy way to make money. The man just cranked his little music box while the monkey jumped around and held out his hand. People couldn't resist. They gave him money as fast as they could dig it out of their pockets. I wanted a monkey.

"Saturday Evening Post, Ma'am?" The lady smiled, but kept right on walking. That kind never bought anything anyway. Her deeply lined face was framed in stray strands of gray hair and her soot colored shoes were split from too much wear and not enough polish. She looked like my mother – weary, worn and broke. Only ladies with bright red lipstick and finger waves ever bought the Saturday Evening Post.

Sometimes they even bought the "Post" and the "Journal," if I had them to sell. I used to wonder how any woman could be that rich. If Mama ever had a nickel, she used it for bus fare or to get some kind of weird herb medicine.

"Saturday Evening Post, Sir?" Another turn down. The man looked at me like I had just burped without saying "excuse me." I adjusted the sack of magazines slung over my shoulder, trying to regain my dignity. I hated to be turned down. It made me feel like a beggar.

It hadn't been a bad week for selling, actually. In fact, it was about the best week I'd had so far – six magazines the first day and two the second. The eight nickels in my pocket felt thick and round like Spanish doubloons. Only eight cents of it was really mine, of course, but it made me feel rich just to carry around all that money, even if most of it belonged to the company.

I turned over in my mind all the possibilities available with my eight cents – four jaw-breakers and four licorice whips, or one package of gum and a big peppermint stick, or a single-dip ice cream cone and three caramels.

There was always the option to save the eight cents by putting it in the one-pint, cardboard ice cream carton I had set aside at home for savings, but there wasn't much incentive for that. Family members were always "borrowing" from my cardboard bank, especially Mama. I had my savings clear up to a quarter once, but Mama needed it for some slippery elm or ginger root or something, and that was the last I saw of it.

If I could just sell two more "Posts," I'd have enough for an ice cream soda, but that was unlikely. It was getting late, almost time for me to go home for supper. I had never had an ice cream soda, but I had thought about it a lot. I had watched people drink sodas at the ice cream shop on Valley Boulevard, as they sat up to the marble counter on swivel stools. I wondered what it would be like to be that rich to sit there guzzling away that much money as though there was lots more where that came from. The glasses were the biggest I had ever seen – lots bigger than Coke glasses. The frothy liquid inside was pink, or light brown, or white, depending on the flavor you ordered. Someday, maybe, I could afford one, but probably not this week. It would be a waste of time to try to sell any magazines after today. No one ever seemed interested if the magazines were more than three days old.

"Saturday Evening Post, Mister?"

The man walked by, hesitated, then turned around and came back.

"Sure, I'll take one," he said. He fished into his pocket and pulled out a fist full of change, nickels, dimes – even quarters. I couldn't imagine what it would feel like to carry around that much money loose in your pocket instead of in a cardboard ice-cream carton. He dropped a nickel into my upturned hand and I handed him the magazine.

"Thanks, Mister," I said. He smiled, folded the magazine under his arm and walked off.

I sold one. I actually sold one. I had nine whole cents. It was a miracle for sure. Could I sell one more today? It was really time to leave for home, but maybe if I stayed at Crawford's Market just fifteen minutes more. What could it hurt? Mama wouldn't mind.

"Saturday Evening Post, Ma'm?" The lady stopped and looked at the cover.

"Is that the latest one?"

"Yes Ma'am. Sure is."

"Well I don't know. It will be just a few days now until the new one comes out. Will you be here next week?"

"Yes Ma'am," I said, "but—"

"I think I'll wait, then." She turned and walked away. It was worse to have someone almost buy one than to have someone just ignore me. Maybe I should have pleaded with her. Argued. Looked hungrier.

"How about a Saturday Evening Post, sir? It's got lots of good stories in it." That's it, I said to myself, be more forceful. But the man I was speaking to only smiled and turned away. What a shame to be so close to having ten cents of my very own and not make it.

"Here's your Saturday Evening Post, Mister. Not many left. I'm just about sold out." Use the scarcity approach. That might work. But it didn't.

"Get your Post here!" I shouted. "Only five cents for the Saturday Evening Post!" I would try shouting, like the kids did who sold newspapers when an "extra" came out. The manager of Crawford's moved toward me and glowered over the top of his glasses like he was going to fry me in oil. I got the message. No shouting. But then how was a guy supposed to sell anything? If I could just get rid of one more before I had to go home.

I began to feel sorry for myself. Everyone in the family had a different idea about money, but what it all came down to was that I didn't have any. Even money that I earned wasn't mine to spend. I was told what I could and couldn't spend it on, what was foolish and what was practical, what was smart and what was dumb.

"A penny saved is a penny earned," Papa said. That was fine for him to say, but he kept his money in the bank where other people couldn't get to it.

"Spend your money wisely," Mama said. She meant spend it on haircuts and shoelaces, but never anything you enjoyed.

"Save your money and invest it," my brother Raymond said. Being in college, he wasn't around very often to give me advice on money matters, but his route of gum-ball machines up in Bakersfield was helping to put him through U.S.C. As a matter of fact, that's what I thought I might do as soon as I was old enough. Just going around once a month or so and scooping piles of money out of machines was the easiest way of making a living that I could think of. It sure beat selling Saturday Evening Posts in front of Crawford's Market. The idea of gum-ball machines had an added appeal. I could chew gum the whole day long.

My sister Mildred never had much more money than I did, but she sure had her own ideas about how I should spend mine. She thought marbles, secret de-coder pins and bubble gum had no practical value. She bought jars full of cream to rub under her arms and rouge to dab onto her face. At my young entrepreneurial age, having just turned eleven, that seemed a total waste of money. Everyone in the family was convinced that I was too young and too inexperienced to know how to spend my own money. That made me furious.

All of this was going through my mind when a blimp-shaped man with a rust-colored dog on a leash came down the sidewalk and headed into the store. "Hello there, young man," he said, pausing beside me. "Wonder if I could ask you to do me a favor?"

"Guess so," I said.

"Would you mind watching Tillie here, while I duck into the store for a minute?" He held out the leash to me.

"Sure," I said, "but I have to go pretty soon."

"I won't be long," he said. "It will only take a second." He patted the long-eared, rusty dog on the head. "Nice girl," he said. "You stay right here 'til I get back."

"She doesn't bite, does she?" I asked

"Goodness, no. She's tame as a goldfish. I'll be right back."

The man shuffled away and squeezed through the turnstile. I wrapped the leash around my fist and looked at my new responsibility. "Don't you run away," I said to Tillie. How was I supposed to sell magazines and watch a dog at the same time? I reached down to pet her, but when she just stared at me, I thought better of it. What if the man was fibbing when he said he'd be right back? What if he didn't come back for a whole hour? What would I do then? Worse yet, what if he just disappeared? What if he left by a rear door or something? What if he was only trying to get rid of his dog and figured I'd take care of it for the rest of my life? What would Papa say? My hand began to perspire where the leash wrapped around it. This sure wasn't helping me sell magazines.

At last, the big man came through the check stand carrying a small, brown sack and came over to get his dog.

"You wouldn't like to buy a Saturday Evening Post, would you?" I asked. Why did I put it so negatively? I could have kicked myself.

"Yes," the man said. "I wondered if you were going to ask me." He pulled out a nickel and gave it to me. I handed him the magazine with a smile and watched as he shuffled off with his rust colored dog.

Success was sweet. Ten cents. It had been a great three days. I shifted the near-empty sack over my other shoulder and headed for home feeling the heavy jingle of all those coins in my pocket.

To get to our house, I had to walk right by the ice cream parlor. There was plenty of reason to hurry past – supper was ready, no doubt, and Mama was waiting. It was "Lone Ranger" night on the radio, and I didn't want to miss any of that. On the other hand, if I went home and showed everyone my money – put it in that ice cream carton – how long would it be before I could spend it for myself – on anything I wanted? Most likely never. Like the taxes Papa said he paid to the government, I'd never see it again.

Over the door of the ice cream parlor, a huge neon ice cream cone, tilted at an angle over the door, beckoned like the sirens singing to Odysseus. As twilight shifted to dark, the pink, blue and white outlines of the cone beamed their invitation. I stepped slowly past the glass door, hesitated, turned back and opened it. Why not buy that soda? When would I get another chance like this one?

I approached the counter with the swagger that only wealth can produce. Putting my half-empty sack of magazines on one of the unoccupied stools, I sat down on the one next to it. I leaned my elbows on the counter and felt the cold marble on my skin, a silent sensation of fortune and luxury.

"What will it be for you?" said the man behind the counter. He wore a white, short-sleeved shirt, white cap cocked sideways, a white apron tied around his waist and, for the moment at least, was my servant. He was waiting for my order, my direction, my wishes. The sense of my power was intoxicating.

"Ummmmm. I think I'll have an ice cream soda," I said.

"What flavor?" he asked.

"Let's see – what flavors do you have?" I knew I wanted strawberry, but I was savoring the moment and wanted him to run through the list.

"Vanilla, chocolate, strawberry, cherry and pineapple."

"Ummmmm . . ." I stared up at the circular fan on the ceiling, watching the slow movement of the blades. I reviewed my choices, touching each finger of my hand as though it were a flavor. The man rolled his eyes in a gesture of impatience, but I would not be rushed.

"I think I'll have strawberry," I said.

"You got ten cents?" the man asked, in a tone of doubt.

"Sure," I said with a bit of insult in my voice. I pulled out one nickel and then another, letting them click authoritatively on the marble counter. The man scooped them up and went to work putting the ingredients into a tall, ribbed glass.

I hunched over the counter and clasped my hands in front of me, the way I had seen Jimmy Cagney do it in the movies. I had entered the unfamiliar world of the well-to-do and I loved it. I was making choices, buying service, paying for luxury. I was a wage earner.

"Here you go, son." The man placed the beautiful drink in front of me, majestic in its pink foam with a tall straw pointing skyward, waiting for my lips to draw up the sweet elixir. I sat savoring the sight of it for a long moment before I began to drink. There was a zing to it at first that backed up into my nose, but soon the mellow ice cream and strawberry syrup dominated. The smooth liquid stroked every taste bud in my head as it made its way down my throat.

The gentle whisper of the overhead fan was a soothing lullaby while I turned slowly from side to side on the swivel stool. The posters on the wall blended with the soft lights of the jukebox to make this spot a corner of heaven. I was part of the real world now, no longer just looking in through a window. I was a productive member of society, a seller of goods, a consumer, making and managing my own money. Success was mine.

I seemed older somehow, a bit taller, too. Affluence displaced frustrations. All things were possible and obstacles to happiness vanished in the cool ambiance of the ice cream parlor. There would be other times – lots of other times. Next week, if I sold another ten magazines, I would try a chocolate soda, or maybe a double-dip cone. I could even imagine asking a girl to share a sundae with me. The opportunities before me unfolded in a kaleidoscope of delicious dreams.

My reverie was soon broken by a nerve-jarring slurp as I sucked up the last bubbles of the soda through the straw. I had hit bottom. Why did it have to end so soon? I wanted this experience to last forever. I wiped my mouth on my bare arm, picked up my canvas bag and ran the rest of the way home.

"Where in the world have you been?" Mama asked. "I've been worried sick about you. Dinner was ready an hour ago. Everyone else has eaten."

"That's okay, Mama. I'm not hungry anyway."

"Well, you have to eat something." There was impatience in her voice.

"What are we having?"

"Beets."

"Beets?" I pictured the crimson little spheres lying cold on a plate, ugly in their loneliness. How could they compete with the heavenly cocktail I had just consumed?

"Beets and hamburger patties," Mama said.

"Maybe later," I said.

"Well you must have had a good day at Crawford's Market."

"Yeah, pretty good."

"You didn't spend all your money on candy, did you?"

"Nope," I said.

"Well something took your appetite away. It's just not like you to turn down dinner."

I shrugged my shoulders, grabbed a sofa pillow and lay down on the floor to bathe in the light of our rose colored lamp shade. It cast a pink glow, like the tint on the glass of that tall soda. The taste in my mouth was still cool and sweet like strawberries. Turning on the radio, I tuned the dial until I came to the familiar strains of the William Tell Overture. I was just in time for the Lone Ranger.

CHAPTER 18

IS THERE A DOCTOR IN THE HOUSE?

"Given one well-trained physician of the highest type
he will do better work for a thousand people than
ten specialists."

-Charles Horace Mayo

Had you asked me my impression of medical doctors back in the 1920's and early 30's, I would have told you they belonged in the same category as dragons, monsters and bogeymen. Despite their white coats and all the faith that fawning adults seemed to put in them, they always spelled trouble for me. They had a penchant for needles and knives and nasty tasting liquid that they told you to swallow. "This is good for you," was a phrase I learned to distrust at an early age. How could some monstrous pellet that gagged you when you tried to swallow it be "good for you?" And how could these white-coated ghouls have your best interest at heart when they punched through your skin with sharp instruments? I didn't believe them. Adults were such hypocrites about doctors, too. If I played "doctor" with any of my young friends and poked around on their bodies in places where doctors poked around on mine, I got lectured or spanked.

"Hate" is not too strong a word to describe my feelings about doctors. They had unlimited power. They could take me away from my family and put me in a gray-walled warehouse called a hospital or they could lace me up in a strait-jacket type contraption that inhibited breathing and gave me a bad case of claustrophobia, and they didn't even have to ask permission to do these things. They used to wear little round mirrors on their foreheads like a cyclops. Whenever I saw one, I knew I was in for a bad time. Just the sight of one turned me into a kicking, screaming tiger.

Much later on, I learned that there are good doctors and bad doctors. That didn't conquer my reaction to them. The initial impression was too deeply ingrained at too early an age. I came to understand, however, that sometimes the doctors actually did help me and make me feel better. Mostly, it was the "good" doctors undoing the work of the "bad" doctors.

I was too young to remember the first "bad" doctor I encountered, but the results of his botched diagnosis are clearly evident today. I was three years old, or a little less, when the gland on the right side of my neck began swelling. This alarmed Mama, so she and Papa decided it was abnormal enough to consult a doctor. The doctor, whose name has been mercifully forgotten with the passage of time, dismissed my obvious problem with a wave of his hand and told my concerned parents that they were "typically over-anxious." They were told to ignore the swelling and not worry so much. I would "get over it." The swelling, in the meantime, increased to the size of a hen's egg.

As the swelling grew and I got sicker by the day, my "over-anxious" parents decided that it might be wise to talk to another doctor. Second opinions were rarely sought in those days. It showed a certain lack of faith and was an insult to the doctor in charge. The "doctor in charge," after all, was no more to be questioned that Moses or the Angel Gabriel. It gives some indication of my parent's concern to say that they would even consider going to another doctor.

The new doctor took one look at my swollen neck and enlightened my parents rather quickly on the urgency of the situation. "Any time there is a swollen gland like that, it is serious," he told them. They had not been "over-anxious parents." They had not been anxious enough. "We must lance this gland immediately," he said, "and hope and pray that it's not too late."

It was.

I don't remember the actual slashing of my neck. I was too young. The scar remains, however, so I believe my parent's account of it and, although this new doctor was one of the "good ones" – I'm sure I didn't think so at the time.

By the time this second doctor got to me, the swelling had already ruptured and the tubercular infection had settled into my spine to do its dirty work. This would destroy two vertebrae and alter the slant from which I viewed the world for the rest of my life. For the next five years, I would lie flat in a cast and stare at the ceiling. So much for "bad" doctors.

The next parade of doctors who looked in on me at the Children's Orthopedic Hospital and subsequent doctors who treated me for the next ten years or so, flew by in such rapid succession that I do not remember their names. I remember nurses more than I remember the doctors, for they had a more regular contact with me. I assume that these orthopedic doctors did the best that they could for me, under the circumstances and with the medical skill which was available at the time. One of the doctors told my parents that a team of specialists could attempt a spinal fusion, but the whole procedure was very "iffy" and I would only stand a 50% chance of living through it. My parents decided to let nature take its course rather than take a chance with a fusion.

The next doctor that I distinctly remember treated me when I was early into my fourteenth year. He was one of the bad ones. Not "bad" in the sense of evil, but "bad" in the sense of incompetent. His cold, patronizing demeanor sent chills over me every time he made a house call. All doctors made house calls in the 1930's.

For some unknown reason, when I turned fourteen, I developed severe headaches, spinal pain and heart palpitations. I suppose it all had something to do with hormones and a surge in growth, but I'm only guessing. When this particular doctor listened to my heart and thumped around with his fingers on my chest and back, he determined that I should go to bed and stay there. This meant I had to drop out of school and go back to home teaching, if and when I was able to have a teacher come to the house. As a treatment regimen, he had one medicine – phenobarbital. I think he had controlling stock in the pharmaceutical company that produced it. He put me on a heavy dosage and, understandably, I was soon in a mental fog. When I complained, he increased the dose. I became more lethargic by the hour.

Papa had found a new friend in that doctor, one who understood his plight and the misery of his life. The two of them used to sit out in front of the house in the doctor's limousine and talk away the morning. As I peeked out the window through my drug-induced fog, I used to wonder what they were talking about and wondered if Papa was being charged extra for the doctor's counseling sessions. I suppose it didn't really matter. Papa had found his own personal psychotherapist.

Mama wasn't convinced of the worth of the doctor's treatment plan. He kept increasing my intake of phenobarbital until I became a bedridden zombie. I was drugged into a virtual catatonic state. To top it off, the doctor told Mama, "He will never be able to walk again. Keep him as comfortable as you can and have him join a 'shut-in club.' Try to create as much interest for him as possible, but he will be an invalid for the rest of his life."

Mama refused to accept that verdict and argued heatedly for a second opinion. At first, Papa saw no need to change doctors. After all, he and the doctor were mutual friends by this time. With Mama's continual agitation, he finally agreed to let someone else at least examine me. The new doctor was one of the "good" ones. I don't know where he got his training. I never saw his framed credentials, but what he may have lacked in specialized education he more than made up for in experience and common sense.

After listening with his stethoscope and thumping around with his fingers, as all doctors do, he had me get up on my feet and walk around our ugly, green pool table. I came stumbling back to the couch, gasping for breath. He listened again with his stethoscope.

"Now the first thing I want you to do," he said to Mama, "is throw away those phenobarbital pills. Don't let him take another one. Then I'm going to prescribe some iron pills to build up his blood."

Then he turned his eyes on me. "And as for you, young man, I want you to walk around that table two or three more times today. It isn't going to hurt you." He moved his plump hand through his gray, thinning hair. "Then I want you to keep increasing the number of times you walk around that table every day. All you need is exercise. It is absolutely ridiculous for a fourteen year old boy to just lie down and not get up." That was it. In just few days I was up and about again and back in school. This doctor with the kindly eyes and practical wisdom saved me from a drugged stupor and membership in a "shut-in" club.

Ten years earlier, in 1929, the artist Norman Rockwell painted a cover for the Saturday Evening Post. It depicted a ruddy cheeked country doctor in a rumpled, black suit tending to a little girl. The little girl held up her doll and the doctor was listening with his stethoscope up against the doll. The picture captured in visual form a doctor's compassion, experience and dedication. My new doctor could have been a model for that very picture. He looked and acted the part in every way. There are, of course, the good and the not-so-good, the wise and the not-so-wise in every walk of life. Why should it be different with the healing arts?

CHAPTER 19

SORT OF A MIRACLE

"Whatever a man prays for, he prays for a miracle.
Every prayer reduces itself to this: 'Great God,
grant that twice two be not four.'"

-Ivan Sergeyevich Turgenev

"Prayer changes things," the wall plaque said. Mama didn't actually put it on the wall because she didn't want to argue with Papa, but she kept it loose on the table or under a stack of magazines so it would turn up every once in awhile. She believed what it said and I wanted to believe it, but I wasn't always sure.

"God does so answer prayer," I said emphatically to my sister Mildred. "That is, if you pray hard enough."

"Sometimes," she said. "Not always."

"Uh huh! He does so."

"Does not."

At fourteen, Mildred was our resident skeptic. My brother, Raymond, was away at college so I couldn't argue with him. Anyway, there wouldn't be any use because he knew everything.

"I suppose you don't pray?" I said, challenging my sister.

"I didn't say I didn't pray. I just said you don't always get what you want just because you pray for it."

"Oh yeah? Then what about Marietta's cat that had kittens?"

When you're losing an argument, it's a good idea to pull in a star authority. Marietta was a friend about my age whom both of us knew. Her large, innocent eyes exuded honesty.

"Okay, so what about Marietta's cat?" Mildred asked.

"Well all four of the cat's kittens were born blind. So Marietta prayed that God would heal them. Nothing happened at first, so she prayed even harder. Four whole days went by and nothing happened. Those poor little kittens just stumbled around blind as ever. She prayed harder and harder. Then on the fifth day, a miracle happened. Their eyes began to open just a tiny bit. Marietta got real excited and prayed harder than ever. An' know what? All the kittens' eyes opened clear as anything. They could see. All of 'em! Boy! You'd have a hard time telling Marietta that God doesn't answer prayer."

Mildred laughed right out loud. Obviously, she didn't believe me.

"It's true!" I said. "You just go ask Marietta."

"All cats are born blind, silly," Mildred said.

"That's not true!" I lashed out at her with the vehemence of a true believer.

"It is so," she said. "Just ask Mama. Ask Papa. Ask anybody except Marietta. Everybody knows kittens are born blind. After five or six days, their eyes open." She began laughing again.

"Ay-theee-ist," I screamed, wrinkling my nose into the most pugnacious expression I could muster. "You're nothing but an ay-theee-ist!"

After checking it out with Mama, I discovered to my embarrassment that Mildred was right, so I avoided the subject of prayer for quite awhile. I hated it when my zeal outran my knowledge. I still believed Mama's plaque, but tried not to pray for things that were going to happen whether I prayed for them or not.

A miracle was Mama's trump card. She continually hoped for it, prayed for it, expected it. Usually, she was not public about her praying. "Go into your closet and shut the door," Jesus said. She took it quite literally. The pantry, just off the kitchen, was her "closet." The tall, green stool was her altar. There she beseeched God for miracles – a new personality for Papa, enough money for her herb medicines and a straight spine for her youngest child. I didn't always know what she prayed about, but I could guess. If I had a way of checking off how many times she got what she asked for, I might have rejected prayer flat out, but I didn't. I imagined that God must be something like Papa, sitting up there in heaven someplace with all this power, waiting to see you grovel and beg before He let you have it.

There was more to getting your prayers answered than just wanting something and pleading for it real hard. Mama said you had to have "faith." This "faith" business was sort of like believing that something was going to happen even when your better judgement told you it wasn't – like Santa Claus coming down a chimney or the Easter Bunny laying eggs. You knew it was impossible, but you believed it anyway. You just shut your eyes, gritted your teeth and believed it. Those that were real good at "faith" always got what they wanted. Mostly those people were in the Bible. I wasn't that good at believing. I prayed that God would save our canary after the cat got hold of it. Mama wrenched it out of the cat's mouth and blew into its face to try to revive it, but when I saw its limp, broken neck, I knew that my prayer was as useless as hauling water in a sieve.

But Mama believed in miracles. Her turn would come just like it did for Abraham and Joshua and Daniel. To give a boost to her faith, Mama would take Mildred and me into Los Angeles to hear Aimee Semple McPherson, the charismatic evangelist and faith healer. Angeles Temple, Aimee's church, was a Mecca for miracles. Its huge auditorium with two balconies, seating five thousand, was a miracle in itself and a sight-seeing attraction for tourists. One whole room was given over to the evidence of past miracles. Walls were hung with crutches, canes, braces and wheel chairs proving beyond a doubt the supernatural power of prayer and the extraordinary healing energy which flowed through Aimee's electrifying hands. Angeles Temple was the "Lourdes" of Southern California in the 1930's.

One day, when Papa had gone away on one of his "vacation trips," Mama took us to the Temple. It was more than just an outing – it was a faith pilgrimage. All those braces and crutches in that miracle room were discarded by real people – who had come in crippled and walked away healed. If it happened for them, it could happen for us. "Prayer changes things," the plaque said.

I did not have a chance to discuss or question it. I found myself that afternoon waiting in a long "healing line" leading up to a high platform where "Sister Aimee" was praying for the sick.

At nine years old, I was unnerved by new experiences, especially medical ones. But this was different from going to the doctor. This would not hurt, Mama assured me. It would be a wonderful, happy event where I would feel God's power go through me and I wouldn't be sick anymore. My back would be straight and I wouldn't have to wear my brace ever again.

I watched spellbound as Aimee fervently pronounced her incantations over the sick. Sometimes she clapped her hands together in front of the invalid and at other times she simply laid her strong hands on the person's head. In almost all cases, the sick ones, after Aimee touched them, dropped to the floor as though given a jolt of electricity. That's what it must feel like, I judged, an electric shock just like when Papa would stick his thumb in one of the outlets in our fuse box. What was it like for these people? Why did they fall on the floor like that? What would I do? In any case, it would be worth it. I could throw away that cursed brace, my back would be straight as a flag pole, I could go to public school, I could eat all the sugar I wanted, and they'd probably let me play first base instead of right field when we chose up sides for sandlot baseball.

The line grew shorter and I moved closer and closer to Aimee. With her flowing, blue cape and crisp, white uniform, she was a mesmerizing figure somewhere between a nurse and an angel. Her blond hair was neatly coifed in stylish finger-waves and her strong voice was authoritative without losing its feminine touch of compassion.

At last, I stood directly in front of her. The previous sick person fell to the floor and lay to one side with all the others. Some were twitching uncontrollably while others lay perfectly still. It reminded me of some of the battlefields I had seen in the movies, but these people were not bleeding. Most had their eyes closed, but others stared wide-eyed at the ceiling as though transfixed by some heavenly vision. Suddenly, Aimee's full attention was focused on me. I was speechless. Something the size of a baseball had lodged in my throat and cut off my voice as effectively as a tourniquet. I could not have spoken my name if she had asked me. She turned to Mama and asked what my problem was. Mama explained about my tubercular spine and pulled my shirt taut to show my deformity. Mildred stood below the platform trying to disasso-ciate herself from what was going on, looking at the toes of her shoes and trying to blend in with the crowd. Sister Aimee explained loudly to the people about my disease and enlisted resonant waves of sympathy from the audience. I was the focus of attention, surrounded by white-uniformed attendants, fallen bodies and wailing members of the congregation. It was as though I had wandered onto a movie set and suddenly found myself to be the star.

Aimee laid one hand on my forehead and raised the other hand to heaven. The warmth of that hand on my head sent shivers down to my toes and the blaze of white light from her uniform was a heavenly radiance. She called on God as though He were only one floor up and the crescendo of voices from the congregation almost drowned her out. Every nerve and muscle in my body was so quickened that had she said, "Fly!" I would have immediately soared into the air. Without warning, she clapped her hands together and pronounced me healed. I crumpled to the floor like a broken necklace.

I'm not sure how long I lay there or when the service ended. I don't remember getting up or leaving the building. An emotional trance blotted out all recollection. I do remember walking to the train station to take the trolley home. It was afternoon and we were not staying for the evening meeting.

"I'm healed," I kept telling myself, but I didn't dare reach back to feel of my back. That would be a lack of faith. My spine was straight now. It had to be because Aimee and all those people had prayed for me.

Mama walked on ahead with the shopping bag she always carried on these pilgrimages, a bag stuffed with dried fruit, bread, peanut butter, apples, bananas and extra sweaters. We probably could have lasted a week from the contents. Mildred and I walked a few paces behind, just out of earshot.

"Nice show," Mildred said under her breath.

"What?" I asked.

"I said, 'Nice show.'"

"What do you mean by that?"

"You know what I mean," Mildred said. "Collapsing up there on the platform like you'd been hit by lightning. What made you do that?"

"How do I know? God I guess."

"Hmmph!" Mildred grunted in disgust.

"Come on." Mama hurried us along, not listening to our conversation. "Let's make this traffic signal."

Mildred and I still hung back. "I was healed," I said. "That's all I know."

"Well, you don't look any different to me," Mildred said.

My faith took a momentary nose-dive. I reached back in a reflex action and felt the angle in my spine. It was still there, but was it getting straighter? Maybe these things didn't happen all at once. Maybe the hump would be gone by the time we got home.

"You're just jealous," I said, trying to find some defense against superior logic.

"Jealous?" She laughed. "What have I got to be jealous about?"

We crossed Spring Street on the way to the station while traffic waited for the light to change.

"You're jealous because Sister Aimee didn't pray for you."

"What are you two arguing about?" Mama asked.

"Nothing," Mildred said.

"She says that—"

"Nothing," Mildred said again with emphasis.

"Well, let's hurry or we'll miss the train."

"Ay-theee-ist," I whispered to Mildred. She gave me a look that would have frozen molten lava as we fell into silence behind Mama.

I did not speak the rest of the way home, as though talking about what had happened might break the spell. The angle in my spine was still there. I could feel it against the back of the trolley seat. I had not worn my brace to Aimee's temple. Mama had me leave it at home. Maybe she thought that if I wore it to the healing service, someone would make her leave it in the miracle room at the temple and that would certainly enrage Papa. He had paid a lot of money for it and so it was really his property.

That night my sleep was filled with white-robed angels. They were all smiling and had blue wings and passed me around from one to the other like an inflated ball in some sort of game. I was lighter than air and floated freely among them. I felt loved and happy and best of all, my back was as straight and strong as a California Redwood. One of the angels was Aimee and another was Mama. I could tell, because below her white robe, Mama wore the black shoes with the cube heels that Papa had bought her.

The next morning the sun shone through the clear windows of our back sleeping porch and I covered my head to keep out the light. The dream seemed so much better than life. Maybe I was healed, but it didn't feel like it. I still couldn't lie flat on my back.

Maybe it was lack of faith, but I had to see for myself. I jumped out of bed and ran to the bathroom. Standing on a stool, I turned sideways to look into Papa's shaving mirror. Sure enough, my back was as crooked as ever. What had happened? Surely God heard Aimee's prayer and Mama's prayer. It must be my defective faith. I didn't believe hard enough. I did my best, but it wasn't sufficient. There must be something wrong with the part of my soul that believes. Maybe if I had taken my brace and put it in the miracle room for all to see. Because I didn't do that, maybe God wasn't going to heal me.

I ran to the kitchen to confront Mama. "I'm just the same," I said. "God didn't heal me."

"Don't say that," she said. "These things take time. Not all miracles happen right away. Just be patient."

"But Sister Aimee said I was healed."

"I know. Maybe God is testing our faith."

That was something I didn't understand. God surely knew already how much faith I had or didn't have. So why did He have to test it? Was it like the oil in our Buick where Papa had to measure it with a dip-stick? And if my soul was low on faith, how did I get more? It was all so confusing.

"Well . . ." I hesitated, not wanting to destroy any more faith than I had already, "should I put my brace on again?"

"I expect you'd better," Mama said. "Papa will wonder why you're not wearing it."

As the days passed, my expectations of a miracle faded. I didn't question prayer, or God, or Aimee. I just figured I was one of those people born without enough faith. I accepted my lot and didn't think much more about the supernatural. My mind was preoccupied with other things – comic books, building a club house for "boys only," playing kick-the-can on summer evenings. I had no need for God to bail me out – until I started high school.

It was the summer of 1940 and I had just turned fifteen. There was plenty to frighten a teenager. A world war was brewing, President Roosevelt had been elected for an unprecedented third term and Mama's radio evangelists said the end of the world was near. But my own fears that summer were centered around entering high school in the fall. This was a personal crisis that knew no bounds.

I had never attended a public school before. On the doctor's orders, I had been tutored at home by teachers employed by the public school system for those too sick to attend regular classes. I wasn't really "too sick," but the thinking was that the unsupervised rough and tumble of the playground would do further injury to my spine. The result of it all was that I knew English and Math as well as any kid my age and could find the Tigris and Euphrates Rivers on a map, but I was mortally afraid of competing with other students and was sure that I would come out looking like Mortimer Snerd, one of Edgar Bergen's dummies. I didn't know anything about what went on in a normal classroom. When should I raise my hand? Where would I put my lunch? What if I had to go to the bathroom? What if I had to undress in front of other boys in the gym class? I heard from others that you had to change clothes in the locker room and all the boys walked around naked. I wouldn't mind taking off my pants, but my shirt? First, they would see my long underwear. Then, after the laughter had died down, they would stare at my crooked back and ask how I got that way. I could hear them now. "Hey, Humpie, how'd you get that hump on your back? Were you a freak in the circus?" Or maybe, "Look at this freshman, guys. He zigs where he should zag. I think his Mama was a camel." I shook when I thought about it.

We were given a list of things to buy before starting high school: ring-binder, paper, pencils that sort of thing. Then there were gym shorts and an athletic supporter. "Athletic supporter?" The guys I knew never called them "athletic supporters." They were "jockstraps." I didn't own one. I didn't even know how to put one on. How could I ask Papa for money to buy a jockstrap? What if he asked me what one was? How would I explain it? "It's some kind of elastic thing that holds up your balls, Papa." I could never describe one to him. And how could I go into a store and ask some clerk, "Where are your jockstraps please?" Worse yet, what if a woman waited on me? I'd die!

The most fearsome thing was what seniors and juniors did to freshmen. Freshmen were "scrubs." They could always tell "scrubs" by the way they looked – wide eyed, baby faced, hunted. I knew that they would spot me in a minute. Mildred told me what happened to "scrubs" and her girlfriends embellished her stories with graphic anecdotes until I trembled all over.

"I'll never make it through the first week," I confided to Mama. "They'll kill me for sure. I just know they will."

"No, they won't," Mama said. "Jesus will be with you."

135

That was little comfort. I wanted an armed guard, not a white robed guy with a lamb slung over his shoulder. I didn't think Jesus would have slowed them down much. After all, the bunch that crucified him was not much different from high-school seniors and juniors, I reasoned.

"You don't know what they do to you," I said to Mama. "They paint your face with lipstick and they put a belt around your neck and lead you around like a dog and they make you carry their books home and – and – all sorts of awful stuff."

"You'll be fine," she said.

"That's not the worst of it." I wrung my hands together, wondering if I should tell her the absolute worst. "Sometimes they 'pants' you."

"'Pants' you?"

"Yeah. A bunch of guys gang up on you right there on the school grounds and pull your pants off. Then they hide your pants or run 'em up on the flagpole. You have to run around in your underwear in front of girls and everybody. It's awful! Really, really awful!"

Mama went right on peeling potatoes like she didn't even care. Why didn't she understand?

"Sometimes they even take away your underwear!" I wailed. "Everybody laughs at you. What would I do, Mama? How would I get home? I couldn't walk all that way without any pants. I don't even want to go to school."

"I'll pray for you," she said. Just like that. "I'll pray for you." She was totally unaware of my own lack of faith. It would be an unmatched miracle for me to get through the first week of highschool without being initiated. It would be as great a miracle as Jesus' walking on water or turning water into wine. Miracles never happened at our house. Talking to God wasn't any more productive than talking to Mildred through tin cans strung together with wire. Prayer never rose past the ceiling.

On the first day of school, I stood in the hallway of Alhambra High School waiting for the bell to ring. I turned back the cuffs of my long-sleeved shirt exactly two folds. It was the way the older kids wore theirs. I scribbled designs and fake signatures on my three-ring binder so that it wouldn't look new – sort of a battle camouflage and I tucked a stub of a pencil behind my ear. I chewed on a toothpick, too. I don't know why, but I had seen some seniors do that and figured it would help me blend in.

The bell finally rang and I simulated a saunter down the hall to Mr. Scanlon's room, my Orientation Class. Mr. Scanlon was a no-nonsense sort of man, heavy-set with black hair, who brought the class to order by crashing a blue paperweight down onto his desk in a way that stopped all conversation and made many swallow their chewing gum. The class was entirely made up of freshmen, but somehow they all seemed more sophisticated than I. Mr. Scanlon was of the opinion that a new freshman class was like a new colt that needed breaking in. Once you established who was boss, the rest was easy. He lost no time in firmly establishing who was boss. If I was nervous before, I was terrified by the end of that first session.

At the end of the day, I slid out the side door and walked as casually as my taut nerves would let me, sneaking glances behind me to be sure I wasn't being followed. Once I cleared the school grounds, I ran the entire two miles home, stopping only to catch my breath when I felt it was safe.

"I made it!" I said to Mama. "I made it through the first day!"

"I told you that you would," Mama said. "I prayed for you."

She talked like the whole ordeal was over, but I knew different. This was only the first day. There were four more fear-filled days to go. I felt like a bird in a turkey-shoot. With so many out to get me, how could I possibly escape for four more days?

The next three days were repeats of the first one. Mr. Scanlon putting the fear of the administration into all of us and my own desperate attempts to appear two or three years older than I was. The first week, we didn't have to dress for gym, but I did have an "athletic supporter" in my gym locker and had even raised enough courage to go to the store and buy it myself, carefully avoiding all female clerks.

The last day would be the real test – Friday – the day notorious for "scrubs" to feel the scorn and derision of juniors and seniors. I arrived at school as late as I could without being marked tardy. I had almost perfected the art of acting blase. I clasped my "worn" ring-binder loosely with one hand and stuffed my other hand into my pocket and clicked keys together. No matter that the keys didn't fit anything. They made a nice, grown-up sound. I didn't drink anything all day, figuring that dehydration was a more acceptable consequence than going to the boys restroom. The restroom was a sure trap for unsuspecting "scrubs."

After the last bell had rung, I skipped going to the locker. No use inviting trouble. Knots of older boys formed in the halls and there was plenty of evidence of their work – boys and girls, but mostly boys, with bright, red lipstick scrawled on their faces and kids carrying huge stacks of books for jeering upper-class students. I hoped – I prayed – that it wouldn't happen to me. The older students were prowling the hallways like prides of lions after helpless prey. I slipped out a side door and headed for home.

I hadn't walked a block when I glanced over my shoulder to see a red-haired giant running after me. My heart took on the staccato beat of a Latin drummer. I knew what he would do if he caught me. My nose would glow with crimson lipstick and "s-c-r-u-b" would be blotched on my forehead like a neon sign. Maybe he would even steal my pants.

"Hey, kid!" he yelled. I quickened my pace, calling on every ounce of adrenaline in my body. He was gaining on me and there was nothing I could do.

"Hey, kid!" he yelled again. "Wait a second."

I froze. He had closed the gap. I was a goner.

"What are you running for? Are you scared or somethin'?" he asked.

"Me?" I protested. "Why would I be scared?" I knew my heavy breathing betrayed me.

The red-haired kid tipped his head and gave me a disbelieving smile. "Here are your keys," he said. "They must have fallen out of your pocket. I thought you might need them."

"Ahhh – yeah – sure," I stammered. "Thanks a lot."

"Next time, don't be in such a big hurry," he said. He shook his head, turned and left in the opposite direction. I stuffed the useless keys back into my pocket and walked on my way slowly, then quickening my stride as soon as he was out of sight.

From then on, I didn't use the heavy traffic streets – Main Street or Atlantic Boulevard. I dodged south on side streets, zig-zagging blocks like a fugitive trying to lose the police. If I saw some other student, I cut across a lawn, acting like my own house was the very next one.

It took me a long time to get home, but there it was at last, that yellow and brown, wood-frame house, with its untrimmed lawn and wild red-berry bushes and clusters of yellow dandelions and the dirty litter blown against the retaining walls, looking more like a castle than it ever had before.

I bounded up the front steps and through the door, shutting it hard behind me. I gasped for breath like a marathon runner. Mama heard me and came out of the kitchen, wiping her hands on her apron.

"Well, how did it go?" she asked.

I grinned. I could relax now for the whole weekend. "It's

over," I sighed. "Nothing happened. Absolutely nothing. It's a miracle."

"I'm not surprised," she said, as though she hadn't been worried at all – as though it had been no serious matter anyway. "I knew you'd get through it all right. I prayed for you."

She went out to the kitchen again to shell peas or make meatloaf or whatever she had to do to prepare supper. She passed it all off so easily. Maybe I had made too much of it. Maybe all those stories I had heard from others were exaggerated. Maybe it wasn't such a big miracle after all.

I laid my three-ring binder on top of the clutter that stood in a heap on the table. The extra weight was more than the pile could bear, causing magazines and papers to slip to the floor in a cascade of paper. There, sticking out between the Saturday Evening Post and Liberty Magazine was Mama's plaque, "Prayer Changes Things."

I remembered the red-painted faces in the hallway and the taunting of the students as short freshmen carried large stacks of books. I remembered, too, the giant red-haired boy running after me with something waving in his hand. Well – maybe it had been a miracle – sort of a miracle, anyway.

CHAPTER 20

A TOURIST IN BAKERSFIELD

---

*"Hip is the sophistication of the wise
primitive in a giant jungle."*

-Norman Mailer

The word "klutz" had not yet entered our vocabulary, but that's what I was, back in the late thirties. As far as social acumen was concerned, I could have come from another century. Mama and Papa were not exactly social sophisticates themselves, so they had little to pass on to me. Besides, I was the "sickly" one and had no need of such things. In their overzealous, protective parenting, I was kept away from much of the worldly wisdom that my brother and sister picked up by the osmosis of everyday living. Some of that was about to change in the early spring of 1940. My brother, Raymond, would guide me through what amounted to a "rite of passage."

Raymond wasn't a "bum" anymore. This miraculous transformation was accomplished through the innocent charms of a gorgeous young woman by the name of Hazel Morton. Raymond met Hazel at U.S.C. in the fall of 1939 and brought her home to "meet the family" shortly thereafter.

The fateful meeting took place one evening in our living room amidst the pervasive, green aura of the monstrous pool table. Mama and I were the first ones to be introduced to

141

Hazel. After the introduction, Mama excused herself to go summon Papa, who was ensconced, as usual, in his hideaway "office." As she knocked on the door, I could hear his subdued growl like the flush of a stubborn toilet.

As Papa entered the living room, the first thing that surely struck him was Hazel's extraordinary good looks. This outstanding example of feminine pulchritude brought a smile to his face like a rainbow after a rain shower. Hazel, with her dark, coffee-colored hair and sculpturesque form were enough to grab his undivided attention, but link that with her undeniable intelligence and academic prowess and it was enough to erase all past grudges Papa might have held against his oldest son. Now Raymond was not just the prodigal returned home; he had never even been away. Papa was totally "won over" and, at long last, Raymond was part of the family again.

Hazel lived in Bakersfield, California, which, to my unsophisticated mind, was close to the end of the civilized world. Raymond, as a true entrepreneur, had invested in a number of peanut and gum-ball vending machines to help himself through school. As good fortune would have it, these vending machines were also concentrated in Bakersfield with a few stationed on up the valley toward Fresno. When Raymond periodically serviced his machines, it was more than convenient to include a few dates with Hazel on his agenda. It was all of this that prompted Raymond to invite me to go along on one of his trips to Bakersfield to help service his machines and to meet Hazel's family.

Just a few months before, Papa would not have let me go on such a long trip, especially with Raymond, but now that Raymond was not a "bum" anymore, it was okay for me to go with him. This was adventure of the highest order. Not exactly travel to a foreign country, but close to it. "Bakersfield is a whole different culture," Raymond impressed upon me. "Not all that far from home, but you'd be surprised at how unlike

Los Angeles it is. Little mannerisms and customs; Bakers-field – is just different." I wondered if I would be able to pick out the differences. Did the people speak with accents? Did they wear their hair in a different style? Hazel certainly was not all that different better looking than most, but not strange in any way. I wondered about all that.

It was early spring in 1940 and I was, without doubt, the most unsophisticated fourteen year old in the state, maybe the world. The prospects of the long trip ahead filled me with both excitement and apprehension. I looked forward to the new sights and sounds of a different city, but I also knew my proclivity toward social blunders and was deathly afraid that I would embarrass myself and my older brother.

Two days before the trip, I started packing. "What shall I take, Mama?" I asked.

"Take your good suit," she said. "You want to look nice when you meet Hazel's parents."

"I know that, Mama, but what else should I take?"

She was not much help. When she first married Papa, she had traveled to Brazil. Surely she must know more about travel than "take your good suit." I would be gone for three days. So how would I pack for that? I wasn't growing any hair on my face, so I wouldn't need a razor, but would I need that cream stuff you rub on under your arms? Should I take soap? A towel? And what would I put it all in? Papa had a brown, expandable bag with straps across the top. The big, ugly valise was roomy enough, but it was so antique looking that I wouldn't carry it even if he'd let me.

"I'll need something to keep my hair in place," I said. "Wildroot Cream Oil is nice. Could I get some of that?"

Mama sighed. "I suppose so," she said, "but you'll have to use some of your own money. I don't have any right now."

"I know," I said.

With the care and anxiety of an Arctic explorer, I laid out

my travel necessities as best I could – tooth brush, comb, socks, underwear. Lacking more appropriate travel gear, I stuffed these items into a Bullock's Department Store shopping bag. Who would know? I would be staying in an honest-to-goodness motel. Only Raymond would see the makeshift suitcase. My greatest concern was my lack of sophistication. I would be with refined college students, citizens of the world and those who were at ease in refined society. This both excited me and terrified me. I was well aware of my lack. Papa's idea of high adventure was a trip to Grand Central Market in L.A., and his notion of culture was a Johann Strauss waltz played on our Victrola. I thought "eggs Benedict" might be eggs laid by a chicken named Benedict.

I was up early on the day of our departure. The excitement of travel drove all sleep away. As Raymond pulled into the driveway with his 1936 Ford coupe, I hugged Mama as though I were headed for a tour of duty overseas. I was worried about leaving her alone. She was not well. My enthusiasm for travel, however, overruled for the moment the concern I had for her health.

"Got your things all packed?" Raymond asked, bounding up the front steps.

"Sure do," I said, handing him the Bullock's shopping bag. "Mama said you could probably fold up this suit in the trunk of the car."

Raymond took my things and placed them beside his suitcase in the trunk. Raymond climbed into the driver's seat and I moved in beside him. As we backed out onto Atlantic Boulevard, the twelve years between us seemed to disappear. Being temporarily free of any parental control instantly added at least ten years to my age. I rolled down the window to feel the warm California breeze whip against my face and to drink in the sophistication of the moment.

As we wound our way through the streets of Pasadena toward the foothills and Highway 99, I began to envy Raymond's independence and wondered what it would be like to be free – really free – to be able to pick out your own clothes, have your own transportation, go by your own time schedule and make your own decisions. To me, Raymond had it all. He had found the good life. I wondered if I ever would. I did not consider the responsibility or work that went with that freedom.

Soon we were out of the city and became part of the long-haul traffic that wove through the California hills toward points north – Bakersfield, Fresno, Modesto and Sacramento. It was a revelation to see just how many there were, truckers, bus drivers and commuters, who drove this route week in and week out through fair weather and foul. I felt part of a great fraternity of travelers.

The trucks pulling up the grade toward Gorman and Lebec through the Tehachapi Mountains seemed almost standing still as we passed them. Soon we were at the top of the perilous "Grapevine." Here it was, Raymond said, that brakes failed, engines burned up and cooling systems went dry. Coming back up the Grapevine from the other direction, we must take extra water and put the car in second gear around the steep, treacherous curves. The danger of it all added to my excitement and sense of adventure.

After we twisted and turned down the tangled path of the Grapevine, the road straightened out into a line that stretched from here to eternity. I had never in my life seen a highway that continued mile after endless mile until it simply disappeared into the shimmering heat waves on the distant horizon. I was sure that it would take us far into the next day before we found a bend in the road. Raymond assured me it wouldn't. I sat in awe pondering the fact that my brother made this trip, on average, once a month and managed to remain so blase about it all. The landscape began to take on a different form. Fields of green were sprinkled with white puffs like popcorn. "Cotton," Raymond explained to me. I had never seen cotton growing before. And oil wells—hundreds of them. This must be the richest country this side of Baghdad. This was, indeed, like a foreign country.

At last we reached our motel in mid-town Bakersfield, a modest affair as motels go, but it was majestic to my young eyes. As Raymond pulled his Ford into the asphalt parking area, heat rose to meet us as though we had rolled onto a griddle. I had experienced heat in Alhambra, but nothing like this as early in the year as it was. The hum of the air conditioner beckoned us inside.

That air conditioner was another reminder of the luxury of this travel experience. They were not all that common in 1940, and I was duly impressed. I wasn't sure how I could sleep through the noise of it, but who needed to sleep anyway? I had slept in a hospital bed, of course, away from home, and I had slept on the ground in a tent in the backyard of a friend, but I had never slept in a motel. The bed was made up with a bedspread, clean towels hung in neat rows in the bathroom, a tidy desk and chair was at our disposal with a complimentary note pad and pencil, there were several lamps, all of them working and even a telephone. I was overwhelmed by the splendor of it all. I hung up my suit on the coat rack, unpacked my Bullock's shopping bag and walked around the room in wide eyed amazement.

Raymond settled into a chair, picked up the phone and called Hazel. We were to eat at her house that night and he wanted to confirm the time and let her know that we were in town. It was about then that the panic set in. What was expected of me? What was I supposed to do and not do? I didn't want to confess to my apprehension, but I didn't want to embarrass myself either.

Raymond directed me to the bathroom and showed me the

tiny, wrapped bar of soap. He said he would take a shower after I was finished. Shower? I had just taken a bath last night. Why did I need to take another bath? I didn't voice my objection. Of course this is what one did in the sophisticated world. One bathed after a long trip and especially before dinner.

"While you're at it," Raymond said, "cut your fingernails. They're dirty and I don't like the looks of them." I scurried into the bathroom and shut the door. I had not taken particular notice of my fingernails before. Now they appeared to be ugly, black claws, unfit for proper company. What else was wrong with me? I had polished my shoes before I came, so that didn't need to be done. Had I put in any deodorant cream? No! I forgot the deodorant cream! Oh, well, maybe if I used enough soap no one would notice. Anyway, I had brought the Wildroot Cream Oil for my hair. It had a nice scent to it and would probably cover up most anything else.

I shut the bathroom door and undressed for the shower. Strange how small differences can unnerve you. We did not have a shower at home, only a tub. No matter. Adjusting the flow of water and getting it to come out the shower head instead of the spigot couldn't be all that complicated. I experimented with the faucets until I got the right water temperature coming out of the spout. I discovered a little knob over the spout and pulled it. The water burst forth from the shower head in a blinding spray while I drew the shower curtain forward and fiddled with the shower head to adjust the direction. Pretty swell. A shower all our own for as long as we wanted. I took my time. Only when I finally turned off the water and stepped out of the tub did I notice that something must have leaked. There was enough water on the floor to form a habitat for ducks.

"Raymond, the shower leaks," I called out in alarm.

Raymond opened the door and sized up the situation through the steamed up bathroom. Hands on hips, he exhaled a great sigh and shook his head. "You're supposed to put the shower curtain inside the tub. If you let it hang outside, the water runs off onto the floor. I thought you would have picked that up somewhere along the way. Haven't you ever taken a shower before?"

"Sure. Lots of times," I lied, "but this never happened before."

"Well, let's mop it up," he said.

"What with?" I asked.

"The towels, of course. What else is there?"

The steam dissipated through the open door and my ego right along with it. How could I be so dumb? What would we do with the soaking wet towels? Would the manager of the hotel yell at us for making such a mess? Would Raymond be charged extra for the room? Now he would probably feel that it was a mistake to ever bring me along.

After we had sopped up the water and thrown the soaked towels into the tub, I fished out my clean shirt and socks from the Bullocks shopping bag and pawed through my other belongings for the bottle of hair oil. Without it, my dry, blond hair would fluff out like cotton candy on a stick.

"I can't find my Wildroot Cream Oil," I said. "It must have dropped out of the bag. It's probably in the trunk of the car. Could I have the keys?"

"I'll go get it," Raymond said. "I have to go get my jacket anyway."

He trotted through the door of our room that opened onto the parking lot. The hot, Bakersfield heat radiated off the asphalt like waves on the Sahara. He opened the trunk of the car, retrieved his jacket and quickly spotted the bottle of hair oil. I took a few steps out onto the pavement.

"Here you go," he said. He half squatted to the ground and slid the bottle toward me. It was an innocent flourish of geniality meant to contribute to our bonding, like a slap on the shoulder or a knuckle rub to the head. How could he know that the rough, hot surface of the asphalt would burst the bottle as cleanly as a hammer blow? Well, it did. The white cream oozed out onto the blacktop in a viscous puddle of goo.

"I'm sorry," Raymond lamented, holding his hands to his head. "I'm really, really sorry."

"It's okay," I shrugged, trying hard to be nonchalant. "It wasn't very expensive."

How could I say that? It cost way more than a loaf of bread or even a gallon of gas. And it wasn't just the cost, either. How was I going to keep my unruly hair in place?

"I'll buy you another bottle tomorrow. I promise," Raymond said. "I'd buy you a bottle tonight, but we're already late for dinner at Hazel's house."

"Don't worry about it," I said, mustering a weak smile. "I'll just use water. It works just as well."

I knew that wasn't so, but I didn't want to be anymore trouble than I already had been. It was an unforeseen accident, but I felt guilty for it anyway. Guilt was going to be my chief companion for this whole trip.

We climbed into the Ford coupe and rolled down the windows to prevent being cooked alive in the ferocious Bakersfield heat. We pulled out of the parking lot and headed toward Hazel's house on 19th Street. I don't remember any nervous gestures on my part, but there must have been some because Raymond told me to "just relax." How does one "relax" on command? I tried.

"Now Hazel's Dad is Ross Morton and her Mom is Grace Morton. Remember that," Raymond emphasized, "because names are important. Nothing is so important as a person's name. You like people to call you by your name, don't you? Huh?"

"No."

"What?"

"I don't really like my name," I said. "Kids name their goldfish 'Wilbur.' I don't really like my name."

Raymond sighed and I could see him work the muscles of his jaw . "Well, you'd better like it, because it's going to be yours for as long as you live. And believe me, everybody likes to be called by name. But don't use first names with anyone that's a stranger, okay?"

I tried to absorb the strange advice he was giving me. "So what do I call them?"

"'Mister' or 'Misses.' You don't say, 'Hello Ross,' you say, 'Hello Mr. Morton.' You don't say, 'Hello Grace,' you say, 'Hello Mrs. Morton.' Got that?"

"I think so."

"Don't think so; know so. Let me hear you say, 'How do you do, Mr. Morton.'"

"How do you do, Mr. Morton." My repetition sounded stilted and unnatural.

Raymond shook his head. I was afraid he would give up on me. Why couldn't I just be myself? Learning this stuff was such a pain.

"And another thing," he continued, "don't bow like you did the first time you met Hazel. That's kind of dumb. No one does that anymore. It's old fashioned."

"I thought it was proper manners."

"It's affected. Too formal. Way out of place."

I sat in silence, but the more I tried to absorb the simple social graces, the more panic stricken I became. The air blowing in the window was cooling some, but it was still warm. My hair was thoroughly dry, by this time and was flying about like straw in a windstorm. There was no way I was going to be able to comb it into anything but a feather duster.

Raymond rounded the corner onto 19th Street and we slowed down. We passed several houses until we came to the brown, shingled house that was the Morton residence. It had a wide front porch, just as our own house did, and a sturdy foundation made from large, gray stones. Papa would have called it a "substantial house."

My pulse quickened as I got out of the car. I could feel my unruly hair sticking straight out from my head, porcupine style, and I was afraid I might trip over my own clumsy feet before I reached the front steps. When we got onto the porch, Raymond rang the bell. "Just relax," he said, "and remember what I told you." How I could do both at once was a mystery.

The door opened and Grace Morton stood before us with open arms. She smiled broadly as she greeted Raymond and then turned to me. "And this must be Wilbur."

"How do you do Mrs. Morton," I said. Ross Morton walked into the room. "How do you do Mr. Morton," I added. Hazel was by her father's side. "How do you do . . ." and then words failed me. What should I say? Hazel? Miss Morton? I held out my hand in a weak gesture. That brought a burst of giggles, even from Raymond. Why? Why were they laughing? My face was a chili pepper. They thought I was "cute." If there was anything I did not want to be, it was "cute."

Raymond moved over to the couch and Mr. Morton to the easy chair while Hazel and Mrs. Morton retired to the kitchen to put the finishing touches on dinner. I sat on the opposite end of the couch and smouldered.

Soon, Mrs. Morton stepped into the living room, removing her apron, to announce that dinner was ready. As we approached the table, I was both awe struck and terrified. The candles were lit, the fine china in place, water glasses, coffee cups, linen napkins with little rings around them and more silverware at each place than I would ever use all day long. Why were there two forks at each place and an extra spoon placed crosswise above the plate? The opportunity for social blundering was enormous.

At home, we had china too. Mama had hand painted it herself, but it was never used. It was too nice. It was like the engagement ring that Papa bought for Mama. Good to look at from time to time, but much too expensive to use. Our "dinners" at home were catch-as-catch-can affairs, never around the table. Mama took Papa's dinner to him in his room, where he ate alone. The rest of us heaped up our plates and took them to the living room where we could listen to the latest fifteen minute installments of serial adventures on the radio. Meals were practical and utilitarian, not social events.

I decided that in this situation, the best course was not to make a move until I observed what others did. I certainly did not want to bring further embarrassment to my brother or myself. I did not speak unless spoken to and I did not lift a fork or a spoon unless I saw someone else do it first. To add to my self consciousness, my hair was so full of static electricity that it fairly crackled if I touched another surface.

As we drove back to the motel from the Morton's that night, there were some fine pointers from Raymond on the subject of conversational skills of which I had none. I cannot recall all that was said, but the gist of the lesson was that I should be interested enough in other people to ask pertinent questions about their work, hobbies, family, interests, likes and dislikes, but I was to avoid like poison the subjects of politics and religion. It was all too much for me to learn. I longed for bed and a new day.

That new day dawned bright and clear as we started out to service the gum-ball machines. Raymond took a quick inventory of supplies in the trunk of his car, reviewed his list of locations and slid into the driver's seat. I thought my day would consist of learning the inside secrets of the gum-ball business and it did, of course, but it was also to be a rolling classroom to inculcate social savoir-faire as well. My first lesson began before we had driven a scant mile down the road.

A man out for a morning stroll waved at us. Raymond waved back, but I sat like one of the stone faces on Easter Island.

Raymond gave me a look of disapproval. "Why didn't you wave?" he asked.

"Because I didn't know the guy." The answer seemed obvious to me.

"That doesn't matter," Raymond said with measured emphasis. "When someone waves at you, wave back."

"Why?" I asked. "He doesn't know me and I'll probably never see him again."

"Are you part of the human race?" Raymond was an expert at razor-sharp sarcasm. "Civilized people wave back. It's a simple greeting. It's like saying 'hello.' Do you only say 'hello' to people you know?"

"Yes." Sometimes honesty was my downfall.

Raymond shook his head. "I don't know where you've been, Wilbur, but I think it's time you hatched. Maybe the guy who waved at you knew you and maybe he didn't. When you just sit there like a tree stump, it's an insult. What does it cost you to be friendly? Not a darn thing. When you wave back, you're saying, 'Hi there. Nice day.' When you don't, you're saying, 'I don't care about you.' It's rude. So crack out of your shell and be a little more friendly. You'll get a lot farther in life."

I slid down in my seat a little. I hoped another stranger would pass by so that I could wave to him. No one did and I had nothing to wave to but the trees.

There was so much to learn – how to shake hands with a firm grip, how to smile and make small talk, how to look people in the eye – to say nothing of the business end of the enterprise. I learned how to count pennies and wrap them, how to clean the glass bowls of the vending machines, how to replenish the supply of gum or peanuts, and how to pay the proprietor for allowing space in his store. This was not a work free sight-seeing trip.

In between service calls, Raymond grilled me and drilled me on the social aspects of adjusting to high school. He stressed the importance of good study habits, getting along with teachers, being on time and so forth. He could have saved his breath. I already knew all that. What I didn't know was how to dress more like other kids as long as Papa purchased everything I had to wear. It was embarrassing to wear long-johns and flannel shirts when no one else ever did. And I wanted a new pair of Keds instead of wing-tips and a belt instead of suspenders. Most of all, I wanted some loose change jingling in my pockets.

"You just have to stand up to Papa," Raymond insisted. "Tell him kids don't dress like that anymore. Tell him things have changed." Easy enough for him to say. He hadn't lived at home for a long time and seemed to forget the patriarchal dynasty under which we lived and the "big depression" mentality pervading everything Papa did. Now he had Hazel to run interference for him. He had a new kind of freedom, respect and independence that was almost like someone new coming in from outside.

We finished our gum-ball chores in the early afternoon and went back to the motel to get cleaned up, change our clothes and get ready for supper. Raymond was taking Hazel and her folks and me out to a restaurant. This time, I showered with the curtain inside the tub and plastered my hair down with a new kind of hair oil that Raymond had bought. I was ready for another "learning experience." I had never eaten in a restaurant before.

The restaurant was nice, but not as elegant as the ones I had seen in Hollywood. Nevertheless, all of my senses were on full alert and I was watchful for any faux pas – traps that lurked behind the innocent looking water glasses or the folded napkins.

The piquant odors from the kitchen wafted in front of us as we entered, but I wasn't a bit hungry. I was more like a prisoner on his way to the gallows. How could I be interested in food? All of my energy was focused on appearing suave. We stood huddled in a bunch until the hostess came and led us to our table. Hmmmm. Interesting. Why couldn't we just walk in and sit down? How strange were the rules of propriety. I waited to sit until all the others were seated. Raymond held the chair for Hazel and Mr. Morton held the chair for Mrs. Morton. With a deft forward motion, they nudged the chairs closer to the table so that the ladies could sit down. How smooth. Would I someday develop that art form? I must practice at home. I pulled out my own chair and sat to Raymond's left.

The cloth napkins were folded in front of us like miniature tents. How quaint. I waited to see what others did with them. They did nothing. A buxom waitress approached with five menus and passed them out. I had seen people use menus in the movies, but I had never actually held one in my hand. I opened it with caution, as though something might fly out. The others studied theirs with rapt interest and I tried to do the same. Actually, it might as well have been written in Chinese. Entrees? What was an "Entree?" I couldn't even pronounce it. Appetizers? What were they? And then there were "beverages." Why not just say "drinks" and be done with it? Most of the foods listed I had never heard of – couldn't even spell. What were they? And "A la carte?" What was that? Did that mean they wheel in your food on a cart? The prices were all scattered about in such a way that they made no sense. How much did anything cost? As I tried to understand, I calculated that this little dinner was going to cost poor Raymond the monthly revenue from two or three peanut machines. Outrageous. The silence dragged on as the others weighed the possibilities and pondered their choices. I just sat dry mouthed and mystified.

Soon the waitress returned again, smiled and asked if we were ready to order. Raymond answered in the affirmative. The others nodded in agreement. I froze. I didn't know a croissant from a crocus. I waited.

Raymond nodded toward Mrs. Morton. "You first," he said.

"I think I'll have a breaded veal cutlet," she said, "with potatoes au gratin, and the tossed green salad with vinaigrette dressing."

What strange language are we using here, I wondered? Yes, indeed, Bakersfield was different. They didn't even eat the same food I did.

The waitress made some notations on her pad and looked over to Hazel for her order. "That sounds awfully good to me," she said. "I'll have the same – breaded veal cutlet."

The waitress jotted it down and then all eyes turned to me. Without hesitation, like a hopelessly broken record, I choked out, "The same. I'll have a breaded veal cutlet." I had no idea what I was ordering, only that the safe thing to do was follow suit.

Raymond looked down at me with utter disgust. "Oh Wilbur," he said, in those slow, even tones that registered total disappointment. Hazel and Mrs. Morton giggled and Mr. Morton smiled. I had done it again. I had committed the unpardonable sin. Unwittingly, I had stumbled and fallen on my face. With the best of intentions, I had completely embarrassed my brother.

"No, really" I objected. "That's what I want – breaded veal cutlet. Yes. That's my favorite."

I pondered what I had ordered. "Bread" I understood. So was it something wrapped in bread? Like a sandwich? What was veal? Some kind of meat, I presumed, but whether it came from the range, the sea or the air, I couldn't guess.

Mercifully, the waitress went on to Mr. Morton. I have

forgotten what he ordered, but it most certainly was not a breaded veal cutlet. After the orders were taken, the rest of them unfolded their napkins and placed them in their laps. I wanted to place mine over my head. When the orders finally arrived, I studied the contents of my plate and tested the veal cutlet as a visitor from a rain forest might do. I stabbed it, cut it, smelled it, pushed it about and ultimately tasted it. I probably would have even enjoyed it, had I not lost my appetite. By then, the conversation resumed its normal flow back and forth across the table and I was more or less ignored, which was exactly what I wanted. I had endured the test of my social graces and, by any measurement, I had flunked. By the time we reached the motel again, I flopped into bed, exhausted, and longed to be home again. Foreign travel was just not for me.

Mama and Papa had traveled to Brazil and drunk the smoky dregs of matte. Raymond had clung to the top of freight cars, traveled to Milwaukee and tasted lager from the German brewer's craft. Mildred had sailed to Catalina Island, waved at flying fish and dined on abalone. Now it remained for me to uphold the cosmopolitan reputation of our clan. I had traveled to Bakersfield and eaten a breaded veal cutlet.

CHAPTER 21

THE EQUALIZER

"Guns will make us powerful;
butter will only make us fat."

-Hermann Goering

Papa always slept with a Colt .38 under his pillow. When no one else was around, I would lift the pillow and look at it. Like a coiled cobra ready to strike, it lay poised, chilling, deadly. This was probably the only revolver under any pillow in the whole city of Alhambra, but in the early 30's I did not think it unusual. Although at times the muzzle pointed in her direction, Mama did not complain, so I considered it normal to sleep with a gun. One grows accustomed to the usual. Papa kept it under his pillow in case of emergency – prowlers, gangsters, escaped convicts, that sort of thing. I imagined that this included Catholics and Technocrats who, I had heard, were set to take over the world and ruin the country. In any case, Papa often told me that he would shoot first and ask questions afterward, so I made sure that I was never out behind the garage after dark and that I whistled Yankee Doodle good and loud if I emptied the garbage after sunset. I was impressed by that gun. It was almost alive. Its cold, blue steel and brassy cartridges exuded undisputed power. It was the "great equalizer," Papa used to say. That weapon could make a weakling strong and turn a cripple into a man to be reckoned with.

I used to pretend that I had a gun – all my friends pretended, too. For an eight year old, an index finger made a pretty good gun barrel and a thumb pointed skyward served well as a trigger. Armed with these imaginary weapons, we played cops and robbers or cowboys and Indians. Back then, no one worried much about the socioeconomic forces that shaped some men into robbers or the ethics involved in overpowering Native Americans. The world was all black and white.

The problem with imaginary guns was imaginary bullets – whether a man was hit or not was always open to dispute.

"Gotcha! You're dead!"

"I am not! You missed me a mile!"

This was a dialogue shouted from a thousand young throats in backyards across the city, which often resulted in a more decisive kind of combat involving black eyes and bloody noses.

The squirt gun was a vast improvement in weaponry. These blackened-tin pistols with gold colored tips were filled with water by pulling back on a notched plunger positioned at the rear. A good squirt gun could fire six or seven rounds in rapid succession. Of course, the gun had a relatively short range, but there could be little dispute over who was hit and who wasn't. It took away the guesswork.

The problem was that the squirt gun lacked realism. It made no noise and produced no smoke. A cap-gun did both of these. It was as much preferred over the squirt gun as a revolver over a blunderbuss. Besides, by inserting two caps in place of just one, the "bang" was awesome and the white smoke curling out of the barrel was enough to palpitate the heart of any young lad.

What I wanted was a cap-gun. Not just any cap-gun, mind

you, but the one on display at the local Woolworth's Five and Ten Cent Store. Realism was crafted into that gun like no other. It looked like a real gun, hefted like a real gun and felt like a real gun as I curled my fingers around its simulated ivory handle. The vision of that gun dominated my thoughts day and night. I had made do with finger and thumb long enough. I had a squirt gun, but it was like a toy. I already had a belt and holster, but it hung lifeless and empty from my hip. I had to have that gun.

The big problem was, that particular gun cost fifty cents. That was as much as five Saturday matinees or ten single-dip ice cream cones. This vast amount required going to Papa, who was the source of all grants above ten cents. I rehearsed my plea all Saturday morning, but couldn't muster enough courage to appear before Papa until after lunch. I'm not sure whether it was the whine in my voice or the tears in my eyes which had the most influence on Papa. Maybe neither one. Maybe he was just pleased to see his sickly child plead for such an obvious symbol of red-blooded masculinity. In any case, to my surprise and delight, Papa opened his leather coin purse – the Fort Knox of our family – and handed me a fifty cent piece.

I learned first-hand the meaning of a gun's being the great equalizer. Surely that cap-gun proved the point. With its long, shining, silver barrel and its gleaming white handle, it was the envy of every boy in the neighborhood. I was more than their equal now; I was the leader of the pack. To feel the weight of that gun slapping against my thigh from a low-slung holster was to know unsurpassed power. Overnight, I was the most popular of the backyard cowboys. I was sought after, admired and envied. Once in a while I would loan it to a friend, but only for a few minutes and only to "cops," never to robbers and only to "cowboys," never to Indians. The borrowers, of course, had to supply their own caps.

In time, however, even the cap-guns grew inadequate. There was simply no way to prove that one was a good or bad shot with a cap-gun. For all the noise and smoke, it inflicted no genuine pain. Now that we gun toters were older, something more violent was needed. The rubber-band gun became the weapon of choice.

The rubber-band gun was fashioned from a piece of scrap board. Almost any piece of wood would do, so long as it was twelve to eighteen inches long. A coping saw, some sandpaper, and a spring-held clothespin could form a fearsome addition to any boy's arsenal. The clothespin was mounted near the handle to hold one end of the rubber band while the other end was stretched over the muzzle. The rubber band, mind you, was no puny circle like the paper boy used to hold the Alhambra Post Advocate together – no, it was a three quarter inch section cut from an automobile tire inner tube with a knot tied in the middle. When fired, it packed enough wallop to raise a welt on the skin like a red boil. It was a hazard to the eyes, ears and other vital parts of the body, but budding young warriors are little concerned about real dangers, only courage, prowess and the howls of defeated enemies. That none of us ended up with a patch over one eye is an indication of our lack of marksmanship rather than a tribute to our concern for others.

Then 1943 came and I was eighteen. Squirt guns, cap-guns and rubber-band guns had long since been put aside. It was time for real guns now – the kind that Papa kept under his pillow. My country had been humiliated before the whole world by a small island of a nation with a pint-sized Emperor Hirohito. I wanted vengeance. I wanted to even the score. Papa's lesson about the "equalizer" had proven to be true. Size seemed to have nothing to do with conquest – fire power did. Given enough bombs and enough airplanes, a tiny, postage stamp empire could virtually wipe out our entire Pacific Fleet.

But now it was our turn. Young men, who had only played with rubber-band guns before, would handle real guns now. We would show the "robbers" of the world what the equalizer could do. We cops, we cowboys, puffed with patriotism and propelled by rage, would make short work of these upstart invaders. Many had already enlisted, the rest of us were now eligible. Even a guy like me – small of stature and crooked of spine – could pull the trigger of a gun. I had been doing it for years.

There is something about standing in a long line of naked men that makes one acutely aware of differences. We were not all alike standing there for our pre-induction physical. We were similar, perhaps, but not alike. Small irregularities of physique glared like giant abnormalities. True deformities stood out like the flaws of Frankenstein. Usually clothes can shield the body from curious stares until one imagines himself to be almost normal, but there were no protective shields in that naked line.

As the owner of each stripped body completed the tedious physical exam, he stood before the medic and was handed a small slip of paper that would decide his destiny. Each naked patriot was eager to avenge his country. Each simply wanted a chance to prove his loyalty. Each wanted a chance to pull the trigger, regardless of his naked body's design.

As I stood before the white-coated medic, I wished for something to cover the flawed part of my nakedness – a tee-shirt or a towel, something to drape around my shoulders. Without lifting his eyes, the medic handed me a small slip of paper about the size found inside a fortune cookie. I thought he might say something. "Move along," were the only words he spoke. I stepped ahead and nervously opened the folded slip. The message was in purple letters, all capitals, a quarter inch high. "REJECTED."

The power of one word can be a blow to the head. That's

all it said, "Rejected." What it really said was, "You are physically unfit to serve your country." What it said was, "You are unequal to your peers – even to your enemies." What it said was, "You are not equal and you will never get your chance at the equalizer." What it said was, "You are forever judged unequal." It is well that the slip did not have more than one word, for I could not have read more anyway.

I hurried to the locker to find my clothes and cover my un-equalness. The trip was a long one. In my mind I framed and re-framed ways to tell my friends of my unequalness – ways to make it sound like maybe my country needed me more urgently at home – to be a Civil Defense Block Warden or a security guard. Nothing worked.

When safely at home, I said nothing to Mama or Papa. There was no need. They knew. They knew before I even went for my physical. What I did do was steal into their bedroom for one last look at Papa's Colt .38 – the "equalizer." I carefully lifted Papa's pillow and stared at the gun. It was smaller than I had remembered. It had shrunk, somehow. Lost its mystique. The ominous, cold steel weapon could do nothing to make me equal. Once the symbol of unquestioned power, it lay there pathetically weak, smothered by a soft, feather pillow.

CHAPTER 22

POWER AND WEAKNESS

"Where love rules, there is no will to power;
and where power predominates, there love
is lacking. The one is the shadow of the other."

-Carl Gustav Jung

The great ring of keys on Papa's belt were like the keys on a jailer's waistband. There were keys to the house, keys to the garage, keys to the gymnasium, keys to the car, keys to various trunks and numerous keys to the school rooms where he taught. The keys jingled and jangled with every heavy step that he took as he marched through the house. The ching-chang of the keys delivered a powerful message just as clear and forceful as any spoken one. The message was power. Saint Peter held the "keys to the Kingdom," but Papa held the keys to everything else. The ring of keys was a badge of authority hooked to his belt. All doors were closed unless he unlocked them. All doors were open unless he locked them.

There were other badges as well. His slide rule was one. He kept it strapped to his waist, ever at the ready. It told the world that he could solve any problem in less than an eye-blink. There were no computers or hand calculators in those days, but Papa's slide rule worked about as well. Did you want to know the circumference of the moon? He could figure it for you in seconds. Did you want to know how many cubic feet of air space in the house? He could tell you in a jiffy. Did you want to know how many metric tons of cabbage a farmer could raise on twelve hectares of land if he planted them thirty centimeters apart and each weighed .45 kilograms? Just ask Papa. He could come up with the answer while you were looking up the definition of a hectare. Papa could solve all things algebraic, geometric or physical with his trusty slide rule and if you couldn't solve it with a slide rule, then it wasn't worth solving.

There was his Colt .38 too, of course. That was the ultimate power piece. When he displayed it, as he liked to do, it quelled all challenges to authority. No one doubted his willingness to use it if other alternatives were exhausted.

Our little family of five was, in truth, a fiefdom. "Head of the house" was a title Papa took quite seriously and literally. His control was absolute, total and unquestioned. Part of this control must be understood within the context of the time. In the first years of the twentieth century, it was not uncommon for husbands and fathers to control most of the decision making. What made our situation unique was the extent to which Papa ruled.

His methods were simple and effective. First of all, forbid all telephone service. While our relatives and most of the neighbors had telephones, we did not. "Too expensive," Papa said. We never questioned that there might be other reasons besides money to explain our lack of a telephone. For whatever reason, the results were the same – a severely limited contact with the outside world.

Second, allow no outside transportation. Many, if not most, families were limited to one car, in those days, but for our one car, Papa was to be the only driver. That meant that most requests for transportation must first be submitted to him. The bus line ran right by our house, but what good was the bus if you didn't have any money?

Third, maintain control of all money in the family; pay all bills, buy all clothes, purchase all food and pay medical expenses. At first blush, this might sound like utopia, but it soon loses its luster if all personal choice is gone as well.

Power over the family is one thing, but power over the neighborhood or on the roadway is quite another. Papa was good at creating an atmosphere of invincible testosterone in these areas as well. One way to do this was to harness contraptions that belched fire, noise, smoke or all three. That is why Papa dearly loved our flame-throwing weed burner. It created such an awesome aura of violent subjugation. The neighbors all had yards with a few inherent weeds, but our yard was bigger and had weeds the size of small trees. Incineration was the only cure. Neighbors stood mesmerized as Papa stood wreathed in flame and smoke, fuel tank strapped to his back, wielding a long, metal tube with a large blowtorch device on the end. It may well have been the precursor to the first military flame-thrower. It was a vision of purgatory created right before their eyes. Had someone called the fire department, Papa would have shooed them away with a wave of the hand. Everything was "under control."

Papa controlled the road, too. Our 1928 blue Buick with the wood-spoked wheels was much like other cars of the day – average in size and speed – but what ours had that no other cars had was a horn that could puncture eardrums and break windows into the next county. Papa rigged our Buick with an air horn that would rival anything the Southern Pacific Railroad had on its locomotives. Let an offending driver cut in front of us on the highway or take up more than one lane of traffic and Papa would give him a blast from the air horn that would raise him six inches off the driver's seat and set his ears ringing for a week. Today it would be called "road rage." Then, it was simply "Papa power." Mildred and I used to crouch down on the rear floor of the car when one of Papa's road tirades occurred, hoping we would not be seen and praying that the car would not careen off the highway and roll over. The objects of Papa's wrath were always so startled and intimidated that they eagerly swerved out of the way of whatever maniac was behind the deafening horn. "DUMB BOOB!" Papa would yell out the open window. Then there usually followed a loud observation that the roads were full of nuts and screwballs that never should be issued a license. Mama flushed with embarrassment, but never argued the point.

Papa's greatest opportunity for power, however, came during World War II. After Japan's attack on Pearl Harbor on December 7th, 1941, Americans on the west coast were understandably fearful of bombing raids from the air. After the devastating destruction of Pearl Harbor, anything seemed possible. The rumor mill went into overtime manufacturing stories about imminent attack, sabotage and dive bombers launched from aircraft carriers. This meant that the eerie wail of air raid sirens often permeated the peaceful skies over Southern California. Blackouts were in order. It was expedient that every streetlight, every commercial sign, every automobile headlight and every household light be turned off completely. The resulting blackness was overwhelming. I remember going out into the street during a blackout, unable to see my own hand in front of my face.

For a blackout to be truly effective and instantaneous, however, volunteer enforcement officers were needed to be sure that all households and businesses complied. The job was tailor made for Papa. He quickly signed up as block warden, was issued a helmet, arm band, shovel and a bucket of sand. The shovel and sand were anti-incendiary measures. Now, at last, Papa had "official," government backed, unquestioned authority to march down Atlantic Boulevard yelling, "Douse those lights! Blackout! Blackout! Do it now!"

All the neighbors on the block were loyal, patriotic Americans and more than willing to obey the orders to turn out their lights, but they also knew that Papa meant business. Perhaps they feared his Colt .38 more than the possibility that a Japanese bomb might drop from the sky. For the duration of the war, Papa enjoyed patrolling the streets wearing the legitimatized badges of his authority and reveling in the excuse to bark commands.

Impressed with the macho image of my bantam-sized father, one of my friends said to me, "Wow! He's a strong man. Do you know anyone more powerful that your Dad?"

"I don't know," I said. "God, maybe. I can't think of anyone else."

CHAPTER 23

A SCARF WITH HOLES

"Mother died today, or maybe
it was yesterday."

-Albert Camus

"The Stranger"

"Oh, What a Beautiful Morning" was the cheerful song coming out of the Philco. The day was Friday, September 10, 1943, but it was not beautiful. The day was ugly. The sun was shining as bright as a copper button on a blue vest, but there was a darkness that hung inside of me that blotted out the sun.

Mama was dead. We didn't have a phone, so hours passed before the sanatorium could get word to us.

Most of the night before, I had prayed for Mama, contorting my face, twisting my insides in agony. At eighteen, I should have known better, but I had been taught that God answers prayer in direct proportion to the anguish of the one who prays. Some lessons cling with the tightness of a tattoo.

"Please! Please, God, don't let her die!"

As I prayed, small cameos of memory passed in front of me – moments insignificant when they occurred, but as important as breath now. So many pictures, buried until this night. Mama in the morris chair, peeling an apple with the dexterity of a Donatello, letting the skin spiral down into a bowl in her lap; Mama standing over the heat vent in winter, flannel gown puffing out, making her an inflated angel as she read out words for my spelling lesson; Mama sitting at the piano, filling the room with music from a bygone era and a bygone life. They were tiny shards of memory forming a sharp mosaic to serrate my soul.

"No, God! No!" I wrestled like Jacob with an unseen opponent, beating my pillow with my fist. "I can't let her go. I won't let her go!"

God was my adversary, with power to take away my dearest and best. The Lord was not my shepherd now. The Lord was not my shield and buckler. The Lord was not my defender. The Lord was my enemy.

It was nearly three in the morning when the struggle ended. Exhausted, I fell back into bed. "Okay, God," I said, "have it your way." That was my version of "Thy will be done." I knew that she wanted to go. I knew it was best – for her – but not for me. She wanted to be free of the hell she had lived in – the pain, the poverty, the pools of blood from her body. I hated to admit the truth. I was not praying for her – I was praying for me.

"If it's best, God, then let it be."

The next morning, Papa told me, "She's gone."

Perhaps Papa thought I was calloused, I wasn't sure and didn't care. I did not cry. The news was old to me by the time he told me. I knew the night before that when I awoke, she would not be alive.

I switched off the radio with its lyrics from "Oklahoma" and sat in silence for awhile.

"Can I go to the beach?" I asked. "Some kids from the church are going and they invited me to go with them."

Papa leaned against the door casing and slipped his thumbs into his belt. He arched his thick eyebrows in a reflex of surprise.

"Well, I guess so," he said. "There's nothing you can do here. I'll make all of the arrangements." Of course he would. Since when did anyone else ever make any "arrangements" in the family? There would be no decisions that he had not already made. There would be no consultations or discussions.

I went to my room, put on my swimming trunks under my clothes, grabbed a towel from the bathroom and left without saying goodbye. I wanted to get away from the house and from Papa. Both Mildred and Raymond had married and no longer lived in our house, so I would have been alone with Papa all day. I neither trusted nor believed his grief and saw no point in sharing it. It was all a sham. How many times had I heard him say to her, "If I outlive you . . ." Now he had outlived her and he could get on with his life. Mine had ended.

I was somber as I rode to the seashore with my three other companions, trying hard not to dampen their gaiety, but not in the mood for laughter myself.

My closest friend was with me. Her name was Ruth, a pre-missionary girl with a scrubbed, no make-up face and a soul to match. She was trying all she knew to put me in a party mood, but could only bring wan smiles in response.

At last we reached the shore, parked the car and unloaded the picnic basket, umbrella and blankets. I spread out my towel and quickly stripped to my swimming trunks. Ruth thought I was some kind of saint when she saw the reddish-purple marks on my knees where I had knelt on the hardwood floor for long hours praying for Mama. I could not help but draw the likeness to camel knees, leathery knobs to match the hump on my back. I didn't worry about it today. Let people stare if they wanted to because I was outside the scene any-way, looking down on actors playing their parts.

I headed for the water and stood ankle deep in the receding tide, feeling the sand wash from under my feet. The damp, salt breeze blew cool across my face like the touch of my mother's hand when I had a fever. Death, like a silent thief, had robbed me forever of the one who gave me life, my counselor, provider, comforter and friend. Grandma Elvina Rees had died six years before, but it was nothing like this. I was left with a vacuum that continued to expand like a great, black hole.

In a moment, Ruth came and stood beside me. "You're awfully quiet today," she said.

"My mother died last night."

Ruth put her hand to her mouth. "Last night?" I nodded my head. "And you still came to the beach party?" she gasped.

"I wanted to get out of the house," I said.

Ruth took my hand and squeezed it. "I'm so sorry," she said.

"It's okay," I said. "I mean, she suffered a lot. It was bound to happen, I guess. Only I hoped maybe it wouldn't happen. You know some miracle or something. It just wasn't to be."

"What will you do?"

"I don't know. Keep living where we are, I guess. Me an' Papa. 'Til I finish high school."

"When will the funeral be?"

"I don't know. Monday, maybe. Tuesday. I don't know. Papa's doing everything."

"Would it be all right if I came?"

"Sure. Of course. Only I'll be with the family, I guess."

"I know," she said.

The rest of the day and the whole weekend passed like a thick, California fog, blanketing all activities into a gray sameness. Was this what grief was like? A dullness that muted the pain and made all of life one big blur?

I don't remember much about the service. It was held at the local mortuary on Main Street. Papa had no church, so asked the Pastor of the church I attended to officiate. There was no eulogy that I could remember. How could there be? Dr. Britton, the Pastor, had met Mama a few times, but only to say "hello." He didn't really know her. Papa never allowed her to go to church with me.

I remember the sick-sweet smell of the flowers and the tearless faces that swam before me like a great montage of black and white photographs. There was the sad organ music and defused light and the muffled shuffle of feet as people passed by the open casket. I resented them because they did not know Mama's story. They came for Papa, who sat appropriately red-eyed, playing the part of a grief stricken husband, but they did not know of her entrapment, her anguish, her starvation for love. They did not know that Papa had not slept inside the house in months, preferring to make his bed out in the gymnasium rather than sleep under the same roof with Mama. They did not know of the months of silence that he built around her like a wall of ice. They did not know of his calloused indifference toward her endless hemorrhaging. They did not know of her loyalty and faithfulness in the face of his mountain rendezvous with a school secretary. They did not know of her poverty that compelled her to beg for any and all personal spending money. Most of all, they did not know of the profoundness of my loss. I wanted to tell them all, but could not.

I shed no tears during the service. I felt only numbness. But at the close, walking by the open casket, seeing my mother's body, dressed in a beautiful dress that Papa had purchased for the occasion, her hair styled in a way that it seldom was in life, face rouged to hide the gaunt, pale complexion, my tears spilled from a reservoir of grief to obscure my vision as though looking through distorted glass. I stumbled into the "family car" provided by the mortuary and sat silently for the long, lonely ride to the cemetery. There was no headstone for the grave. Papa could not afford one. They were impractical anyway, he said. Why did everything have to be utilitarian? Just once, why couldn't the alabaster box of ointment be broken and spilled over bare feet? Why couldn't such a simple acknowledgment of a life lived be given without regard to dollars and cents and practicality?

Days passed into weeks. Papa attempted to share his grief with me, bringing small items Mama had touched during life to show to me and to cry over them; broken beads she intended to string, scripture references written on scraps of paper, wads of tissue emptied from her apron pockets. Was he remorseful? Had his grief blocked out the memory of all those nights and mornings he had raved at her? I didn't know, but I turned away each time.

There were bills to be paid, I was sure of that; hospital bills, doctor bills, funeral expenses. There was one obligation which he seemed to forget; the honorarium for the minister. Years earlier, I wouldn't have mentioned it, but this was the minister of my church and I felt it was important to pay him something. It was the custom, I had heard.

"I haven't forgotten," Papa said. "Did I ever tell you about the minister that married your mother and me?"

"Yes, Papa, I think you did," I said.

He went on as though he hadn't heard me. I knew he would.

"This pompous stuffed-shirt that performed the ceremony was a money grubber."

"Uh-huh."

"I was going to give him a fine, hand made, oak chair for his services, but it took a little time to have it made."

"Uh-huh." I had heard the story a thousand times, but there was no escaping. I had to hear it again.

"Do you think the old fossil could wait? Oh no. After a couple of weeks, he came to me with his hand out."

I don't blame him, I thought. I never did blame him. Every time I heard the story, I blamed him less. Had I been this man, I too would have assumed that I had been forgotten.

"'I usually receive a little something for my services,' he said. How's that for a professional attitude? You'd think he'd be willing to wait for a few days."

I sighed. No use trying to stick up for the poor man. He had been tried, convicted and sentenced by Papa every time he got a chance to tell the story.

"Well, I gave him 'a little something,' all right. I gave him three dollars, is what I gave him. I went right out and canceled the order for the chair. He lost out because he was so greedy. He really lost out."

Papa pushed out his lower lip and tilted his head back, the way he did when he made an important point.

"I'm sure Dr. Britton wouldn't ask," I said. "I just wanted to be sure that you hadn't forgotten."

"Needn't worry. We'll take care of him. I have a very expensive woolen scarf out in the trunk. He'll appreciate that."

My insides wrenched. Another relic from the trunk, reeking of moth balls. He probably had a dozen scarves in there, all the same color and all from "Bankrupt Stock Liquidators."

"Money might be better," I suggested. "That way he could spend it for something that – well – that he really wanted."

"He'll like the scarf just fine."

"It wouldn't have to be a very big amount of money."

"We'll give him the scarf. Anyone who wouldn't appreciate a nice, woolen scarf, wouldn't appreciate anything."

That same afternoon, Papa went out to the garage where the storage trunks, all four of them, stood lined up like pirate's treasure chests. He dug into the contents of one and pulled out a gray, striped scarf, wrapped it in red paper, and tied it with Christmas string. If Papa ever gave a wedding gift to the King and Queen of England, it would be wrapped in red paper and Christmas string.

Papa's face radiated pride as he handed the package to me to deliver – pride because he had the foresight to be prepared for these little gift-giving emergencies – pride because of his frugality and shrewd management of money – pride because now he had satisfactorily met his social obligations and paid off the minister for his services with an expensive appearing gift.

My feet felt like someone had poured lead-shot into my shoes as I pushed and dragged them over to the minister's house. When I handed the package to Dr. Britton, I made sure that he understood that it was just from Papa, not Papa and me. Papa picked out the gift, Papa wrapped it, Papa did everything but deliver it. Dr. Britton thanked me and passed along a few words of comfort which I promptly forgot in my haste to get away.

With my task completed, I didn't think about it again until the next Sunday when Dr. Britton pulled me aside, holding the gray scarf in his hand.

"You know," he said, "when I opened the package, I found that this beautiful scarf had a number of moth holes in it."

My face turned the color of boiled lobster.

"See? Look here," he said. "There are quite a few."

I looked at the holes, some nearly a quarter inch in diameter. Why did I have to look at this? Why wasn't Papa here to look at the shabbiness of his gift? Why did I always have to bear the brunt of his faux pas?

"I'm sorry," I said. "I'm really sorry."

"No need to be sorry. Those things happen. I was just thinking that if your Dad had the sales slip, maybe he could return it and get another one. This one, obviously, has been in storage for quite a long time."

"Yeah," I said. "I guess it has." I stood looking at the ugly cloth, dumbstruck. What should I do? Take it back? Confront Papa with the moth-eaten neckpiece? Listen again to another lecture about money grubbing preachers? Would Papa then go to Dr. Britton and give him the lecture about ingratitude?

"I'm sure that if your Dad knew, he'd want to take it back," Dr. Britton said.

"Yeah, sure," I said, "except – well – I don't think he has the sales slip anymore. He never saves that sort of thing."

"Maybe he could just take it back to the store and explain to the clerk . . ."

"I don't think so. I mean he may not remember that is, without a sales slip – you know – it would be really hard."

Dr. Britton gave me a quizzical look and hesitated an embarrassing moment. "Well – of course." He pulled back the scarf and folded it twice. "I understand. Don't worry about it. It's the thought that counts anyway. I appreciate your Dad thinking of me. You tell him 'thank you' for me."

"Yeah sure," I said.

But I never did say "thank you." I never said anything about that hated scarf. I wanted no more lectures or stories with morals or discussions about ingratitude, but that afternoon, I went out to the garage where the large trunks stood full to the brim with blighted bargains and stale merchandise, kicking each one in turn until my toes were sore. I sobbed out curses on surplus gifts that never fit the occasion and moth balls that didn't work.

On cold Sunday mornings in December and January, I used to look for that scarf around Dr. Britton's neck, just the edge of it, maybe, peeking out from his coat. It never appeared. But he never took it back to Papa – I gave him credit for that. He understood – and so did I.

CHAPTER 24

THE GRADUATION PARTY

"It's my party and I'll cry if I want to"

-Herb Weiner

The class of 1944 was a small graduating class – twenty six in all – ten boys and sixteen girls. I was, as they say, a sizable frog in a tiny pond. I had been nominated as student body president, if only I would just continue on at Los Angeles Pacific College for the next two years of college. L.A.P.C. was that small Free Methodist school which I had been attending for the last two years of my high school career. It was accredited to teach four years of high school and two years of college. While it would have been an honor, no doubt, to serve as student body president, I was ready to move on to bigger puddles, or so I thought. I had my sights set, to everybody's consternation, on the University of California at Los Angeles. The reasons I gave tended to center around academic excellence, proximity to home and reasonable tuition fees. While those incentives were plausible enough, the real reason was that my female friend, the prospective missionary to China and the one to whom I had lost my heart, was already attending there. I'm sure my decision was more hormonal that academic.

The pressures were enormous to keep me at L.A.P.C. Faculty members, all my friends at school and, of course, Papa were dead set against my moving on. The difficulty of bucking such a strong current of opinion was exhausting.

No matter. It would soon be over. Graduation was looming on the horizon. The announcements had been printed, the class pins distributed (we were not allowed to have rings – they were too "worldly") and the measurements for the gowns were being recorded. Our gowns were white. I suppose this was to register our purity, for white is really a non-color. In less than four months I would be taking my first classes at U.C.L.A. and all of the pressure about decisions would be over.

Sunday, June 4, 1944 was the date. 5:30p.m. was the time. Perfect. The ceremonies and speeches would be over in a couple of hours and that would leave a full night for celebration. Everyone parties all night on graduation night. Oh, it would not be an immoral affair. There would be no liquor or unbridled sex, but certainly there would be raucous celebration at least as raucous as fundamentalist people ever get. The possibilities seemed infinite – dinner at Chinatown and then a trip to the beach where we could lie on the cool sand and gaze at the stars. Perhaps the importance of the occasion would even prompt a kiss or two. Or maybe a stroll along Hollywood Boulevard. Something exciting was always happening there. Or we might go to an evening church service and then take a trip up into the hills overlooking the city and feast on the dazzling lights while exploring the limitless opportunities for our futures. This would be a night to remember and no one could take it away.

The graduation ceremony took place as scheduled in the newly completed amphitheater, with the slim graduating class bedecked in white robes and solemn faces. Our white vestments made us appear to be a local chapter of the KKK, except that our caps were mortarboards instead of pointed hats. The amphitheater was a modest affair, a shallow basin scooped out of the hillside by a bulldozer, concrete steps leading up the sides to Spartan wooden benches, fifteen rows of them. There were plenty of empty seats available, but still, it was the largest crowd our little school had ever seen, numbering somewhere between three and four hundred. This was a resounding endorsement of our achievement in the academic world and also in the realm of religious faith. A sedate, young female student, dressed in white, stood at attention holding the Christian flag to remind all present that these exercises held eternal weight. There were no bands, trumpets or waving banners; only a simple piano to mark our triumphal entry into the "stadium," but it might as well have been the Boston Philharmonic judging from the nervous tension which gripped the young graduates.

The California sun was leaning against the horizon before the proceedings ended. At last the speeches were made, the diplomas distributed, the songs sung and the eternal blessings invoked. Clutching the proof of my graduation in my sweaty palm, I could look forward to my own private celebration with my girlfriend. I was as eager as a rutting elk.

Sad to say, graduation observances never had amounted to much in our family. No family members even attended the grade school graduation of my sister, Mildred. She had to walk to the school by herself. I'm not sure that anyone showed up at my brother's high school graduation, either. As for my graduation, Papa was the only one who came from the family and he was probably only there to provide transportation. Mama, of course, had passed away, so she was not present, except perhaps in some spiritual dimension. The one I wanted most to be there was my would-be missionary to China. No matter. I would see her afterward. We would join hands later in a post-graduation tryst to discuss the events of the day and explore the meaning of life, the quest for happiness and other philosophical mysteries which young lovers explore. We were not committed to each other in any formal sense of the word, although heaven knows I wanted to be. We were not engaged, almost engaged or even "going steady," but there just seemed to be an undiscussed covenant between us. That unspoken arrangement was motivated by a mutual attraction and sealed by an occasional holding of hands. She was, after all, the reason I was going to U.C.L.A. This is why I was not overly disturbed by the lack of relatives or church friends at the graduation ceremony itself. The rendezvous afterward was the main event. We had so much to talk about, laugh about and maybe even cry about. We would rehearse our dreams and dare glimpses into the future. Perhaps even the word "love" would creep into the conversation. Who cared now about valedictory speeches, diplomas, pious benedictions and solemn marches to "Pomp and Circumstance?" The heart of this day lay yet ahead.

I shook hands with my fellow seniors and a few teachers, exchanging congratulations and good wishes. I did not envy their post-graduation celebrations. My interface with their Free Methodist culture was not a good fit. I preferred the celebration of my own making.

Papa drove me home. I liked it that way. When I drove, I had to put up with his constant "back-seat-driving." I had already asked him for the use the car in the evening and he had reluctantly agreed.

"How long are you going to be out tonight?" he asked me, as we drove down the hill from the school.

"I'm not sure. Probably quite late, I expect."

"How late?"

"After midnight, maybe."

Papa clinched his teeth and looked hard at the road ahead. "Where are you going?"

"Out to eat, probably," I said. "Don't really know yet. Nothing you need to worry about. It might be even just a friend and me."

Papa drummed the steering wheel with his fingers. There was that palpable tension between parent and teenager which is as old as time. The young one struggling against the fetters and the old one seeking to reign him in.

"You're pretty tired," Papa said. "You shouldn't be driving around late at night when you're tired. You've had a busy day."

"I'll be fine, Papa. I'm not all that tired."

Papa drove the rest of the way in silence. When we finally reached home and pulled up into the driveway, he sighed in resignation, but did not drive the car into the garage.

I had been holding the graduation tassel retrieved from my mortarboard, running my fingers through the silken strands. Before I got out of the car, I hung it from the rear view mirror. It was a casual act, one which Papa didn't even notice, but it was a momentous act of triumph and achievement. The word "cool" was not yet given to such acts. "Swell," I think, was the word we used. But that long, white tassel looked absolutely swell hanging down into the middle of the windshield. It would be impressive as I drove with the girl of my dreams at my side.

I raced into the house, grabbed a few nickels and dimes from atop the dresser, and raced on foot to the corner phone booth. With trembling hands, I inserted the coins and dialed her number, listening for the ring.

"Hello?" There she was. She must have been sitting by the phone waiting for my call.

"Hi," I said. "Well, it's over. I am officially graduated."

"Congratulations!" Her voice was warm and friendly. "How was the ceremony?"

"It was okay. Kind of boring. The main thing is, it's over."

"It's a good feeling, isn't it?"

"Sure is." I waited a moment. "So – are you ready to go help me celebrate?" The line took on an awful silence. "You still there?" I asked.

"Yeah – " she said. "But you know – I'm awfully tired. Aren't you tired?"

Fear gripped my throat. She was beginning to sound like Papa. "No. Not really. I'm not tired at all. I mean – this is graduation night and I thought – "

"Yes, I know, but it's Sunday night and I have to get up fairly early tomorrow. I have school and – "

"We don't have to stay out late," I said. "I thought maybe we could just drive to the beach or something."

"The beach?" She gave a slight laugh that cut like a razor. "That would take an hour just to get there."

"Well, how about just a hamburger at Bob's? That would-n't take long. You know, just a chance to get out of the house. I've got the car and I could pick you up in a jiffy."

"I'm sorry," she said. "There will be other times we can do that. I promise. Tonight, I'd just like to go to bed early and get some rest. You understand – don't you?"

"But you promised "

"Promised? No, I didn't promise." Her voice took on a coolness. "We talked is all. We said we'd see how things turned out. Remember? I don't think that was a promise."

"But I thought – "

My stomach felt like I had swallowed a handful of red-hot rivets. How could she do this to me? How could graduation be so insignificant? Was there someone else in her life? No. It couldn't be. I knew almost all of her friends. Besides, she wouldn't lie to me. But tired? How could that be?

"I'm just not in a celebration mood. It's been a long day. You do understand, don't you?"

"Well – sure," I said. "I understand." But I didn't under-stand. "It's just that I was hoping maybe – "

"Listen, I know that you've had a big day too. You're probably more tired than you think you are," she said.

Why was everybody suddenly an authority on the state of my energy? "Yeah," I said. "It's been a busy day but I'm really not tired."

"Well, anyway – congratulations. That's really swell."

"Yeah," I said. "Swell – sure – swell."

Disappointment is hard to mask. I tried. I feigned relief that the ordeal was all over and made some inane comments about the ceremony. The conversation dribbled on for a few moments and then we hung up. I dragged myself home, put the car in the garage, lifted the tassel from the rearview mirror and headed for the back door of the house.

"Thought you were going out tonight," Papa said, as I banged the screen door behind me.

"Guess not. Like you said, I'm tired. Guess I'll just go to bed."

"Good idea," Papa said.

Hurrying quickly to my room, I felt a shapeless block of something in my throat which is sometimes a precursor to tears. Don't cry, I told myself. This is not the time. This is not the place. I went into my room, closed the door and threw the tassel in a heap on the writing desk. I stared at it transfixed. How could such an inert bunch of threads be mocking me? It took on a persona of its own, like some court jester. It was a symbol of pride and joy that suddenly turned into a tangled wad of meaningless silk strands.

The next morning, Papa was up early, clattering around the house. I slept in. School was out and there was no special reason for me to get up on a Monday morning. When I finally shuffled out to the kitchen in my bare feet, Papa was putting away some groceries.

"Hungry?" he asked.

"Not too," I said. "I'll fix myself some toast."

"Everything all right?"

"Yeah, sure."

"I thought maybe – that is – I thought I heard you – "

"Heard me what?" I asked. I had visions of his crouching by the bedroom door, listening.

"I thought maybe I heard someone crying."

"Me?" I laughed a weak laugh. "Why would I cry? – No."

"Everything okay then?"

"Sure. Just a little tired. You probably heard me sneezing or coughing, or something."

Papa nodded, turned and headed out to the car to bring in another bag of groceries. I went back to my room at the front of the house. The gleaming, white tassel still lay on the desk in sardonic splendor. I yanked it from its taunting perch and tossed it under the bed. I needed no trophies or laurels to remind me of the day. I was sinking fast into the dark, toxic morass of self pity. I had "graduated" into the real world.

CHAPTER 25

SURROGATE FAMILY

---

*"Home is not where you live, but
where they understand you."*

- Christian Morgenstern

We were stuffed into the car like pickles in a jar, Esther, her Mother, her younger brother, her little sister and me. Esther had invited me home to Sunday dinner after church and her Mom had seconded the invitation. I was eager to accept. Now that Papa and I were alone in our old house, weekends home from college were as gloomy as visits to a mausoleum and I welcomed the opportunity to get away.

I had noticed Esther Smith at church many times. But then who wouldn't notice her? She stood out like a chorus girl in a nunnery. Her full, sensuous lips and almond eyes were framed by shimmering sepia hair and animal magnetism extended all the way to her toes. She had many friends, but they were mostly boys. Girls were either jealous, judgmental or both.

"Here we are. Home sweet home," Esther announced as we rolled up to the curb in front of her house. "Mom calls it the 'doll house.'"

"Well, it's not very big," Esther's mother said, "but it's big enough for us, and besides, it's what the Lord prepared for us and so we're grateful." I wondered why God always provided just the minimal, but I didn't say anything.

The house was a shoe box kind of structure nestled in the middle of the block on Electric Street in Alhambra. It had a small living room and dinette, Pullman sized kitchen and a bedroom barely big enough for a small bed. For Ruth Smith and her three children, there was not an inch to spare. Esther slept on the couch in the front room, Sam, her younger brother, slept on a cot in the dinette. The cot also doubled as one of the seats at the table. Ruth and her baby daughter, Gracie, slept in the diminutive bed room.

As we entered the house, the aroma of savory pot roast filled every square inch of the small house. "Sure smells great," I said.

"Yeah. Roast is Mom's specialty," Esther said. "We'd have it every single Sunday, if I had my way."

Ruth Smith's oval face beamed satisfaction. Her cooking was plain, but hearty and she loved it when her children praised her efforts. Her eyes, small and black as peppercorns, radiated a strange amalgam of pride and humility.

"C'mon. Let's eat," Sam said. "I'm hungry."

"Gracie, you set the table. Esther, you and Sam come and help carry things from the kitchen. Many hands make light work," Ruth said.

"Can I help?" I asked.

"Sure," Esther said. "C'mon back, Willy."

Willy? No one but close friends ever called me "Willy." No one in my own family ever did. It meant I was accepted. Confirmed. I was family. From then on, I was always "Willy."

I can't remember what I sat on that day as I pulled up to the table, but it wouldn't have made any difference to me had it been an empty orange crate. My sense of abandonment disappeared like sand castles under an ocean wave. It wasn't just the food, although that couldn't have been more delicious. The relaxed family chatter, the honesty, the instant inclusion into the family was medicine for my soul and convinced me that I had "come home."

I found it curious that there was no "father" at the table, but was too polite to ask questions. Had he died? Was he away on a trip? Was he working? Esther told me later that it was none of the above.

Ruth's husband, Ernest, had left her when they lived in Chandler, Arizona. He took the car and every dime in the house and left her with the three kids to take care of. It was only through the generosity of a friend that she was able to pack up her few possessions and move to Los Angeles to be with her mother. Soon after she arrived, she took a job opening and answering mail for a religious broadcaster, Charles Fuller, who produced the "Old Fashioned Revival Hour." She was only paid $40 per week, but it was the kind of work she liked.

In the mid 1940's, World War II was in full swing. This made it possible for Ruth to double her salary working for Douglas Aircraft as a riveter. At first, she hesitated to take the job as the company had a dress code requiring female employees to wear slacks. This went directly against Ruth's strict interpretation of the Bible which forbade, as she believed, the wearing of men's clothing. She prayed long and hard about the matter and entered into a fierce internal struggle with her fundamentalist conscience. At last, she concluded that wearing slacks might be permissible under the extenuating circumstances of the war and her dire need to support her family. She took the job.

After the war, the Douglas plant closed down and she was able to land a job with Thermadore in Alhambra. She worked there for a number of years on an assembly line winding armatures for electric motors. Right after she took the job, she moved into "the doll house." The tiny dwelling was hardly big enough for two people, let alone four, but it was all she could afford on her meager income. The Smiths, by any standard, were poor, but you would never have known it by their level of hospitality. Ruth had a philanthropist's generosity and never a trace of self pity. It was not long until those Sunday dinners became more than an occasional event. I was there every week as a bonafide member of the family. It should be noted that despite the paucity of her income, all of her children graduated from college and went on to pursue highly responsible careers. Esther became a high school teacher, and later on, a magazine editor/writer for a seminary graduate school, Sam became a minister and Gracie finished as a public school speech therapist. I, of course, became a minister as well, and owe much of my early college experience to "Mom's" encouragement and guidance.

What was it about this family that was different? On the surface, they seemed just as prone to social and emotional disaster as my own. There was usually trouble brewing of one sort or another. Ruth's husband, Ernest, came home periodically, but only for short stays. When he did come home, his visits put a strain on the budget. He never contributed a penny to the household for food, rent or utilities. He came and went at will until finally Ruth put a stop to it. At one point, after he had returned from a long absence, she told him that he was no longer welcome. In response to her ultimatum, Ernest took a bus to Texas, stole a truck, drove it over a state line and then announced to the police that he had committed a federal offense so he should be locked up. The police obliged. He then wrote Ruth several "see what you made me do" letters from prison, blaming her for driving him to such extremes so he could find food and shelter. In spite of Ernest's constant trouble making, "Mom" never allowed any of her children to openly speak against him.

But Ernest was not the only ingredient for family distress. Esther always had some wild, self destructive romance going on which tore at her mother's insides and kept the family in an uproar. Sam worked part time in a hardware store to help keep food on the table while struggling to keep up his grades in the midst of family turmoil and Gracie had to cope with growing up in a single parent family which, at the time, was as unusual as a train without a caboose. Added to all this mix, there was me – constantly worried about grades and deadlines, hiding my dilapidated 1931 Nash so Papa would not discover it, paying off traffic fines and then the ever present love affairs that always ended with broken hearts and crushed egos.

The great difference between this family and my own was acceptance coupled with equality. Never once was I seen as a drain on the family income. "Mom" always welcomed me with open arms and when there was only a small meatloaf for the entire family, she simply tore up another slice or two of bread and added it to the hamburger to make it all stretch a little farther. If there were not enough potatoes, everyone took a smaller portion and if the table was a little crowded, and it always was, then everybody squeezed closer together to make room.

I was never treated as an outsider. I was included in all the family affairs as much as any blood offspring. Nor was I ever considered handicapped, either. The angle of my spine seemed of no importance. My opinions were respected and sought after. "Mom's" wise counsel was evenly distributed among all of us as her children and it was always undergirded with love. Some of her favorite aphorisms were, "never quit under fire" and "all things work together for good." Her faith was simple, honest and strong. These were elements that I desperately needed in my late teens and early twenties and I drank of them as a thirsty man gulps water. In a difficult and unfriendly world, I had found someplace where I belonged.

This may sound like I had stumbled into the perfect family unit "where seldom is heard a discouraging word and the skies are not cloudy all day." But the perfect family it was not. A casual observer might even say I had traded one dysfunctional family for another. Ernest, the husband and father, was both negligent and abusive. He invented his own twisted version of religion which, among other things, demanded that his wife address him as "Lord." This was only one of many demands with which she refused to comply. On those rare occasions when Ernest was home, he drained the meager household income and contributed nothing. He had his own private visions of getting rich quick and was, in a strange way, an entrepreneur of sorts. One scheme after another failed, but one that I particularly remember was his founding of the "Fair Deal Stamp Company," an enterprise engaging in the selling and trading of postage stamps. For this business venture, he dubbed himself "Captain X." Needless to say, it fizzled before it ever got off the ground. His bizarre business ventures became the butt of numerous jokes from his children, always, of course, without his knowledge. But it was his own son, Sam, who took the brunt of his abuse, both verbal and physical. It took years for Sam to recover from the emotional scars which he suffered. It was Sam, too, who at an early age had to assume the responsibility of being the only male about the house.

I only met Ernest on a few occasions and was uncomfortable at each meeting. Without his actually coming out and saying so, I could tell that I was most definitely an intruder. I had no business imposing myself on a family which already had more physical, financial and emotional problems than it could handle. Under normal circumstances, I would have taken the hints and beat a hasty exit never to return. It was Ruth, however, who said loud and clear to Ernest and anyone else within earshot that I was "as much a part of the family" as her own flesh and blood and that I was always and forever welcome. Why I deserved such kindness, I will never know.

I always considered it appropriate that Esther lived on "Electric Street," because she was truly a "high voltage" girl. She was, understandably, a "feature attraction" with the boys. Those boys which she drew into her orbit were not always of the most desirable sort. This became a constant concern for her mother and a perpetual topic for parental advice and lectures, not to mention prayers.

But for me, Esther was always "just a friend." Well much more than that. She was like a true sister. I always had a hard time convincing others of that fact. In the college dorm, I had Esther's picture prominently displayed on the shelf. It received many "Ooohs" and "Aaaahs" and numerous comments about my uncommon luck and extraordinary taste in women. No one quite believed me when I said that our relationship was purely platonic. It was a beautiful arrangement, actually, for when she was in between boyfriends, we could go out together. Likewise, when I was between disastrous love affairs, I had Esther on my arm. The truth is, our relationship never, ever got out of the brother/sister mode.

I wondered at times why this was so. The answers were not hard to find. In the first place, I considered myself out of Esther's league. Her dates were always bronzed, Adonis type males from "Muscle Beach," while I was "Quasimodo the bell ringer." My relationship with girls always ended up in the sink and I was smart enough to know when I was outranked in the physical appeal department. The other reason ran much deeper. I knew that if the love affair failed, and all of them usually did, then I would lose not only a romantic partner but my best friend as well. If that happened, I would also lose my new found family. I couldn't bear the thought of it.

If "Mom" Smith provided stability in the family, it was Esther who sparked the spirit of adventurous rebellion. Esther always pushed the boundaries between the acceptable and the sinful. Her mother's uncomplicated faith defined the world in stark zones of black and white, while Esther was far more interested in the multiple shades of gray. Entertainment was one of those areas under dispute. "Mom's" idea of a good time was a church picnic, while Esther leaned more to the night club experience or parking on a hill with a passionate male. Their differences made for heated conversations and long prayer sessions. I was caught in the middle, wanting surely to keep Esther more or less on the straight and narrow, but at the same time increasingly willing to question some of the injunctions laid down by our fundamentalist church.

Before television rendered the whole discussion moot, movies of any and all kind were on the "verboten" list. They were the Devil's playground where immoral actors and actresses portrayed shocking bedroom scenes and scandalous sexual fantasies, to say nothing of the profligate use of tobacco and alcohol. Movies were definitely on the "sin" list. That is why a moral dilemma was set off within me when Esther suggested, "Let's go to a movie tonight, Willy."

I scowled. "I don't think so. You know I don't go to movies."

"C'mon. It'll get you mind off your breakup. Besides, it's Saturday night and it's boring around here. It would do us both good to go to L.A."

"What would Mom say? I don't think she'd approve."

"She won't care. She's not that narrow," Esther said.

"I don't know. There are other things – "

"Like what? Miniature golf? I've played so much miniature golf I can't look at another windmill," she said.

"We could go down to Echo Park and rent one of those boats and—"

"And putt-putt around the lake three times and spend all our money? Come on."

"Do you know how long it's been since I've been to a movie?" I asked. "Years. Really years. You're asking me to spoil all that?"

"All the more reason," she said. "It's time you found out what you've been missing."

"That may be okay for you," I said. "You might get away with it, but I'm president of Youth Fellowship. What if somebody saw me?"

Esther threw her hands up in exasperation. "They won't. Besides, what if they did? Don't tell me that none of them ever go to shows. Not going to any movies just because there might be a bad one or two is like not reading any magazines because there might be a bad one or two. That's silly."

I couldn't fault her logic, but the wickedness of the whole enterprise sent a flood of guilt coursing through my veins. "What movie did you have in mind?" I asked.

"Well, there are lots of 'em we could go to, but 'Going My Way' ought to be a pretty good one. It's up for a couple of academy awards."

"I just don't know – "

"It's about a couple of Catholic Priests – "

"Catholic?"

"Now don't tell me that's going to keep you away," she said.

"Well, no, it's just that – "

"Honestly, Willy, it's starring Bing Crosby and Barry Fitzgerald. Now that's about as sinful as Jello and whipped cream. It's a religious movie, for gosh sakes." She blew away a wisp of hair that had fallen across her forehead.

"I don't have enough money for both of us," I complained.

"I'll pay my own way," she said. "If you drive, I'll even take us out to Bob's for a malt afterward."

All the way down to the heart of L.A., Esther was humming "Rum and Coca Cola." The tune was catchy. I wondered what a rum and Coke would actually taste like.

After we had parked the car, Esther took my arm and we

walked the two blocks or so to the theater. Before we ever stepped inside, the blended smell of popcorn and musty theater carpet wafted out over the sidewalk. It was the smell of sin. I glanced right and left over my shoulder as I stepped up to the box office. Soon we were following the usher's dim flashlight down the aisle to a section midway down. I hoped that the darkened auditorium would conceal our identity.

Soon I forgot where I was and became caught up in the story being played out on the screen, Father "Chuck" O'Malley's interaction with Father Fitzgibbon and the kids of the inner city parish. If you could overlook the lighting of a cigarette or two, it was a heart warming story with a good moral tone to it. I had to admit it. I was hooked.

After the movie, Esther clung to my arm tightly as we walked to the car. She looked at me with inquiring eyes. "Well," she asked, "how did you like it?"

"Fine," I admitted. "Really, really fine. I liked it a lot. I don't see how anyone could object to that."

"See?" she said, "I knew you'd like it."

"Yeah, you were right. You can't knock them all just because there are a few bad ones out there."

We walked about a block in silence, rehearsing again the scenes of the movie.

"And Bing Crosby. He made a good priest," Esther said.

"Yeah – great acting."

"Some people think a movie isn't 'holy' unless it's boring."

We waited for the light to change before crossing the street. I tried to analyze the current rearranging of my long held taboos. Sometimes decisive changes occur through small incidents – like going to a movie with a friend.

"I've got to remember that line by Bing Crosby – I mean when he was playing Chuck O'Malley," Esther said. "How does it go? Something about what religion should be like?"

"Oh – yeah. 'Full of light and life.' I think that was it."

"Yes, that's it. 'Religion should be full of light and life, not dull and drab.' That's a great line."

The light changed and we headed for the parking lot, arm in arm.

"Yeah," I said. "Great line."

CHAPTER 26

FIRST CARS

*"I think that cars today are almost the
exact equivalent of the great Gothic
cathedrals: I mean the supreme creation
of an era, conceived with passion by
unknown artists, and consumed in
image if not in usage by a whole
population which appropriates them
as a purely magical object."*

-Roland Barthes

The Thomas Flyer was not much for aerodynamic design. It resembled a tin chicken coop with wheels. The headlights in front were the size of two dishpans and the driver and passenger seemed to sit on top of the car rather than inside it. Nonetheless, the automobile was fast, powerful, and one of the forerunners of today's sleek limousines. It was the winner (albeit with considerable dispute) of the round-the-world race from New York to Paris in 1908 and Papa helped build it. He worked for the E. R. Thomas Motor Company in Buffalo, New York. He never tired of telling about that and it was the beginning of his great love for the automobile and the internal combustion engine. He did not own the Thomas Flyer, but he invested a considerable portion of his time and energy into its production.

The Thomas Flyer's appeal for Papa was its power and speed. The 60 horsepower engine could propel the car over fifty miles per hour in the open spaces. Not only that, there were many people in the early 1900's who had never even seen a car, let alone driven one. That was a plus for Papa. He liked being the first with things.

The first car that Papa actually owned was a Willys-Overland, a black, efficient, four-passenger vehicle with a collapsible top and a split-level windshield. It was this car that Papa loaded with provisions and, with Mama by his side and his five year old son, Raymond, in the back seat, started the drive from Boston to Los Angeles back in 1918.

This trip proved Papa's sovereignty over the machine. He reveled in making gears mesh, pistons drive and wheels spin like the wind. The soot colored car was an extension of himself. He made it purr over the vast wastelands of mid-America where not so much as a telegraph pole broke the endless horizon. He sent it growling over the 9000 foot peaks of Colorado and the sun-baked gullies of New Mexico. Three times he knocked out the oil pan on rutted roads and once he broke an axle. Through sand, mud and washouts, usually without the benefit of road signs and sometimes without adequate water, he pressed that first car to the limit until at last, on October 12th, 1918, he and his small family arrived in the promised land: Los Angeles. It had been exactly 40 days since he climbed into the driver's seat to begin the hazardous journey.

"Would you look at that, Cora?" he said, driving up and down the palm-lined streets. "Look at those houses. Imagine what the folks in Boston or Buffalo would think of those. We'll have one just like that, Cora. You wait and see."

It was the automobile that made it all possible. No – more

than that. It was Papa's self-sufficiency, his competence and skill with all things mechanical. He was more than a match for any machine. If the engine balked, he took it all apart, found out why, fixed it, and put it all back together again. If the wheels got stuck, he unstuck them. If there was an obstacle in the road, he went around it, over it or through it. There was grease on his hands and oil in his veins. Driving that car across the continent was not simply a test of the vehicle, it was a test of Papa's mastery over stubborn machines and he had proved himself.

"The streets are so wide and beautiful," Mama said.

"And there are over 250 miles of them," Papa exclaimed. "Think of that! It's heaven! I told you it would be worth it when we got here."

"Is this where we're gonna live?" Raymond asked.

"This is it," Papa said.

Mama craned her neck as they rode down of the busier boulevards. "There are so many people," she said.

"Would you believe it?" Papa said. "It's increased fifty times over since 1880."

With the arrival of the Rees family, the population had increased by three; it would soon increase by five.

If Papa had complete confidence in his own mechanical ability and driving expertise, he had absolutely no faith in anyone else's. He would not allow anyone in the family to own a car or touch a steering wheel. Mama never drove a car nor did she have a license. That was not uncommon in the twenties and thirties. The kitchen was a woman's domain; the garage was a man's.

Male members of our family, too, were forbidden to own a car. In the first place, Papa believed that anyone with a license to drive ought to be able to take his vehicle apart and put it together again, bolt by bolt and gear by gear. Neither Raymond nor I could quite do that. In the second place, there was the matter of insurance, liability and the real possibility that the driver of the car might escape to freedom from Papa's control.

It was this latter, the innate desire to be free, that drove Raymond to buy his first car. I was only six at the time, but I will never forget the family brouhaha caused by his bid for emancipation.

The 1927 Oakland coupe looked like a passport to liberty to Raymond. He was tired of depending on friends for transportation, waiting for buses, walking and begging for rides. He was eighteen now, old enough to make his own decisions, he thought, about where he would go and how he would get there. The flashy, green Oakland was only four years old and was priced at $95 by the present owner, a fellow classmate at Alhambra High School, who played saxophone in the band.

"Kind of high priced, don't you think?" Raymond said to the boy.

"Worth a lot more than that, actually," the boy said. "Look at that paint job. Like new. Most guys would soak you over a hundred dollars for a car like that."

"Tell you what," Raymond said, putting on his most sophisticated air, "I'll give you fifty dollars for it."

"Fifty!" The boy scowled in hurt and disbelief. "I might as well give it to the Salvation Army. I'm not gonna sell it half price."

"Well, I'm not exactly rich, you know."

"Okay, I'll come down to eighty five dollars, but that's as low as I'll go."

"Seventy five and we've got a deal," Raymond said.

"Gosh, that's awful low." The boy began rubbing the back of his neck.

"Cash"

"Cash?"

"Seventy five cash. My very own money. I'll take it out of

my savings account today," Raymond said.

"It's a deal."

Later that day, Raymond climbed behind the steering wheel of his very own car with a sense of primal pride in ownership. The Oakland, as he soon discovered, had a better paint job than engine. It barely started and then left a cloud of black smoke as he pulled away from the curb. No matter. It was his all his. There would now be two cars in the Rees garage.

"Look at that pile of scrap metal," Papa raged as he walked around the Oakland parked in the driveway. Raymond was pacing in short steps behind him. "How long do you think that'll run before it falls apart? A week? A month? I'll give it two days."

"I think it's in pretty good shape," Raymond said.

"What do you know about automobiles?" Papa put his hands on his hips and shook his head. "Did you have a compression test done on it? Did you pull the wheels and check the brakes? The bearings? No! Of course you didn't! You don't know the first thing about a car. You liked the paint job, so you bought the whole damn car."

Raymond clenched his teeth, raising the muscles on the side of his face like steel cables. The pride of ownership was draining out of him. "It runs good."

"Runs good?" Papa sneered. "Start it up – if you can – let's see how it 'runs good.'"

Raymond climbed behind the wheel and turned the ignition key. The motor barely turned over. Clearly the battery was dying and might expire before he could demonstrate the efficiency of the engine."

"Battery's dead!" Papa roared. "You haven't even got a decent battery."

Raymond pulled out the choke lever and gave it one more try. "Come on come on," he whispered desperately, as though the engine were a dear friend who had let him down. The starter growled, paused, and growled again. Then, in a cloud of black smoke that billowed from the tail pipe like a mid-west tornado, the engine turned over, and the Oakland began to quiver and shake like a palsied, old man.

"Good Lord! Look at that smoke!" Papa was coughing and waving his hand in front of his face. "Do you know what that means? Huh? Do you have any idea what that means?"

"I've probably choked it too much," Raymond shouted above the rattling engine.

"Choked it too much? In a pig's eye! You need piston rings! Rings! With this old wreck, you'd probably use more oil than gas. Probably need a new gasket, too. The whole engine has to be rebuilt."

Raymond pulled on the hand brake and put the gears in neutral. He stepped out of the car and watched as black clouds continued to belch out the rear.

"Do you know how to rebuild an engine?" Papa asked sarcastically. "No. Of course you don't. And I certainly don't have the time. How much money did you sink into this junk pile?"

"Only seventy five dollars," Raymond confessed, "but it was my own money. I earned it."

"Seventy five dollars," Papa slapped his own forehead as though the whole State of California had just declared bankruptcy. "You threw away seventy five dollars, just like that. It must be nice to be rich. It must be just great to have so much money that you can just throw it around on a bunch of tin and bailing wire that won't even get you around the block. Great! I wish I had cash to burn."

Raymond kept working his jaw muscles, trying to maintain a residue of pride. He said nothing.

"Great Caesars's ghost!" Papa bellowed. "Why didn't you give me the seventy five dollars? We could have gone out and bought you a real car."

"I didn't think you were much in favor "

"No, I wasn't in favor. I'm still not in favor. You don't need a car, you can't afford a car, and you don't know anything about a car. But if you just had to have one, seventy five bucks could have bought you something that would at least run. The question is, now what do we do?"

Papa walked to the front of the car, lifted the hood and peered down at the vibrating iron and steel. He shook his head again as a doctor might look at a dying patient.

"I'll haul it down to school," Papa said.

"School?"

"Down to the auto shop at Roosevelt High. Maybe they can work it over so it will last a year or two."

Thus began an extended impounding of Raymond's newly acquired Oakland coupe into the auto shop at Roosevelt High School where students worked at glacial speed to rebuild the engine. Raymond didn't see the car again for months. Every inquiry concerning the status of his automotive investment was met with a stern lecture from Papa about the folly of his purchase. A small puddle of oil seeped into the driveway where the Oakland had parked for a little more than a day. That was the only reminder that Raymond had of his new-found "freedom."

At last, Papa hauled back the Oakland from the shop and it rested again in the Rees driveway as crisp and green as a new dollar bill. The battery had been replaced, the valves ground, new rings installed, wiring, spark plugs, distributer, the works. Raymond was grateful enough, but guilt took the edges off his gratitude.

It was March 10th, 1933, late in the afternoon when Raymond eased the car into our double garage after coming home from school. Inside the garage, Papa had separated the shop, tool and storage section from the automobiles by a non-bearing wall made from 1 X 12 shelving. It was Raymond's habit to gently touch this wall with the front of his car when he parked it inside. The wall had a slight spring to it when nudged by the bumper. On this particular day, at the precise moment that Raymond bumped the wall with his car, the whole garage began to sway and tremble like a skid-row drunk. Raymond's first thought was that the shaking and vibrating was caused by Papa's coming down the stairs from the second story of the garage. He was probably in a rage because the car hit the wall too hard. When Papa did not appear, Raymond's second thought was that he had bumped the wall with such force that the whole garage had been knocked from its foundations and would soon collapse on top of the Oakland. Vivid pictures of Papa's reaction flashed before him as the garage began to rock and roll and seemed sure to shake down in a huge pile of broken beams and split timbers. It would be one more catastrophe to chalk up to the renegade Oakland. How could he face the shame of it?

The shaking, of course, was not a result of Papa's stomping down the stairs, nor was it caused by Raymond's bumping the wall with his car. It was the devastating earthquake that left the cities of Compton and Long Beach in piles of rubble with 115 dead and many of the buildings in Southern California cracked and damaged. But then, how was Raymond to know that the quake would occur at the precise moment that he pushed Papa's wall with his car?

Soon after that episode, Raymond took a job with the Monterey Park Progress, a small newspaper not far from home. He had parked his refurbished Oakland in front of the shop while he worked late at the printing press. It was work that he enjoyed and gave him a renewed sense of financial independence.

As he reflected this night on his freedom and the bright prospects for the future, his reverie was interrupted by a deafening crash. He rushed outside the building to investigate.

What greeted him was his cherished Oakland, looking like a green, metal accordion, smashed by another car filled with drunken men returning from a party. There it was, new pistons, rings, battery and all, crushed beyond recognition. He sold it the next day to a junk dealer for $15.

I was a sophomore in college before I had a car I could call my own. Papa had two cars by then: his 1937 Buick and a small, 60 horsepower, 1937 Ford coupe. The coupe was his "loaner." He loaned it to me on occasion, but I always had to trump up some cause, as good as taking a dying friend to the hospital, before I could get my hands on the keys. Anything so frivolous as a date was out of the question. I always had to give a full accounting afterward of where I had been, how many passengers I took along, how much mileage I put on the odometer and how much gas was left in the tank. I chafed at these restrictions. Romance was so severely limited by taking a girl on the bus or the streetcar. My desire to have a car of my own became an obsession.

Mildred was married before I started college. My new brother-in-law, Wayne, had a 1931 Nash that he was having trouble selling. Little wonder. Rust was blossoming on the fenders like lichen on a river rock, the wheels were so badly out of alignment that the car seemed to travel sideways down the highway and there was no gear shift. It did run, however. By thrusting a stout screw driver down through the floorboard, one could manipulate the gears. To me, it was still a dream car. The only problem was that he wanted two hundred dollars for it. It might as well have been ten thousand dollars. I didn't have ten cents of my own. There was no use asking Papa for money. "You don't need a car. The bus is good enough," I could hear him say.

Wayne, on the other hand, was approachable. He was young enough to know that one person's frivolous fancy is another person's desperate need. And he could see me eyeing that car like a cat watching a mouse hole.

"I'll tell you what," he said one day. "It wouldn't be right to just give you the car, but I could sell it to you and you could pay me later without any interest."

I had never bought anything on credit. According to Papa, buying on credit was very close to robbery. Our family ran on cash-and-carry. Still, the vision of sitting behind the wheel of my very own car was pulling me as irresistibly as a shark to blood.

"I don't know," I hesitated. "It might be quite a long while before I could pay you." I could see two hundred silver dollars stacked as high as the pyramids in Egypt.

"I know that," Wayne said.

"I might even have to wait until I finish college."

"That's okay," he said, "I can wait."

Imagine! My own car! What leverage it would give me on the social scene. No more scheming to ride along in someone else's car. No more checking of bus schedules before asking a girl for a date and no more begging Papa for the use of his "loaner."

But that brought up another problem.

"What about Papa?" I asked with a sigh. "He'd go through the roof if I drove it home. I remember what happened to Raymond."

"So?" Wayne said with a slight smile. "Why would you have to tell him?"

Conspiracy! Now conspiracy was being added to the sin of buying on credit. I felt deliciously wicked.

"Where would I keep the car?" I mused. "I couldn't keep it at your house. Tujunga is too far from Alhambra, and that's a pretty big car to hide at our house.

"Don't you have any friends close to home?" Wayne asked. "It seems to me you could leave it at a friend's house until you thought your Dad got used to the idea of your driving it."

"Sure!" My face lit up like a theater marquee. "Esther Smith. Her Mom wouldn't mind if I parked it in front of her house. That's what I'll do. Hey! It's a deal!"

My first purchase, after taking possession of the car, was a knob for the steering wheel. That was as essential as gasoline for the tank – maybe even more essential. The boys called them "necker's knobs." It allowed the boy to steer the car with his left hand while his right arm was around the girl sitting next to him. She, in turn, snuggled close and shifted gears as he worked the clutch. It was a ritual as universal as hamburgers and drive-ins and produced an intimacy unattainable in any other way as the vehicle maneuvered through traffic and negotiated stop signs. This all presented a problem with the old Nash, because it is one thing to learn how to synchronize shifting gears with the driver's foot movements, and it is quite another to do it with a screwdriver.

The girl who learned to shift gears flawlessly, even with a screwdriver, was Betty June. Ah, Betty June! She had breathtaking sapphire eyes and lips that begged for kisses the way daisies beg for bees. That first ride in my "new" car, with Betty June by my side, was a trip into Omar Khayyam's paradise. I did not have a book of verse, a jug of wine or a loaf of bread, but I had something much better, my rusty, green Nash. With Betty June shifting gears, it turned any wilderness into Shangri-la.

For Papa, the automobile was a rebellious piece of machinery to be tamed, conquered, subdued. A wrench and a screwdriver were to Papa as a lasso and spurs are to a cowboy. The motorcar afforded an opportunity to demonstrate mastery and power.

For Raymond, the automobile was total liberation. Driving was a right of passage. It meant independence, freedom and adulthood. It was a life-boat away from our Titanic of a family.

For me, it was different. I learned to distinguish between a sparkplug and a distributer cap only because of necessity. I was not interested in mechanics or technology, I was only interested in making the car run. I recognized that unless the motor worked, the chassis was of little worth in the dating process. The automobile was a social tool by which I could enter competitive courtship on a more equal footing, and much more. It was a magic chariot by which I could transport Aphrodite to the hills to overlook the lights of the city and drink the sweet wine of love. My '31 Nash may not have had chrome trim or a radio, but it did have a "necker's knob."

CHAPTER 27

THE BROTHERHOOD

"Brothers all
In honor, as in one community,
Scholars and gentlemen."

-William Wordsworth

I was as lonely as a field mouse in a falcon's nest. The year was 1944. I had passed my entrance exams and was accepted as a student at the University of California at Los Angeles. The excitement and thrill of it all should have been enough to keep my spirits flying high, but it wasn't. To save expenses, I lived in a student Co-op, which was a pretty good facsimile of a gulag. The rooms were small, cramped and smelled like dirty socks. To help pay for room and board, I washed dishes – mountains of them – every night until nine o'clock. After that, it was difficult to focus on studies. It was "character building," I'm sure, but tedious and miserable. To make matters worse, I was friendless and devoid of social skills.

I remember Halloween night of that year in particular. My roommates, who had already found their place in the sun, were getting ready for the big night of costumed revelry. With black eye masks perched on their foreheads, flasks in their pockets and condoms in their wallets, they were ready to roll. Already the cacophonies of the big bands were floating on the night air from the many club and fraternity parties on campus. When my festive friends bolted out the door, it was without so much as a "see 'ya later." I could have been an empty beer bottle for all the attention they paid me.

After they left, I climbed onto my top bunk, lay on my stomach and stared out into the black night. Twinkling lights in the distance advertised that there was, indeed, fun and excitement somewhere, but I was certainly not a part of it. My erstwhile girlfriend was now with somebody else, what other friends I had were all miles away in Alhambra and my own family had flown the nest. I lay there bathed in self pity and wallowing in loneliness. I had discovered the black hole of the universe and it was right there on the top bunk of the co-op on the U.C.L.A. campus.

A more adventurous soul might have crashed some party here or there or maybe hitched a ride into L.A. to find some excitement or at least gone to a movie, but not this one. I resigned myself to my misery and refused to find solace anywhere. Social isolation, I determined, was the high price one must pay for holiness.

To find a cure for the loneliness of that particular night was hopeless, but in the long run, perhaps there was an answer. Even in wartime, the enrollment at U.C.L.A. was still over 20,000. Finding friendship in such a gigantic melange was next to impossible. I needed to find some smaller group – a sub-stratum of students – like a fraternity. But what fraternity?

The only investigating I had been able to do revealed three things about fraternities: they were expensive, exclusive and depraved. But wait. I had heard of one which was, perhaps, different. It went by the Greek letters "Alpha, Gamma, Omega." It had the reputation of being a "Christian" fraternity. The juxtaposition of those two words did not strike me as oxymoronic at the time, so I decided to investigate.

Being a slow learner in matters of social grace, I was especially lacking in my knowledge of proper protocol regarding "Greek row." I did not know, for example, that one does not just march up to the door of a fraternity house and say, "Hi there. I'd like to join your fraternity." The prospect must be "rushed" and then "pledged" and then "voted upon." Things are a little more complicated than that, but that is the general idea.

This explains why the student who answered the door at the A.G.O. house stood there with mouth agape after I, with the utmost aplomb, announced that I had come to join the fraternity. Astonishment is too mild a word for the look on his face. It took him more than a little time to decide that, no, I wasn't some sort of joke and, yes, I really was from the planet earth. After he regained his composure, he gave me some sort of card, told me to write down my address and assured me that I would be contacted before "rush week." Was that laughter I detected after he closed the door?

During the next few weeks, I decided to broach the subject of fraternities with Papa. I dreaded it. I had painful memories of Raymond, white-knuckled, waiting outside Papa's study door to talk about money for school.

"No, no, no. Joining a fraternity is not a good idea." That was Papa's first response to my suggestion.

"But I'd get more time to spend with my studies," I said. "I wouldn't have to wash dishes every night until nine o'clock and I'd have lots of Juniors and Seniors to help me."

Papa kept shaking his head. "Fraternities are just glorified party groups on campus. They're more concerned about boozing it up than studying."

"Not this one," I said. "This one is a Christian fraternity."

Papa's thick eyebrows arched like dueling caterpillars and a smile crept over his face. "Yes, I suppose they all say that."

"No, really," I said. "I've heard they have ministers and

211

missionaries in the fraternity and everybody goes to church."

Papa scowled. "That may be, but fraternities are expensive. I don't have that kind of money. You have to pay dues on top of everything else."

I studied Papa's face, looking for some softness, some weakening of his determination. "I've thought about it a lot," I said, "and I found out that it wouldn't cost me anymore to live in the fraternity house than it does in the Co-op. If you figure in all the help I'd be getting, it would actually be cheaper. I would be getting what amounts to free tutoring."

"I just don't think fraternities are a good influence and—"

"You belong to one," I interrupted.

Papa looked surprised, searching for a reply.

"You belong to the Masonic Lodge. That's a fraternity."

"That's a lodge," Papa said. "Quite different."

"What's the difference?" I asked. "You pay dues, you go to meetings, you help each other – the only difference I can see is age."

Papa rubbed the back of his neck with his hand. "I'll think about it," he said. "For now, let's just think about it."

As Papa walked out of the room, I congratulated myself. I was getting better at this confronting thing. I went into my room and traced the Greek letters "ΑΓΩ" on my buckram binder.

There were many steps between getting Papa to say "yes" to the fraternity idea and getting the fraternity to say "yes" to me. There were the "rushing" formalities to go through, moving into the house, going to meetings, receiving the "pledge" pin and so on, but by and large, AGO was living up to my expectations. They were certainly straight-laced enough – no drinking, no smoking, no girlie magazines – all the restrictions that I deemed important at the time.

For all of its "blue laws," AGO had a certain broadening effect on my social habits, however. Dancing and movie attendance were now on the "acceptable" list and a little "smooching with the girls" was okay, too, so long as it didn't go too far. It never occurred to me at the time that there might be other issues of more lasting importance. Some of those "other issues" were not long in coming.

One young man with whom I felt a special kinship was a paraplegic confined to a wheel chair. In terms of physical handicap, he was far worse off than I. I admired him for not letting his disability get in the way of his education or his social life. He was a serious, intelligent, focused guy with a winning personality and high morals. He was just the kind of person that the fraternity was looking for, or so it seemed. He was a Methodist from, he said, a "liberal" church. I didn't give that a whole lot of thought until one of the "actives" in the fraternity presented him with a "statement of faith," which he had to sign before becoming a member. In the statement was a line about believing in the "virgin birth" of Christ. No big deal, I thought at the time. It seemed standard doctrine and presented no problem. To this young man, it was a very big problem.

"I'm sorry," he said, "but I can't sign that. I would be less than honest if I said I believed in the virgin birth."

"I'm sorry too," the fraternity man said, "because it means that you'll be automatically 'black balled.' You can't join."

I was stunned. I was shocked first of all because my friend would not sign. It deepened my respect for his integrity and unabashed honesty, but I was dismayed that his honesty would automatically exclude him. I was disturbed, also, by the fact that a list of doctrines could be so weighty as to disqualify one who, in every other respect, was unquestionably a "Christian."

I argued vehemently with the both of them. I wanted my friend to change his belief system to conform to the fraternity and I wanted the fraternity to relax the rules so that he could join. Both arguments were to no avail. While, at the time, the doctrine under discussion did not challenge my own core beliefs, I began to question the importance of any credo that could pass such unreasonable judgement upon one so obviously qualified to be a saint. I still maintained my intention to join, but my faith in the whole fraternal system was severely shaken.

My second disillusionment came from that quaint right of passage euphemistically called "initiation." The week preceding that event is more accurately described as "hell week." The incongruity of "hell week" in a Christian fraternity never seemed to cross anyone's mind. For the most part, the week consisted of menial tasks such as carrying books for active members, washing dishes, scrubbing floors and the like, but there were also painful and humiliating experiences such as sitting naked on a block of ice until one could not take the pain anymore and then, as a relief, being swatted with a stout wooden paddle. When the paddling was over, one was compelled to sit on the ice again. All of this was mild compared to the initiation itself.

Before the initiation ever took place, there were plenty of rumors about what it would be like. All of this, of course, was part of the plan. Strike great fear and dread into the hearts of the lowly "pledges." While it seemed to me that some of these wild tales had no place in a so called "Christian" fraternity, I was determined to make it through initiation even if it killed me. I would never be called "chicken." Then, if I deemed that reform was necessary, I would push for it from inside the fraternity as an active member.

The fated night began with the usual high jinks that one might expect – a diet of raw oysters, fat earth worms, nauseating drinks of pepper sauce and vinegar and then there were the "hot seats" wired with electricity to shock unsuspecting rear ends and endless rounds of paddling. The culmination of the evening came with my stripping naked and being painted with various colors of oil based house paint from the top of my head to the soles of my feet. In that condition and without a dime to my name, I was dumped at the corner of Hollywood and Vine at one o'clock in the morning, with a pair of under-shorts as my only clothing, and told to find my way back to the fraternity house as best I could.

There were always flocks of people at the intersection of Hollywood and Vine, so my fraternity "brothers" knew that I would not want for attention. This was during wartime, so I remember two sailors passing me on the sidewalk. One poked his buddy and said, "See? I told you you'll see anything and everything in Hollywood." I asked people for money so I could get some sort of transportation back to the campus, but most just looked at me like I was an escapee from an asylum. Finally, two students from our rival school, U.S.C., spotted me, understood the situation and gave me enough money to take the trolley to the end of the line. I had a hard time acting nonchalant as I boarded the Pacific Electric streetcar, dropped my coins into the box, and endured the stares of fellow passengers all the way to the turn around. When I got off the trolley, I spotted a cab, explained the circumstances and promised him the cab fare if he would just take me back to the fraternity house. The driver must have figured that no human being in my miserable condition could possibly be lying.

When I finally arrived at the house, it was close to 3:00 in the morning. At that point, I took one of the most stupid actions of my entire life. In my total naivety, recognizing that my paint covering was oil based and was crusting all over my body, I took a can of turpentine, went into the shower and proceeded to scrub off the paint. You have never experienced hell until you have taken a shower in turpentine. I spent what was left of that night in absolute agony.

Did any of that really hurt me? I suppose not, although I'm sure the extensive paddling might be called abuse and certainly the paint and turpentine did not enhance the condition of my skin in later years, still I survived and much of it I can look back upon and laugh. I did, however, exert what little influence I had in toning down some of the more objectionable and dangerous elements of initiation.

A challenge of a more serious nature came soon after that. I was responsible for recruiting a pledge to the fraternity which I thought would be a splendid addition to the brotherhood. He was a fine athlete, intelligent, clean-cut, courteous and an excellent student with high marks. In addition to all that, he was a devout Christian with great recommendations. There was no difficulty in getting him to pledge. Everybody liked him and related well to him. There was only one problem. He was Black.

Race didn't evolve as a drawback until he had completed his pledge period and was about to be inducted into the fraternity. It was then that one or two of the active members brought up the possibility that at some point the fraternity might sponsor a dance. If this particular man came and danced with one of the white girls, this would be totally unacceptable. I was furious. If there was some objection, why hadn't it come to light earlier?

Doctrinal differences are one thing. Any religious or quasi-religious organization might argue that it has the right to set its own religious requirements. Hazing is yet another moot question. It could be argued that, as long as no one is hurt, initiation rites are just good, clean fun. It is quite another thing, in the name of Christian brotherhood, to defend blatant bigotry and racial prejudice. How anyone in the fraternity could call himself "Christian" and refuse membership to any man simply on the basis of skin color was more than I could understand or stomach. I voiced my objections loud and vigorously. To their credit, many others did too.

To add insult to injury, those who opposed his membership asked me, as sponsoring member, to inform the young man of his rejection. No way. I told them I wanted no part of it. Since they were the ones with the problem, they would have to deliver the message. I would not.

That particular fraternity may have revised its policy over the years. I certainly hope so. But at the time, I felt I could no longer be a part of the fraternal system and I have remained of that opinion to the present day. The fraternity taught me much and I benefitted from the friendships I formed. I am not sorry that I joined. At the time, it filled a need in my life. Since that time, however, I have realized that the whole fraternal concept is exclusive not inclusive and I cannot lend my support to that philosophy.

CHAPTER 28

MARKED

"Before I formed you in the womb
I knew you,
and before you were born
I consecrated you . . ."

-Jeremiah 1:5

"That shows that God has marked you," Grandma said. She held my left ear lobe between her thumb and finger. Since birth, that ear lobe looked like someone had taken a knife to it – notched it like a sow's ear. No one had an explanation for it except Grandma Elvina Peet Rees, Papa's mother. "That says that you belong to Jesus plain as anything," she said. It was not the first or the last time that she would say this to me or to anyone that would listen. I felt like a branded calf.

"What does it mean to 'belong to Jesus?'" I asked.

"Well, I don't know every little thing that Jesus has planned for you," she said, "but it's something special. Something big. You'll just have to wait and see what it is." I was six or seven when Grandma first started telling me this. At the time, all I wanted to be was a streetcar conductor. What if having a notched ear meant God wouldn't let me do that? What if I had to go to Africa or China as a missionary – eat monkey heads and boiled zebra meat? I had no stomach for that. What did it mean to be "marked by God?"

Mama, when she was alive, used to tell me much the same thing. One time when I was in the hospital, I contracted pneumonia and Mama thought I was going to die. She went into the pantry just off our kitchen, knelt down at the green stool that she kept there and promised God that if He would just spare my life, He could have me to do with as He pleased. Like Hannah turned Samuel over to God in the Old Testament, I was signed over to God like a house reverts back to a bank after foreclosure. That's a pretty strong revelation to lay on a kid who hasn't even reached puberty.

I was too preoccupied with toy soldiers and my collection of bubble-gum pirate cards to worry much about it, but more and more I was being forced out of my neutrality on things religious.

There was a holy war that raged in our family. Mama and Grandma held to the faith side while Papa and my Uncle Clayton were staunch defenders of science and reason. Until I was fourteen, I vacillated between the two, not caring a whole lot for either side. Papa had fact and logic going for him and a lot of impressive scientists and writers like Galileo, Darwin and Robert Ingersol. On the other hand, Mama had a faith that made anything in the universe possible and a love and tenderness to go with it. She, too, had a lot of impressive patriarchs and saints to back her up: Abraham, Isaiah, Saint Paul and Aimee Semple McPherson. It was a sort of "yin-yang" affair.

Where did I come out in all of this? In ever larger increments, I took on my mother's faith-imprint. For all of its "hellfire," Mama's religion seemed to have a gentleness to it – a softness and concern that was lacking in Papa's outlook. There was science and reason on his side, to be sure, and I wanted to embrace that, but it was as cold and unfriendly as a steel meat cleaver and pointed to an empty universe devoid of anyone who cared. It made me shiver.

The continual sound of hymns and homilies from the radio was also beginning to knead the dough of my soul. Whenever Papa was gone from the house, Mama tuned the radio to one of the many kilowatt clerics who ministered to the "folks out in radio land." It was her way of coping with the hopelessness and frustration of her locked-in role as nursemaid and char-woman. If there was nothing for her in this life, maybe there would be in the next.

The urgency of the messages brought by these radio evan-gelists and the authority of their dogma began to mold my mind, but it was a tent revival meeting that came to town that finally tipped the scale. I was fourteen when I wandered alone into that tent, more out of curiosity than anything else, and listened to an impassioned preacher fill each listener's ears with the horror of sin and the fear of hell. Like many others that night, I tearfully shuffled down the sawdust aisle to repent. At fourteen, my "sins" were still in the incubation stage, but I was convinced that they were more horrendous than those of Jack the Ripper. When I arose from my knees, I was "born again." I was more "born again" than a reptile shedding its skin or a polliwog changing to a frog. From then on, there would be many who might question my sanity, but no one could question my zeal.

There were only two Bibles in our house: Mama's shabby, worn-out Bible stuffed with notes, dried flowers and "blessed" handkerchiefs, and a small "Christian Science" edition with type so small it was almost impossible to read. I wanted a Bible of my very own. By contacting one of the radio preach-ers, I received a Bible through the mail. I read it through from Genesis to Revelation, wading through the interminable genealogies of the book of Numbers, puzzling over obscure verses in the prophets and worrying about the fiery predictions of doom and destruction in Daniel and Revelation. With Bible in hand, I set out to convert the world, beginning with my startled neighbors and bewildered friends. Never was I more convinced that I was plucked out of the mainstream of the human race, for whatever reason, by the Divine Power. I was marked by God.

All of this "specialness" had good and bad sides to it. On the bad side, it alienated what few social contacts I had managed to cultivate during my freshman year in high school. My closest friends were sure I had started chewing peyote and casual acquaintances saw me as a hopeless fanatic.

I started carrying my Bible to school and planting it squarely on my desk as a "witness" to the world. My teachers ignored it and my classmates shot amused glances at one another, but I considered these social indignities as valuable vouchers that I would cash in someday at the heavenly portals. Those first few months as a zealot did not do much for my personality or popularity with my peer group.

That is not to say that no good came of it. For one thing, my new-found religion gave me a way to rebel against Papa, and I had reached the age where I needed a cause to flaunt and a banner to wave in Papa's face. If Papa believed that the Bible was nothing but fairytales, then I would read it as the irrefutable truth of all ages. If Papa said that prayer was talking to the fence post, then I would make a point of bowing my head before every meal. If Papa said that God was non-existent or unknowable, then I would be God's personal friend and loyal subject. If Papa said, "You can't go to church today," then it was to church I would go.

Attending church was my first significant rebellion. Since I had no transportation, just getting there was a big problem. I learned of a "true-to-the-Bible," fundamentalist church out in El Monte, a city adjacent to Alhambra, which was close to the bus line which ran along Valley Boulevard. El Monte was twelve miles or so out, but at least I could get there by bus on my own. The bus fare was fifty cents – a small fortune in those days. Papa didn't want me to go to church and wouldn't give me money for such a waste of time. That made me more determined than ever. I saved every nickel and dime I could get my hands on until at last, I had enough to make the trip. I could see no way to afford that on a weekly basis, but at least I could attend once in awhile – maybe once a month.

When Sunday arrived, I laced up my polished shoes, buttoned the clean shirt that Mama had starched and ironed and started out early for the bus stop. It was about 7:00 on Sunday morning. By the time Papa missed me, I would be long gone. I pitied Mama. I knew he would rant and rave, but when I got home, I would stand up to him. With all the self righteousness of a John Huss going to be burned at the stake, I boarded the bus for El Monte.

I arrived at the church before 8:00 in the morning and climbed the few steps to the church door, but the building was locked tighter than a saloon on election day. The minister must be around somewhere. Standing next to the church was a house that looked promising, square and colorless, the way I imagined preachers and their houses were supposed to look. Maybe the minister lived there. I had heard that sometimes they lived in houses close to their churches. I took a chance and knocked on the door. No one answered at first, so I knocked again. I was surprised at what happened next.

A man came to the door in his undershirt holding a glass of orange juice in his hand.

"Yes?" he said.

"I'm looking for the minister," I said. "Could you tell me where I could find him?"

"I'm the minister." The man looked more like a wrestler than a minister and didn't seem too pleased at having his breakfast interrupted.

"Oh," I said, stepping back off the first step to the house. "Well I came to church – that is – I'm from Alhambra and I want to start coming to your church.

The man looked at me as though I might have just arrived from outer Mongolia. "Well, Sunday school doesn't even start for an hour and a half, son. You're a little early, aren't you?"

"Yeah, I guess I am," I said. "I'm sorry. I didn't know when church started or how long it would take me to get here. I just wanted to be on time."

"Well, why don't you just sit down over there on the church steps and wait. I'll open up the church in about an hour. I haven't even eaten breakfast yet. Where did you say you came from?"

"Alhambra. I came on the bus."

"That's quite a ways, son. Don't they have any churches in Alhambra? There must be one close to where you live."

"Maybe so," I said, "but I don't know of any. And anyway, I don't have a way to get there. Your church is just off the bus line."

"Well now, I think I can give you the name of a church closer to where you live. In the meantime, you just be patient and wait right over yonder. The church won't be open for quite awhile yet."

I sat down on the church steps and cupped my chin in my hands. Where was all the love and welcome I had heard the radio evangelists talk about? Didn't this minister know who I was? Didn't he know that I was hand-picked by Jesus? Didn't he see my notched ear? Didn't he notice my crooked spine? I was special. So why did I feel like a bank robber trying to break into the vault?

Eventually, the man came out of the house, dressed in a dark, blue suit and silk tie. He fumbled with the lock and opened the front door to the church. It was musty and clammy inside, like the cellar under our house. I hung back as the preacher turned on the lights and opened the doors to side rooms, directing me to one with folding chairs and a small speaker's stand. "This will be your Sunday School room," the preacher said. "No one's here yet, but you can look over the lesson material in the book here." This was the first time I had seen a Sunday School quarterly. I read the day's lesson like it contained words from a divine oracle. Soon other boys filtered into the small classroom and I could see that the boys were to be separated from the girls. It was a rule I never questioned. Girls, I supposed, distracted one's mind from Godly thoughts.

I sat through Sunday School and the worship service, trying to make myself feel welcome. I was never introduced and, except for a smile or two, no one seemed to notice that I was there. After church, the minister wrote out the name of another church in Alhambra and suggested that I go there. "They're a Bible preaching church," he said, "and they're much closer to you. I don't think you'd better come here anymore. It's just too far for you to travel."

This was my first small, rude awakening to the fact that maybe I wasn't as special as my Grandma had indicated. There were no celebrations at my arrival and no one noticed that I was chosen by Jesus. My notched ear didn't seem all that great anymore. Some might have given up on the whole idea of church at this point, but I was determined. I was on a crusade. I discovered that this "other" church, to which I was referred, had a minister that lived a short walk from our house. With great boldness, I knocked on his door and asked if I could ride to church with his family on Sundays, if I walked over to his house every week. This time, I was received more favorably. I had prepared myself for another refusal, but to my surprise, the minister, Dr. Britton, said that they would be happy to take me to church. By now, Papa had resigned himself to the fact that I was going to go to Sunday worship even if I had to walk through a meteor shower, but he still refused to take me.

There was yet another surprise waiting for me. Dr. Britton was a hunchback – just like me – maybe even more crooked than I. Was this a coincidence? It couldn't be. Here was another "special" person – a marked man. Is this the way God made his choices special? By making them crooked?

For the next few years, Dr. Britton would be my role model and my mentor. I was understandably drawn to him because of the similarities of our common affliction. He understood what it was like to have a twisted spine. Others could not.

The theological and psychological ramifications of "being special" did not occur to me at the time. A God of favoritism did not bother me. Egalitarianism was not part of my gospel.

Neither could I sort out the positive and negative elements of being "chosen." Being "singled out by God" gave me a way to cope with my disability, but it also contributed to my feeling of "oddness." It gave me a strong cause and purpose in life, but it also alienated me from normal social contacts. There were certainly worse ways to rebel than pursuing my "calling," but at the same time, it gave my life a narrow focus.

One Sunday evening, I had just finished giving a short talk at a youth meeting at the church. The Youth Director, a man by the name of Chester McLean, came to me and said, "Have you ever considered becoming a minister?"

My answer was an emphatic "no." My "born again" experience had not included this. I knew I was too dumb, too clumsy, too ill suited and shy for anything so grand.

"Well, you really should think about it, you know. It just could be that this is what God wants you to do."

The question lodged like a tack weed in a cat's tail and wouldn't let go. That remark changed my life.

My freshman year at Alhambra Highschool was a disaster. My fanatical commitment to fundamentalist religion made me the "nerdiest" nerd of all time. My old friends had understandably forsaken me and making new friends was as impossible as mining for gold in the Sahara. My social skills were purely evangelistic and my life view was apocalyptic. I saw the student body as a sea of worldliness and school dances were as wicked as Sodom and Gomorrah.

To make matters worse, the doctors had decreed that I must enroll in "rest gym." That is, instead of dressing for gym and working out on the basketball court or the ball diamond, I must remove myself to a quiet room off the gym and lie down on one of the few cots reserved for students with heart conditions and other "near-death" afflictions such as my crooked spine. This set me apart even further. Was this what it meant to be "marked" by God? If so, it didn't make me "special;" it made me "odd." My sophomore year was spent at a new school in the city, Mark Keppel High School, but my station in life did not improve there. I was miserable – noble and self righteous, but miserable.

I shared my misery in a letter to one of Mama's radio evangelists who, once a week, read letters he had received from listeners in the radio audience. By chance or by divine destiny, a saintly woman by the name of Miss Singleton, living in Long Beach, California, responded to my desperation and asked to meet me. With Mama's blessing and Papa's nescience, I boarded the "The Big Red Cars" of the Pacific Electric Railway and headed for Long Beach.

Miss Singleton and I met at a small restaurant and my elderly hostess treated me to lunch. I nervously picked at my food and unfolded the tale of my spiritual conversion and my thorough dissatisfaction with the public school system in general and Mark Keppel High School in particular. The frail, white haired lady resonated with my spiritual zeal and, by some miracle, saw something in my withdrawn personality that perhaps could be salvaged. She was a woman of some means and had a sizeable investment in a small, Free Methodist High School/College called "Los Angeles Pacific College." Before the afternoon ended, she graciously offered to designate for my use part of the endowment she had placed in the school so that I might finish my last two years of high school in the sheltered confines of that deeply religious institution. I felt I had just discovered Shangri-la. I could now pursue my divine destiny in an atmosphere where my zealotry would be understood – even encouraged. There would be a few hurdles, of course, like the distance of the school from our house and, most especially, the approval of my parents.

There was never any question with Mama. My going to a sheltered, deeply religious school was an answer to prayer for her. Papa had to think it over for a couple of days, but in the end, and much to my surprise, he consented to my changing schools. He even offered to drive me to the bus stop early in the morning so that I could arrive at school on time. I'm not sure what persuaded him. Perhaps he had simply given up on my dogged pursuit of godly things, or perhaps he just couldn't pass up a bargain. After all, "free" is a very good tuition price. In any case, the next two years of my life were spent in the holy halls of a school bathed in prayer, laced with restrictions and far from the rough and tumble moral decadence of public school.

By the end of my two year stint, I began to tire of the heavy-handed holiness that was practiced on campus where girls were forbidden to wear make-up and no one would ever be so brazen as to wear jewelry of any kind. For the seniors, rules were relaxed enough for them to have class pins, but class rings were strictly prohibited. In spite of all of my spiritual zeal, I really didn't think that God cared whether I wore a pin or a ring.

I decided that after graduation I would enroll at U.C.L.A., a decision which brought stiff opposition from both Papa and the President of the school I attended. The President of Los Angeles Pacific College even took me to lunch and used all of his considerable persuasive powers to convince me to remain at the school and finish my first two years of college there. Papa, on the other hand, flew into a storm of outrage, convinced that if I entered U.C.L.A., in four years I would exit as a card-carrying Communist. At the time, there were a few political radicals on campus and the news media were giving much attention to Communist agitation among the students at U.C.L.A. The truth is, I had little interest in politics and would never think of embracing any system that excluded God. At the moment, my main interest had to do with romance and physical attraction. I was determined to go to U.C.L.A. because that is where Ruth was. The object of my affection was a year ahead of me in school and already enrolled at U.C.L.A. Had she been enrolled at the University of Leipzig, however, it would not have mattered. I would have found a way to get there. My devotion to her was second only to God and I was determined to be where she was. My devotion to her was doomed from the start because of my crooked spine, but I did not know that at the time. Soon after I enrolled at the University, she ended our relationship.

Moving from a small, religious school with just over a hundred students into a huge, metropolitan university with a student body of 20,000 was something akin to throwing a pussycat into a wolf den. The word "terror" comes to mind. I struggled vainly to appear confident and sophisticated while finding my way to classes through a sea of strange faces, super achievers and brilliant scholars. I was intimidated and demoralized. The wonder of all is that I was able to struggle through my freshman year without flunking out.

At U.C.L.A., I decided to major in Psychology and minor in speech. Both subjects seemed a pretty good fit for my ministerial ambitions. I majored in Psychology, not because I knew a lot about it, but because it was the one subject I knew Papa couldn't help me with. Had he been aware of the scientific side of the course, he would have quickly jumped in and become an expert. As it was, Psychology had too much speculation and too many unproven theories for him. That was fine with me. The last thing I wanted was for Papa to be my drill instructor in college the way he had been in highschool.

During my last year of high school, thanks to a competent and caring teacher, speech and debate had become my forte. Because of my initial successes, I signed up for a class in "discussion" at U.C.L.A. It was one of the smallest classes offered on campus, and seemed to me to be a good launching pad for further speech triumphs. The results were devastating. I found myself in an out-for-blood swarm of stinging-bee intellectuals bent on proving their prowess as future professors, prosecuting attorneys and political pundits. They had immersed themselves in current affairs, world history and political science. All I knew came from the Saturday Evening Post and the Bible. The best thing I could do was just shut up and I did.

My first shock came at mid-term when my grade was listed as a big, fat "D." How could that be? I attended regularly, never showed up tardy, completed all reading assignments and never disturbed the class. That combination had worked so well in high school. Why didn't it work here? I made an appointment with the professor to find out why.

Most classes were so large at U.C.L.A. that students were merely numbers attached to names. Contacts with professors were rare and you were lucky to even find a teaching assistant who had much time for you. But this class was small and the professor knew each student by name and even what individual students had planned for the future. Because of this, the professor had agreed to meet with me one sunny afternoon out on the lawn in front of Royce Hall.

I nibbled on a blade of grass as I waited for the professor to show up, trying to keep my hands from shaking and my stomach from changing places with my heart. The warm, brick front of Royce Hall might have smiled benignly on the other students in the quad, but for me it was a fitting backdrop for a firing squad. I wished now that I could be magically transported back to the sheltered campus of my holiness high school. Why did I ever leave it?

At last the professor walked toward me across the lawn, his long, brisk paces resembling a football referee marking off a penalty. I stood to shake his hand and manufactured a weak smile. He motioned me to sit down again and squatted beside me in a fatherly stance that enabled him to look down on my trembling frame.

"Now, Mr. Rees, you wanted to see me?" he asked.

"Yes, sir," I answered. "It's about my grade."

"Did it surprise you?"

"Well, yes sir, it sort of did. I mean, I've showed up for all the classes and—"

"Showed up for all the classes," he repeated after me. "And you think that's enough, do you?"

"Well, not exactly, but—"

"I need to remind you, Mr. Rees, that this is a class in 'discussion.' Discussion, Mr. Rees, means that you 'discuss.' You interact, you agree, you disagree, you elaborate, clarify, add to, subtract from. My god, you have to say something. You can't just sit in the back row and listen, Mr. Rees. You have to enter in. I was kind in giving you a somewhat less than average grade because at least you showed up, but you also shut up. Don't you have an opinion about anything? Don't any of the subjects that we talk about interest you in the least? Free trade, the League of Nations, labor and management?"

"Yes, sir, but—" How could I tell him the real reason? How could I tell him that I felt dumb? How could I tell him that I didn't know anything about any of the subjects he mentioned? How could I tell him that if I did speak up, I knew that everybody would laugh at my idiot remarks?

He sighed, looked at the ground, and then looked at me again. "Mr. Rees," he said, "You will never make a minister. Never in the world. I hate to see you waste your time preparing for a career that will never happen. I suggest that you think about changing your majors and look for something that's a little more in line with your temperment and your kind of personality. A chemist, maybe, or a lab technician. Something where you would be working alone. You simply don't interact well in groups. As for your grade, well, you can pull it up some, but not much. Don't expect an "A" or a "B," but I think a "C" is attainable, if you work hard. You'll have to work at it – read, study and, for God's sake, speak up."

He rose to leave. The conversation was over. I stood also, but I couldn't muster a smile this time. "Thank you, sir," I said and shook his hand again. "I'll do that – I mean – I'll speak up from now on and work. Yes – I'll work real hard."

The professor wheeled around and walked away leaving me to feel as though I had been poked with a cattle prod. "You'll never make a minister." The words were acid on my soul. I shriveled under his prediction. Here was the frank evaluation of an authority in the real world. No "notched ear" here. No words from Grandma. No missing vertebrae setting me apart for a world mission. I didn't measure up. That was it.

But maybe not. Maybe the professor was wrong. Forget the nicked ear and the deformed spine and all the special visions of doting family members. Forget all the "markings" and mystic symbols. Wasn't there a passion beyond all that? Wasn't there an inner direction that won out over all human predictions? Wasn't there a strong conviction of the soul that directed the course of a person's life in spite of stammering lips and deep seated feelings of shame?

The good professor's candid remarks turned out to be more of a challenge than a defeat. I had been dealt a blow to my gut that left me nauseous and with blurred vision, but I marched to the library and sat down with the latest copies of Time magazine and the Los Angeles Times. I would read up on inflation in China and the conference in Tehran and the introduction of Polyethylene and John L. Lewis and the politics of Joseph Stalin. I would study the uses of uranium and penicillin and vitamin K and I would do more. I would speak up in class. I would have something to say about any and every subject and I would voice it. Let them snicker if they wanted to. Let them all laugh out loud, for all I cared. The professor would never accuse me again of not speaking up. "The Call of God" took on a whole new meaning. It was an inner drive, not an outer sign and it required the mind as well as the heart.

CHAPTER 29

SOME THINGS PAPA NEVER KNEW

*"No one ever keeps a secret so well
as a child."*

-Victor Hugo

Papa knew everything. He knew the size of the sun, the longitude and latitude of Los Angeles and how to decipher any code I invented with my Little Orphan Annie Secret Decoder Pin. But there were a few things that Papa never knew. Not that I lied to him. Lying was a terrible sin, but just not telling Papa everything that I knew wasn't a sin. Take the hat episode, for example.

One day I found a hat near the curb on Atlantic Boulevard. Probably it blew off the head of someone driving along in a car. I picked it up and saw that it was in pretty good shape despite scuffing around in the street for awhile. Except for the dirty smudges, it was a light tan, the color of beach sand, with a wide, ribbed band around it and a crease down the middle of the crown. It was too big for me to wear and much too good to throw away. So what should I do with it?

My imagination kicked into gear. What would happen if I dropped it on the cement walk that ran by the side of our garage? Mildred would probably see it first and it would scare her right out of her shoes. She would connect it to a prowler, a robber or worse. Maybe Mama would see it and it would scare her too. After I had a good laugh, I would tell them that it was just an old hat that I found in the street.

Just after dark, I crept out to the side of the garage and placed the fedora on its side by the garage. The evening passed. I went to bed and forgot about it. In the morning, Papa spotted it immediately. He came storming into the house with the strange hat in his hand.

"Do you know anything about this?" he asked, confronting Mama.

"No, I certainly don't," she said. I made a hurried exit to the bathroom.

"Do you know where this hat came from?" he asked Mildred.

"Uh-uh," she said.

Until Papa went to work that morning, I managed to stay busy in other parts of the house, out of the line of questioning. I intended that the whole situation would be funny – a practical joke. This wasn't funny. If Papa ever found out where that hat came from, I would have to leave home forever – probably have to change my name and live down by the Los Angeles River with all the other refugees from the law. I should have known that Papa would find it first and I should have known what his reaction would be, but I didn't think ahead.

That night, Papa took his loaded .38 and waited for hours in the shadows of the walnut tree or just behind the garage door. Any human being crazy enough to prowl through the yard that night would have been carried away with a .38 caliber hole through his skull. None of us dared to walk outside. Even though I knew where the hat came from, I kept my ears tuned for a blast from Papa's revolver. Guilt mounted in my chest like molten lava. What if one of my innocent playmates climbed the fence and walked into our yard? What if a stray dog trotted past our garage? What if Mrs. Doyle came over to borrow a cup of sugar? Would their deaths rest on my sinful shoulders?

The next night followed the same routine and my guilt increased exponentially. By the third night, Papa grew tired of waiting and decided that the intruder would not return for his fedora. He put his gun back into its holster and came inside. He never asked me about the hat and I never told him how it came to be there. Did he suspect that it had been my doing all along? Was he teaching me a lesson by this demonstration of armed stalking? I'm not sure, but I am sure that no one ever knew for certain how that hat came to be by the side of the garage. Let George Washington fess-up to chopping down the cherry tree if he wanted to, but I would never tell who planted that fedora.

Most of the time, Papa knew what was going on with every member of the family, but there were times when some event, some adventure or catastrophe, was too dangerous to have it discovered. Papa's reaction would have made the devastating Long Beach earthquake of 1933 seem like only a minor jiggle. That made for a conspiracy between Mama, Raymond, Mildred and me. Some things just had to be kept secret.

My brother's trip to Milwaukee was one of those undisclosed events. After a couple of years of college, his attraction toward a girl in Wisconsin was much too great to keep him studying all summer long. Having no money, but a great amount of passion, he hopped freight trains heading east. Befriended by hobos and gandy dancers, he made it all the way back without losing his leg or his virtue, but to reveal that adventure to Papa would have been unthinkable. That would have only confirmed Papa's often stated opinion, "He's nothing but a bum. He'll never amount to anything. He's a lousy bum."

I used to lie awake at night wondering what it would be like to cling to the top of a freight car, wind whistling through my hair, face black with soot and fingers numb with cold. My brother knew – Papa would never know.

My sister, Mildred, was not so much given to adventure, riding the rails and such, but she had her share of perilous episodes, times about which Papa was totally unaware.

One such episode occurred on the night of March 3, 1939. Mama approved of her date that Friday night. Wayne was a tall, gentle young man with a winning smile and a responsible job working at Ralph's Grocery Store. The occasion was a group picnic in the San Gabriel Mountains. Not much could go wrong there; wholesome young people, nourishing food, a warm campfire on a cool spring evening. Papa paid no attention to it. Monitoring the children was Mama's responsibility. Papa, as usual, was sequestered in his stuffy laboratory-study at the back of the house. The only time he met boyfriends was if they posed a threat of some sort. Otherwise, he wasn't interested.

I wasn't particularly interested either. I was busy putting out a neighborhood newspaper and, at thirteen, hadn't become attentive to serious dating.

I wasn't interested, that is, until Mama woke me up with a gentle "Shhhhhh. Don't say anything to Papa," she said, "but Mildred didn't come home last night."

"Didn't come home?" I was wide awake.

"Shhhhhh! Not so loud. No she didn't come home and I want you to run up to Ralph's Grocery right away to see if Wayne ever came in."

"What if Papa finds out?"

"Papa mustn't find out. Now just do as I say and hurry!"

With my heart pounding, I pulled on my clothes and ran the mile and a half to Ralph's like my pants were on fire. Gasping for breath, I asked the manager and any clerk I could find if they had seen Wayne or Mildred.

For reasons I couldn't understand, they all thought it was

outrageously funny and laughed, slapping their thighs, winking, and distorting their faces in "I-told-you-so" smirks. How could they be so flippant when I was imagining the worst? What if they had dropped into some deep ravine and were trapped? What if wild animals, bears or cougars, had attacked them? What if they were in a terrible auto accident? What if Wayne had kidnaped her? The list of possible tragedies was endless.

I raced home to tell Mama that no one had seen or heard anything of Wayne or Mildred. By this time, fortunately, other exciting distractions were happening at home.

The 2000 pound pool table that Papa had purchased from some Hollywood auction was being delivered that day. The move entailed a van, pulleys, winches, inclines, wheels and an army of men. Papa was in his element, running around like an Irish sheep dog, barking orders and keeping everyone in line. He was much too busy to notice who in the family was out of bed and who wasn't. For all he knew, Mildred was still asleep, although how anyone could sleep through all that racket and confusion would be hard to imagine.

By now, I was worried not only about what might have happened to Mildred, but equally worried about what would happen to poor Wayne, if he and Mildred should happen to pop up now, only to be confronted by Papa. They would most certainly wish they had stayed up in the mountains. I was sure that Papa would pull out his .38 and shoot Wayne. Not right at first. He'd probably shoot into the ground, making Wayne dance a jig the way they did in the western movies. Then he would aim straight for the heart and finish the job. The palms of my hands grew cold and sweaty just thinking about it.

"I want you to go over to Olive's," Mama said. Olive was Mildred's closest friend and lived about a mile away, beyond the grammar school and the Catholic Convent. "See if she's over there. See if Olive has heard anything about her."

Other families might have telephoned her friends, but we didn't have a phone. "Too expensive," Papa judged. Others might have notified the police, but that would have gone over Papa's head. Unthinkable! At all costs, this crisis must be solved without bringing Papa into it.

My legs were beginning to ache from all the running and my lungs felt like they would burst. When I reached Olive's house, she thought Mildred's disappearance was funny too. Why did everyone think it was so humorous? Didn't they understand the gravity of the situation? Didn't they know what Papa would do if she turned up missing? Olive did not know where Mildred was.

I was shaking as I ran home again. What would we do now? Where else was there to turn? We needed a car to go hunting for her – to get to a phone – to drive to Wayne's house and talk to his mother.

By the time I arrived at the house, the pool table was in place, squatting like the flat-bed of a ten-ton truck, smack in the middle of our living room. Papa was sitting exhausted in the morris chair, wiping sweat from his shiny, bald head with a handkerchief.

"Mildred must be awfully tired to sleep through all that," Papa said. Mama smiled and left the room. I was afraid that he'd go into Mildred's room to check on her, but he didn't. I went out onto the front porch to head them off, if I saw them coming.

Mama said it was the Lord looking out for us, but whether it was prayer or luck, Papa went out to the backyard for something just as Mildred came walking across the front lawn. Her legs were bloody and scratched as though she had spent the night in a lion's cage. Her hair was stringy and her eyes were all puffy and red.

"Where were you?" I asked in a hoarse whisper.

"It's a long story. Where's Papa?"

"Out back."

"Good! Just let me get to bed."

She came inside, hugged Mama and headed for the bath-room.

"Where have you been?" Mama asked.

"We got lost," Mildred said. "We spent half the night wan-dering in the mountains trying to find our way out. Every-thing's all right. Papa doesn't know, does he?"

"No, not yet."

"Good!" she said. "Just tell him I'm tired and slept in."

"It's almost noon," I said.

"Aren't you hungry?" Mama asked.

"I just want to go to bed," she said.

Standing over the sink in the bathroom, Mildred held a wet wash cloth to her face.

"Were's Wayne?" I asked.

"He's okay," she said. "I had him drop me off at the corner. He didn't want to. He wanted to come in and explain every-thing to Papa."

"Is he crazy?" I said.

"I know. I persuaded him to just let me handle it. He just doesn't know Papa."

We heard the back door slam and Papa's heavy footsteps. Mildred hurried down the hall to her room and jumped into bed. Mama and I went out to the living room and pretended to admire the green monstrosity that filled it.

"Where's Mildred?" Papa asked.

"In bed," Mama said.

"Good Lord! Isn't she ever going to get up? It's lunch time. Tell her to get out here and look at the new pool table."

"There will be plenty of time," Mama said. "She was very tired when she came in."

"I thought since we worked so hard this morning, maybe we could go to a matinee this afternoon. Wake her up so she can go with us."

"Really, Harry," Mama said. "She's very, very tired. Why don't we just let her sleep?"

"All day?" Papa snorted.

"Well, you know they had this picnic in the mountains and it lasted a long time. It was way after midnight when she got home. I think she needs her rest."

I smiled. Way after midnight. Way after midnight indeed.

We went to the movie. *"Destry Rides Again,"* I think it was, but it wasn't half as exciting as what we'd just been through, Mama and I. We had solved a mystery, located a missing person, prevented murder and helped move a pool table, all in one morning.

There were some things too self evident to keep from Papa. The best I could do under those circumstances was to admit the obvious and dodge all other issues. May 12, 1944 was a case in point. I was eighteen and a senior in high school. The small Free-Methodist school was in a section of Los Angeles called Highland Park. How I came to attend that school is a story previously told, but I spent the last two years of my high school career there. It was a small, fundamentalist school where piety was more important than pedagogy. It fit me perfectly at the time.

Old Doctor Kimber was our English instructor and was teaching us the fine points of Shakespeare: Macbeth, I think it was. On this beautiful spring afternoon, none of us in the class were in the mood for "Duncan, Banquo and Macduff," so we suggested to the teacher that we go for a short walk in the hills in back of the school. At first, of course, he would not hear of it. Such a thing would be contrary to school rules and a violation of class procedures. The pressure from the students, however, was constant, intense and unanimous. We could tell that he was warming toward the idea by the slight smile that seemed to grow broader the more we insisted.

"Well," Kimber said, "I suppose it might be all right, but mind you stay close to the school and if anybody asks what you're doing out there, you're on a nature hike. Agreed?"

"Oh, yes sir!" we all said in unison, slamming our books shut and heading for the exit. The green of early spring on the hillsides was already beginning to turn brown under the harsh Southern California sun. Some of us boys, intent on displaying our adventurous spirits, raced on ahead, stirring up a gritty cloud of dust with our pounding feet.

To our delight, we discovered what appeared to be a cave with an entrance at least six feet high. It didn't look to be a deep cave, but big enough for one or two to enter without being seen.

"Hey! How about this?" I whispered. "Look. I'll go just inside, in the shadow there, where they can't see me. Then the rest of you go out and get some of the girls to come over here. When they peek inside, I'll jump out and scare them right out of their skulls!"

"Wow!" one of the boys said. "That's great, but you do it. I wouldn't go in there for anything."

"I'm not going in very far," I said. "Besides, it doesn't look that big. I'll just step back there into the shadow."

I took three to four paces into the cave. Then it happened. I was free-falling in total darkness. I had heard Mama read from the Bible about a "bottomless pit" and I believed I had found it. The sensation was one of slow motion and the only thought going through my mind was that if the bottom didn't come soon, I would never live to tell anyone about it.

Fortunately, after the initial plunge downward, I began to bounce off unseen objects. I was ricocheting against the sides of the shaft like pebbles in a rock-slide. After what seemed like an eternity, I hit bottom with a sound something like two cars colliding.

I was alive. That's all I could tell at the moment. Cautiously, I moved my hands, arms, feet and legs. They all seemed to work. It was as dark as the inside of a black hat at midnight and smelled of damp earth and rotting garbage. Was I truly at the bottom of this pit, or was I only on a precarious ledge? There was no way I could tell and I was afraid to move. Soon I was aware of a low, persistent humming in the air. Mosquitoes – millions of them.

As my eyes adjusted to the darkness, I could see a faint ray of light high above me. I was amazed to see that I had fallen so far and was still conscious. Then I heard a tremulous voice echoing down the shaft. "Are you all right?"

"I'm not sure," I answered. "I think so."

I heard a clamor of voices from the direction of the light overhead, but couldn't tell what they were saying.

"Can you hear me?" another voice called from above.

"Yeah."

"Just stay put. We're going to get you out of there."

What did he say? "Stay put?" I wasn't about to move even if I could. If I moved, I might continue my fall clear to the center of the earth.

"Well, hurry up," I shouted. The words bounced back and forth up the shaft. "There are tons of mosquitoes down here."

"We've sent someone back to the school for some rope. They'll be here soon," the voice shouted.

In the meantime, with the mosquitoes supplying the counter melody, the classmates huddled at the entrance to the cave began singing religious choruses, led no doubt by Doctor Kimber. I wasn't sure if they sang for my benefit or theirs, but they sang loudly and off-key, "Every Day With Jesus," "There is Sunshine In My Soul," and "We Are Climbing Jacob's Ladder." At this point, I wished that I had Jacob's ladder, or any other kind of ladder.

Eventually, the runners came back from the school, not with a rope, but several lengths of garden hose. No one had any sort of rope that was long enough or strong enough to reach the distance I had fallen. By this time, my eyes were accustomed to the darkness and I could make out shadowy forms at the lip of the shaft lowering the hose.

"Be sure that you tie this around yourself real good," someone shouted. "We're going to pull you up."

"Okay," I said. "I'm ready." I had been ready for at least ten renditions of "Every Day With Jesus."

Finally the hose reached me and with as little movement as possible, I looped it under my arms, tied it in a triple knot and then hung on for dear life.

"Okay," I said. "Pull me up."

The ascent up the shaft took considerably longer than the descent down, but eventually I made it. It was difficult to tell who was more pleased at the rescue, Doctor Kimber or me. Kimber was afraid for his job. I was afraid for my life.

The hole, it turned out, was an old, abandoned mine shaft that had never been covered or blocked. Those who knew of it had been dumping trash and rubbish down it for years. It was about half filled, or I never would have lived to tell about it. As it was, the distance of the fall was a good twenty feet, measured by the lengths of the hoses that were lowered to me.

When I got back to the school, I tried to assess the damage without going to the doctor. My clothes were ripped and dirty, my hip wrenched and sore, there were numerous cuts and abrasions and a "goose-egg" on my forehead that looked like I had butted heads with a mountain goat. The worst, however, was yet ahead. I had to face Papa.

I wasn't dreading what he would say to me, although that would be bad enough – a lecture about foolhardiness and safety precautions as well as the importance of staying in class where I belonged. What I was really concerned about was what Papa would do to old Doctor Kimber and the whole school. He would sue them at least, pull me out of school,

243

threaten all of the Free-Methodists in Southern California and probably go after Kimber with his .38. He must never know what happened.

I rode the bus home, hoping that when I arrived Papa would be out on an errand or secluded away in his study. No such luck. There he was, sitting in the morris chair in the front room. There was no way I could get to my own room or the bathroom without going by him.

"What happened to you!" he yelled as he saw my bedraggled condition.

"I fell down," I said, in a voice that sounded matter-of-fact.

"Well that's obvious," he bellowed. "How did it happen? Where did it happen? What did you fall from?"

"I just fell," I said with a shrug of the shoulders.

Papa looked at me with the eyes of a prosecutor. "Did you get into some kind of fight or something?"

"No. I told you. I just fell down."

"Aren't you going to tell me what happened?"

"There's nothing to tell. Really. I'm fine. I just fell down."

I turned to go to the bathroom to get cleaned up.

"I could find out, you know," Papa said.

I mustered a weak laugh as I disappeared into the hallway. "There's really no mystery. I just fell and bumped my head. No need to worry or make a big issue of it. I'm perfectly fine."

I went into the bathroom and closed the door. I ran cold water from the faucet and splashed in on my forehead while I hunted for the aspirin tablets.

By morning, the swelling had gone down some, but my forehead was turning a horrible blue color. Nevertheless, Papa didn't pursue the questioning after that and I never volunteered any more information. Kimber kept his job, I stayed in school, and the mine shaft was filled in. What amazes me now is that the school never called Papa and Papa never called the school. He never knew how I got so banged up and I never told him.

My "spelunking" days, however, were over for good.

* * *

Secrets have a way of compounding – cover-ups begetting cover-ups – until there is a whole network of concealment. That's the way it was in the case of my disappearance for three days. Not only did Papa not know of my whereabouts, he didn't even know I was missing.

It all started with my purchase of an old, black, 1937 Chevy two-door sedan with a sleek chassis and a knock in the engine. The knock in the motor was more than just an annoying noise; it was symptomatic of a terminal condition for the entire engine. When it coughed its last black, smokey cough, I was left without transportation and without money. It was 1948 and I was a Junior in college, decidedly unwilling to admit to Papa that I was so mechanically inept and such a dolt in business dealings that I would make so stupid a purchase. I needed a rebuilt engine and I needed it fast, but this would cost nearly $500. The only solution was to get a job.

Working and going to school, Papa had said, don't mix. "Give all your time and energy to your studies," Papa told me many times. It was sound enough advice, but didn't take into account the need to cover up my foolish purchase and my need for transportation.

To tell Papa about my job delivering wrapped sandwiches for a company in West Los Angeles would have precipitated a family crisis of major proportions. It was better to keep quiet about it. The job involved being at work at 6:00 a.m. and quitting at 1:00. Perfect, if I arranged for my classes to be in the afternoon.

On a spring morning, one of the delivery men called in sick. "Rees," my boss said, "you'll have to take his route and your own too. Get in that truck and go like hell!" All of the sandwiches had to be delivered by noon or they would not sell.

The red, Dodge panel-truck that I drove for the company

had no rear view mirror and whined like a buzz-saw when you pushed the speed over 35 miles per hour. I took my boss at his word and felt that, Christian conscience aside, I must break every speed limit to get my job done on time. I floored the gas pedal and wove in and out of traffic like a shuttle on a weaver's loom. I was a red blur streaking down Sepulveda Boulevard, a main north-south thoroughfare running through West Los Angeles.

The police didn't take up the chase until about Slauson or so. I certainly didn't notice them until I made a left turn onto Pico. All that way, they had been chasing me with sirens screaming and lights flashing. With my engine yowling and no rear view mirror, I was oblivious to their presence.

By the time they had me cornered and pulled over to the curb, they were convinced I was an escaped convict, smuggler or bank robber – maybe all three. They were in no mood to listen to excuses about bologna sandwiches having to get to cigar stands by noon. With guns drawn, they pulled me from the cab of the truck, spread my hands out on the hood and frisked me.

I had never been inside a courtroom. I knew nothing of plea-bargaining, continuances or any of the legal procedures common to the law and justice system. To me, it would be a simple matter of explaining to the judge about bologna sand-wiches and how my boss told me to "go like hell."

When my name was called, the judge peered down through his black, horn-rimmed glasses as though I had just been identified as an escapee from San Quentin.

"Fifty five in a twenty five zone. That's pretty fast," he said.

Fifty five? I marveled. I didn't know the old Dodge would do fifty five. And twenty five? Since when was Sepulveda a 25 mile-an-hour zone? It couldn't be. I said none of this to the judge – only a simple, "Yes, your Honor."

"How do you plead? Guilty or not guilty?"

Well, it was obvious I was guilty. Why plead anything else? After all, I had borrowed sixty dollars from my boss to pay the fine just before I came to court. If the judge really socked it to me, I would simply pay the fine. It was as simple as that.

"Guilty," I croaked.

The judge looked at me straight in the eye. "Are you ready for your sentence?" he asked.

Sentence? Sentence? What kind of strange legal jargon is that? He must mean fine. What else could he mean? Surely "sentence" is just the legal term for "fine."

"Yes, your Honor," I answered.

"I hereby sentence you to three days in the city jail."

My mouth fell open. He didn't ask about the bologna sandwiches. He didn't give me a chance to explain that I'm a student at the university. Three days could be disastrous. He didn't allow me to tell him that I'm a student studying for the ministry. He didn't permit me to tell him that Papa might miss me and, if he found out where I was, there'd be all hell to pay.

"But your Honor – "

"Sit down."

"But you see – "

"Bailiff, take this man away."

Thus began a three-day disappearance from society. I could make but one phone call and only had presence of mind enough to call my boss to tell him that I would not be in for work the next day because I was in jail. At the time, I could not understand the hysterical laughter at the other end of the line.

The West Los Angeles jail resembled a Nazi concentration camp, or at least what I had read about them. The black coffee was a close match to battery acid, the crust of bread was dry and hard, and a blob of boiled beans were enough to take away anyone's appetite. At night, there was nothing but the concrete floor to lie down on and the jailer threw in half enough army blankets to go around. I didn't want one anyway. They were all encrusted with dried vomit from the prisoners in the drunk tank. For three days, there were no showers or water and only one seat-less toilet in the corner of the holding cell for a dozen men. There was nothing to read and nothing to do except curl my fingers around the bars and meditate on the heinous nature of my crime.

As bad as all that might seem, my biggest fear was that Papa might find out where I was. To disgrace the family name by a jail sentence was the worst kind of traitorous behavior imaginable. Fortunately, the three day period was a chunk taken out of the middle of the week. Had it been on the weekend, Papa most certainly would have wondered where I was hiding.

I was not exactly a child when this three day interruption occurred in my life, but I was still as fearful of calling down Papa's wrath as though I had been ten years old. I spared him the awful truth that his youngest son, the fragile one, the one with a crooked spine and aspirations toward the ministry, the one least likely to offend had now dragged the family name through the shameful slime of a seventy two hour jail term in the West Los Angeles City Jail.

CHAPTER 30

KISSES FOR A CAMEL

"This I set down as a positive truth.
A woman with fair opportunities, and
without a positive hump, may marry
whom she likes."

-William Thackaray

The year was 1932. She had everything: charm, beauty, talent and, for the moment at least, fame. She was dancing on top of the table and all eyes were upon her – especially mine. The occasion was an outdoor picnic. The table was one of those long, wooden plank affairs found in most parks and the dancer was a seven-year-old girl named Valene. I was seven, too. But I was tied into a plaster cast, lying flat on the table, close to Valene's tapping feet and lovely little legs. At the close of the dance, she impulsively stooped down and kissed me on the forehead. It was the wake-up call for every latent hormone in my small body. I felt the hot blood rush to my face – a grand and puzzling mixture of embarrassment, surprise, delight and frustration – most of all frustration. I wanted to respond. I wanted to demonstrate that the feeling was mutual, but I couldn't because of the infernal cast that held me captive like an upside down tortoise.

In hindsight, it was the cast that prompted the kiss. It

would be some years before I learned that an amorous kiss and a piteous kiss are as different as a bald-eagle and a buzzard.

The kiss in the park was only the first exercise in a long and difficult lesson – no one craves kisses from a camel. I was a slow learner, but the Valene episode was a harbinger of all that was to come.

As I approached the teen years, there were all the innocent sexual adventures of childhood: post office, spin-the-bottle and the dares of other young swains. One such dare placed me in a large cardboard box – a Buck Rogers space ship it was – with a blue eyed charmer named Joan. I was supposed to kiss her before we reached the moon. I did, but Joan took off into outer space like a wayward asteroid. I could never understand why her mother was so angry and watchful, but that ended my Romeo instincts for four or five years.

The sexual sap began to flow again during my junior and senior years in high school. The primal attraction of girls was absolutely irresistible. I entered the arena of male competition with all the fervor of a mountain goat at estrus. I faced several drawbacks in this contest, but most of them were common to other young males as well – no money, no car, a changing voice and acne. The biggest obstacle of all, however, was one which no one wanted to talk about – the hump that transformed me into a dromedary. I was a camel in a stable full of race horses.

The next few years were seeded with land mines disguised as love affairs. There was the little girl with the snapping, brown eyes and the lilting laughter. She had everything I wanted in a girl and I was ready to settle down for life with my first ever true love. I plied her with gardenias, hamburgers and starlit walks in the park. I even gave her a gold-filled locket to demonstrate the depth of my devotion. Although she was destined to become a missionary to China, I would have followed her to Antarctica for the pleasure of one small kiss. It was not to be.

I should have seen it coming, of course, but my eyes were blinded by rapturous explosions of love. One evening, seated in the front seat of Papa's 1937 Ford coupe, she explained to me that while she enjoyed my company, liked my personality and admired ever-so-many things about me, she was concerned about my health. That "concerned about your health" would be a phrase I would hear more than once. It was a euphemism for "Your hump scares the hell out of me." In less than fifteen minutes, my "eternal bliss" was reduced to "can't we just be friends?"

Then there was the girl with the coffee colored hair and sapphire eyes as large, deep and mysterious as Crater Lake. No missionary to China, this lass, but she delivered kisses that could ignite Mount Vesuvius. They drew from me a passionate plea for her hand in marriage. In a moment of youthful abandonment, she agreed. What could be more simple? We were in love. Then there came the inevitable conversations with her family, friends and advisors. After she had been duly warned and admonished, I heard for the second time that, while I had a pleasing personality, mind, character and all that other good stuff, my backbone was the wrong shape. With all the other fit "animals" in the coral, why should she settle for a camel?

You would think that by this time I would get the picture, but I didn't. The next romance, however, was the clincher. She was a hot-blooded blond with a figure to match her gorgeous face. Between us, we generated more electricity than Grand Coulee Dam. After a torrid few months, we were both ready to say "yes." We talked about invitations, announcements, dates, colors, patterns, flowers and all those planning issues that fiances discuss prior to a wedding. I had met her parents and most of her family and assumed, unwisely, that all of them were in favor of the idea. Wrong. There must have been

251

discussions far into the night about my unsuitability as a groom. I was attending U.C.L.A. at the time, so I am reasonably convinced that it was not my education that came into question, nor was it my character or personality. No, it was my angular spine that was the problem. This time I could see it coming. It was the "nice personality" bit again. I was tired of having all those sterling qualities that people admire from a distance, but not the attribute that girls wanted most of all – a great physique. Twisting a kid's spine may do wonders for his character, but it sure does nothing for his sex appeal or his ego.

When she handed back my fraternity pin, my world ended. I had tasted of love and passion and I longed for both, but like Quasimodo, I was destined to admire feminine beauty only from a distance while confined to the duties of the "cathedral." There was a rage burning deep inside – a rage born of having intense desire while not being intensely desirable.

At this point, I probably would have joined a monastic order, except for the fact that I was not Catholic and my cynicism about girls would have disqualified me. How could God create beings so attractive and yet divest them of hearts? The female Praying Mantis, I had heard, ate its mate while the hapless male insect was in the very act of copulation. Were human females any different?

Despite my squabble with God, I plunged with renewed vigor into my religious calling. Perhaps the Catholic priests were onto something. Maybe celibacy was a good idea after all. Perhaps I could simply ignore my galloping gonads. My male friends and adult mentors all told me that sex was not all that important. They should know. They all had wives or girl friends. Perspective was the only important thing, they said. Keep a positive attitude. What they didn't understand is that perspective is a direct function of the angle of a person's spine. That's why it does little good to tell a man with Pott's disease to "keep looking up." His head is pointed down.

Regardless of the lectures, advice and the hump, the male chemistry was still working. It was a Sunday evening youth meeting at the First Baptist Church when I first noticed her – shy, young girl that she was, blond hair cascading in ringlets over her shoulders like shiny gold coins from a pirate's treasure. The indented waist of her gray suit gave a subtle hint of the sensuous body beneath. The suede pumps with the scooped out toes awakened some dormant fascination with feet. She was delivering a simple homily to the group and even her halting speech attracted me. Dare I heed my instincts again? There was a response from her eyes, or was it only my wishful thinking again?

The girl was introduced as "Reba, new here from Texas," although the soft drawl in her voice announced her birthplace long before she was formally introduced. She was working at the telephone company and living temporarily with the preacher's family right there in our own city of Burbank, California.

The courtship was not a smooth one. How could it be? There were so many differences to sort out. She was country bred with country music coursing through her veins and cowboy philosophy entrenched in her brain. I was a city boy hungry for the sophistication of Hollywood and the hustle-bustle of Los Angeles. Her hands were calloused from picking cotton in the fields; mine were soft from reading books and typing term papers. Being abandoned at the age of sixteen, she had gone to work to put herself through high school. I was about to graduate from college. Because of an abusive father, she was suspicious of all men. Because of my disastrous love affairs, I was suspicious of all women. It was hot and cold from the start. It was hard for friends to tell at any given point whether we were in the midst of a growing relationship or a total break up. The whole romance was confusing to those who watched and to both of us as well. There were those who said, "it will never work," and they had a good basis for saying so. How could two such disparate souls ever get together?

The biggest threat to our relationship, however, was not our upbringing or educational disparities – it was the hump. Eventually, the questions had to come up. "Was it life threatening? Was it contagious? Would it be passed on to children?" I had answered the questions so many times before. They were fair questions, reasonable questions, honest questions, but I had answered them so often that I was sickened by them.

"I hardly even notice it," she reassured me. "It doesn't bother me. I was just wondering, that's all. I don't even see it most of the time."

Never tell a camel that you don't notice his hump. It only confirms his suspicions that you are either blind or a liar. Maybe both. Could she really be saying that it didn't make any difference – that she loved me regardless? Somehow she convinced me of this. Neither of us could foresee the difference that my crooked spine would make, but for a few months, at least, I lost my "camelness." We set the wedding date for a night in June.

Two days before the wedding, Reba's family drove out from Texas to California to participate in the wedding rehearsal and inspect the groom-to-be. I had never met her family and they had never met me. Our first meeting was a shock in both directions. Reba's father fit every Texas stereotype I had ever seen or heard. His face had the deep lined surface of sun-baked sandstone. Beneath a ten-gallon Stetson, his eyes glowered an intimidating stare that would melt granite. It was obvious that he worked hard, fought hard, and drank hard. Reba's mother was the soft spoken spouse who agreed with all that the male members of her clan would say because she dared not do otherwise. There were also two, strapping teen age boys and a thirteen year old younger sister.

Reba's oldest brother and his wife had already moved out west and lived in Southern California, not far from Burbank. If I suffered from culture shock, so did they. They described me as "a hunchback version of Mickey Rooney."

It was Reba's sister-in-law that was the fuse to the impending explosion. By virtue of the fact that she wore a white smock and worked in a factory stuffing vitamin pills in bottles, she passed herself off as a medical expert. She took one look at me and kicked her imagination and creative phobias into high gear. Here was an excellent chance to display her biological expertise. She promptly informed the rest of the family that since tuberculosis had deformed my spine, I would soon die, Reba would be dead within five years and all the children conceived in the meantime would look like little camels.

With the rage of a pit bull that has burrs under its tail, Reba's father stormed the church and threatened to kill the minister if he went through with the wedding. Furthermore, he was going to forcibly take his daughter back to the cotton patches of Texas where she belonged. The fact that she was nearly twenty two years old made no apparent difference.

The scenario was a familiar one to me. The only difference between this one and all the rest was the threatened violence and the proximity to the wedding ceremony. The invitations were out, the tuxedos rented, the church reserved, the cake ordered and all was in readiness. The only trouble was that now there would be no bride, a dead minister and probably a dead groom as well. Her father, I had been warned, was a throw-back to the days of the Alamo, where the gun was the law and no prisoners were taken. Rumor had it that he had killed a dog at one time for his own entertainment and, on another occasion, had ripped out a horses tongue in a fit of rage. Whether the stories were true or apocryphal, you had to take the man seriously.

One might think that I would inform my own father of

what was going on and bring him into the volatile situation, but I did not. I certainly did not want two madmen waving guns around. I could imagine the two of them ducking behind church pews sending bullets ricocheting off the chandeliers and puncturing the sanctuary walls like Swiss cheese. This was beginning to rival a John Wayne movie. But what should we do? Cancel the wedding? That would be unthinkable. Elope? Impossible. We settled on a workable solution at least for the two of us.

Mildred and Wayne now lived in a rock-gully up against the hills between Pasadena and San Fernando – a place called Tujunga – no one but the natives had even heard of it. The night before the wedding, we drove our not-too-dependable Ford up through the foothills and stayed at Mildred's place, nestled among the boulders and Yucca trees, where not even the Texas Rangers could find us.

The minister of the church, however, had no place to hide. How could he escape this gun-slinging vigilante from the Lone Star State? His salvation lay in the fact that he had several high-ranking policemen in the congregation. These he summoned and explained to them the threat against his life. This was the most excitement the City of Burbank had seen since the movie studios were built there. The whole police department rallied to the cause. On June 2, 1950, a cordon of uniformed officers was thrown around the church and a bodyguard was assigned to the threatened cleric. It was difficult for me to fathom the excitement that a couple of missing vertebrae could make throughout a city the size of Burbank. Ah, the power of the hump.

I wanted to keep Reba's whole family away from the ceremony. "Lock them up" would have been my solution. Reba saw no need to penalize her younger sister and brothers just because she had a maniac for a father and a bubble-head for a sister-in-law. That made a lot of sense to her, but then, she didn't have to stand up there in front of the whole congregation waiting for the wedding party to make its way to the front of the altar and the bullet to find its way to my head.

The Police Chief tried to restore my shredded nerves. "Just point him out to us as he comes through the door," he said. "We'll surround him with plain-clothes men in front, back and either side. If he so much as sneezes, we'll carry him out before he knows what hit him." It was small comfort. How long does it take to fire a six-gun? About the same time as a sneeze, I judged.

Eight o'clock came. My execution drew near. My apprehension grew. I had heard the old saw about how your entire life flashes before you as you are about to die. It was happening to me now, except that it was my love-life that was flashing by and it was taking much too long. I remembered Valene, and Joan, the blue-eyed girl in the cardboard spaceship, the adorable missionary to China, the girl with the bedroom eyes and passionate kisses, and the blond bomb-shell that steamed up the windows of my '37 Chevy, and all the other truncated love affairs. How could they all end so badly? Now this was ending the same way only worse. It would soon be over. I would be shot down gangland style from the front pew of the First Baptist Church and all because of a crooked spine. It made no sense.

I was at the church early that night – not because I wanted to be, but because I needed to make sure that the Police Chief identified the hit man correctly. I stood in the corner of the narthex, hands jammed into my tuxedo pockets, pulling the jacket taut over my dromedary hump. I was trying to look calm and dignified.

At last, the bride's family came through the front door – a plump little sister, two young brothers, a teary-eyed mother and the scowling father – hate radiating from his face like heat from the Texas sun. A lifetime of rancor had sculpted itself into his sunken cheeks leaving deep, downward slashes. He was not dressed for a wedding – no tux or fancy suit. Reba had decided upon their first arrival that he would not escort her down the aisle. She would go it alone. What was the bulge in his pocket? What did he have hidden under his jacket? I would soon know whether it was a pistol, a machete, or just a Texas bandana.

I looked at the Chief and nodded my head, Humphrey Bogart style, toward Reba's father. A covey of Burbank's finest followed him into the sanctuary and surrounded him in the pew. I had put my finger on the killer. Whatever happened now, they would at least know who did it.

Finally the sanctuary lights were dimmed and the candles lit in all their shimmering glory. Candles create a certain ambiance at weddings – also funerals. The minister and I took our places at the front of the congregation. I admired his bravery, for we both would soon die in a volley of bullets. We had stricken from the ceremony the phrase, "If anyone present knows of any reason why these two may not be joined together in holy matrimony, let him now speak." No use inviting trouble. I could picture the mad Texan standing up and yelling, "Yer damn right! That little bastard is a contagious hunchback! He has nothing but little hunchback genes to pass on to my precious daughter." I shivered at the thought. It didn't really matter, though, whether he said anything or not. He could stand up anytime, guns blazing, to mow down the minister and me and anyone else who stood in his way.

The beginning of the wedding march was, for me, more like the drum roll for a firing squad. I was shaking. Most of the smiling parishioners thought I was simply nervous. As the bridesmaids made their intolerably slow march down the aisle, beaming and winking, I felt that I had a bulls-eye painted on my forehead.

There was a crescendo as the congregation rose and the

bride started her long journey down the aisle. Now was the time. Now was the place for the shots to ring out and for the people to start falling like tenpins in a bowling alley. Nothing happened – no blood, no screams, no shots, only the noisy blubbering of a pathetic old man, blowing his nose in his bandana, convinced that his daughter would soon die of Pott's disease. The ceremony was not over – still plenty of time for violence – but my mind was not on the guns, the police, or potential screams of objection. For the moment, I had forgotten the hump, too. My attention was all on the alluring young woman coming toward me. She didn't walk – she floated. Wrapped in candlelight and aglow with love, this diaphanous portrait of loveliness drove out all other concerns. This was reality. All else was a fitful dream.

The vows were repeated, the rings exchanged, the pronouncements made. We were husband and wife. The congregation faded into the background and the minister seemed to disappear as I gathered her into my arms for the kiss. The camel, at last, was kissing and being kissed.

EPILOGUE

There was a crooked man,
And he went a crooked mile,
He found a crooked sixpence
Against a crooked stile;
He bought a crooked cat,
Which caught a crooked mouse,
And they all lived together
In a little crooked house.

-Old Nursery Rhyme

A good eighty years later, the house that Papa built on Atlantic Boulevard still stands, although he would not recognize
it now. The front yard has been cut nearly back to the door-
step to make room for a wider highway. The wood siding has
been torn away and replaced by pink stucco. Cheap rental
units stand where the woodpile and the walnut tree used to be.
It is now in what demographers euphemistically call a "changing neighborhood." Knock on the door and you will see it
open a scant two inches while a dark eye peers out across a
stout, double chain. You will not be invited in, for there is
fear there—a different kind of fear than there was when I was
growing up. I have smiled as I wondered if Papa would not
enjoy it more now than when he actually lived within. There
would be an increased need for his Colt revolver and perhaps

there would even be those who would return his fire.

Papa would resent any linkage between that house and the word "crooked." If there is any feature of the house that stands out above all others, it is its straightness. It is squared, level and true. Papa would build nothing less. That which was crooked was not its beam or foundation, but the people who crossed its threshold and planted their fingerprints on its doors.

The crooked little people who once inhabited the house have all gone for good—Papa, Mama, my sister Mildred and my brother Raymond. I alone host the memories of what went on within those walls. Much of the extended family has gone, too—my Aunt Mildred, Uncle Bland, Uncle Clayton, Aunt Addie and Grandma Elvina Peet Rees. When I think about these who have passed on, I cannot help but believe that they are not really dead at all. They continue to live in thousands of ways through the personalities of the living—in their mannerisms and values and temperaments and fears and hopes and memories.

Perhaps that is the meaning of immortality after all. Maybe eternal life is not realized in some celestial city, but in the lives of our children and their children and their children after that. We pass on our crookedness and our straightness to all the little houses to come. Those lives wrap us in laughter and bathe us in tears and give us a kind of tolerance for all of the crookedness in the world. All of the fame and foibles which write themselves into our histories are merely examples of our valiant attempts to cope with the outrageous twists and turns of life.

Inevitably, any collection of memories will be incomplete. This series of sketches is no exception. Incidents have been ignored, names have been passed over and important relationships have been slighted. It is like a swift flight over a mountain range where a few peaks and valleys are pointed out and the rest is left for background. I would hope that this cursory overview is sufficient to illustrate the resiliency of our human spirits and the power of the soul to forgive.

ACKNOWLEDGMENTS

For their encouragement, assistance and helpful criticism, I would like to express my deep appreciation to Hazel Rees, Mandy Rees, the late Raymond Rees, the late Mildred Wylie, Esther Brinkley, Joyce Heintz, Ruth Robinson, Marisela Rogers, Marilyn Morford, and members of the Sagewind Writers: Bob Andrews, Joan Emory, Marjorie Fox, Pat Krantz, Betty Liddington, Carol Merrick and the late Milt Lewis. I would also like to thank Randy Rees and Barbara Jenson for their technical expertise. A special thank-you goes to Shauna Rees for the cover art-work. Without their help and support, these memoirs would remain dormant.

Willis Overland auto in which Rees family crossed the country.

L to R: Harry, Raymond, Cora crossing the country.

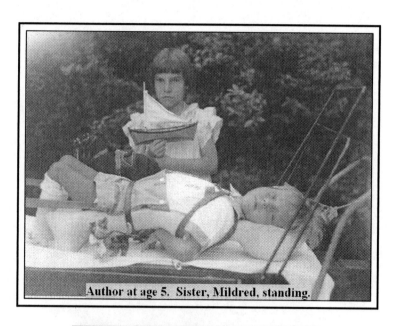

Author at age 5. Sister, Mildred, standing.

Author's Dad, Harry P. Rees

L to R: Wilbur, Cora (Mother), Mildred (sister)

Harry's Mother, Elvina Peet Rees

Uncle Clayton, Harry's brother

Author's sister, Mildred, with bicycle that Harry & Clayton built

Author's brother, Raymond, & fiancee Hazel Morton

Back row L to R: Uncle Bland, Mildred, Cora, Mildred, Harry, Raymond

Front row L to R: Uncle Clayton, Grandma Elvina Peet Rees, Author Wilbur Rees

Alhambra house built by Harry Rees. Picture circa 1935

Alhambra house built by Harry Peet Rees. Photo circa 1990

Reba (Hinds) Rees, High School graduation photo

Reba & Wilbur Rees on wedding day, 1950